THE OCCIDENTAL TOURIST

ISBN: 1536815063
ISBN-13: 978-1536815061

THE OCCIDENTAL TOURIST

A FACEBOOK DEBATE ABOUT
RACE, CULTURE AND VALUES

EDITED BY
PAUL R. GIBSON

Score
Books

FOREWORD

This book is current yet timeless. My sister and I, mainly, discuss race, culture, politics and values. What could at times be consid-ered arcane or futile debate is bracketed by the fact that Donald Trump's run for president of the United States has attracted so many ardent supporters; one such being my sister Sharon. Al-though we only mention Donald Trump a couple of times within our yearlong debate, the same attitudes that radiate from his per-sona cause certain people and their issues to gravitate to his cam-paign. Alongside this push and pull we seem to be witnessing the disintegration of at least one political party while finding concern about what may rise from these ashes.

Although the topics we speak of tend to be emotionally charged, Sharon and I kept our pointed conversation polite. With the rise, however, of the unapologetic rudeness by many of an emboldened right-wing, these issues find new devotees and take on new impor-tance. The anger and belligerence of a great many people is surfac-ing while many believe their divisiveness stands for some moral and/or national unity. Too few people will think critically about their own beliefs yet they shout them from the rooftops. At the same time they damn those who want more reasonable discussion. And make no mistake, this unreasonableness isn't limited to what many call the far right-wing. The same unreasonableness is as prevalent on the far left-wing. Whether you agree with these labels or not, there is a nagging necessity for certain people to encourage that which is most extreme at the expense of civility. Each *side* then calls the other "idiots" who "just don't get it." As a result too many mainstream Republicans and Democrats have come to define the other's party by the extreme idealists on its far wings instead of offering the benefit of some doubt. Having spent years on the far right-wing of our current political spectrum, I can fairly say that I get it. Like others, I listened religiously to right-wing talk radio. Then after watching Fox News on TV there is always the Internet where all of us can search out only those points of view that we agree with. We seem to engage in this sport so as to hone talking points aimed at discrediting others. As it is, we can now read about, watch and listen to the worst that the extremes can dish out about each other for 24 hours a day if we are so inclined. On the right this myopia is often touted as "balance" for that demonic "lame-stream media".

Somehow along the line I sought out another option: Seek out viewpoints I disagree with and then try to find ways to understand them in their best possible light. After all, to seek out and embed yourself within only one point of view can't be justified as balance, it can only result in a self-imposed ignorance. And is ignorance something we really want to value? You cannot fairly learn about your own side when you can't fairly represent the opposing side. Although ideals tend to the extremes, broader reality can reveal the unity that might now appear as distant relations, let alone as brother and sister.

Although I started reading right-wing political books when I was eleven, my furthest right-wing ideals started to moderate in my twenties, and not because liberal college professors were in-doctrinating me. I had simply come to view anti-communism as an awfully narrow and negative basis for my politics. Communism simply wasn't related to everyday issues. My alternative was to start reading history and learning about liberty. Although I soon be-gan calling myself a libertarian, it didn't take long to find out that most libertarians were simply right-wing Republicans who wanted polygamy (I did live in Utah after all) or drugs (or insert your pet desire here) legalized. Most other libertarians were essentially anarchists who saw little if any value in centralized government. As a result, the very idea of freedom began to fall short as a foundation for my political thought. No matter how patriotic it sounded to me, something was wrong with espousing the idea of personal freedom that I couldn't immediately explain.

It normally takes something more than consideration of one's options to spur a major shift in one's thoughts, feelings and values. For me the urgent need for change came in my early thirties while listening to an avowed white supremacist speaking for the KKK. He was using what had become my own best arguments for individual freedom and "state's rights", yet his arguments were targeted against all those *other* people (blacks, homosexuals, Jews, Asians, Mexicans and other mostly non-white "immigrants" or migrant workers) living within *his* America. These people were unworthy of civil and sometimes even human rights. He quoted the Bible while chiding government for protecting those he deemed immoral, illegal or somehow otherwise *less than* himself. He lambasted the judiciary for usurping the role of majoritarian democracy by protecting the rights of minorities who had the gall to demand "special rights". Special rights, it seems, are those rights that the ruling majority take for granted. And while the pests in the minority were asking him to be civil, he said, "What they call civility, I call socialism. This country was built upon freedom not totalitarianism!" He praised democracy while disparaging civility. He referred to this civility with the now common term "political correctness". Perhaps it was his inexplicable use of the terms "socialism" and "totalitarianism" that prompted me to begin understanding just how my beliefs had been guided, or misguided.

How could this man's words and reasons sound so similar to mine and yet be so opposed to the Constitution I valued so highly? What was I overlooking? How should I judge the differences? What foundation could I or should I use for my values and for my politics? While talking to coworkers about this, I came to see that while many people value their own individual freedom, few seem to value the fact that this freedom can't exist when there is no justice to guard and ensure it. Therefore justice must either come first or be woven into the very fabric of liberty. In order to have *liberty for all* we must vigorously promote and defend *equal rights and justice for all*. If we don't do this, democracy is simply a fancy term for the strong ruling over (or constantly overruling) the weak. There is simply no reason to concern ourselves with culture or politics if we refuse to be civil with those we disagree with. If we can't value this simple fact, civil society will come untethered from any greater social morality while society breaks into feuding factions. Within the political climate of 2016 United States, this reality has gained a sense of urgency. We witness the same urgency within the political climate of 2016 Great Britain.

For many on the right today, the term *political correctness* is spat out like an epithet while the left is branded as too sensitive. Of course the sensitivity of the right is on full display when the left dares comment upon certain religious beliefs, holiday rituals and other things that symbolize their brand of patriotism. The right definitely has its own sense of political/social correctness. If they didn't, what would all this hubbub be about? Ironically, some on the right want to rein in the left while claiming that political correctness restrains their free speech. Regardless of the obvious sensitivities on all sides, too many want *others* to watch *their* language while taking little responsibility for their own free speech. Any improvement in this process requires more civility on all sides rather than less. When all is said and done, free speech can only be of value for our society insofar as we are civil with our use of it. Neither side should want their own brand of political correctness to squelch the fair debate that exists within civil, free speech.

I, for one, am very much in favor of free speech yet I regard today's minimal exceptions to free speech to be reasonable. An example of such exception is limiting the freedom of someone who might endanger public safety by shouting FIRE in a crowded theater when there is no clear and present danger. In this way, free speech is not much different from the social health need for vaccination. Health and safety are effected by the social responsibility or irresponsibility of others. So as is often the case, except for those on the extremes, free speech is not what political correctness is all about. Political correctness is not about law so much as it is about social responsibility and respect for others. Many who prefer political correctness are not trying to quell free speech, they are vying for more accuracy within speech. *Words mean things.* They see that our terms are value laden and therefore should be explored for what they may imply. Free speech can be likened to free and fair trade. We can never know if our words approach truth (or if our products approach quality) unless we actively invite and engage in competition; a competition geared toward quality rather than sloganeering. I hope this book is an example of this free and fair exchange.

Freedom tempered with the equal justice necessary for maintaining everybody's civil rights remains the beginnings and ends of liberty. This civic responsibility values civil and human rights over majoritarianism no matter how boisterous those against this equal justice may become. Concern about "the tyranny of the majority" as voiced by John Locke, John Stuart Mill, Thomas Paine, John Adams, James Madison and Alexis de Tocqueville is foundational to liberty within America's classical liberal tradition.

One thing that struck me while reading history as an adult is how most of my own ideas about politics had seemed so negative whereas our forefathers had sounded hopeful and forward thinking. Theirs was a *liberty for* rather than simply the *freedom from* we hear so much of today. I had been so focused upon what was wrong with the system that I had only been quoting Thomas Jefferson when his arguments seemed to buttress my negative views. Inadvertently I had been ignoring greater values that I'd not properly studied. It still strikes me as ironic that I had to study liberty in order to value the concerns that existed beyond my own individual freedom. While learning about liberty I started to look toward potential and I slowly became more positive. New values began to solidify. As I studied America's traditions it began to strike me, as it still does today, how odd it was that I had once assumed the foundations of our American traditions were somehow conservative or even right-wing. The American experiment has been imperfect but its greatest strides have been liberal and quite revolutionary.

INTRODUCTION

After a number of years on *Facebook*, in July of 2015, my sister Sharon found me and *friended* me on my 57ᵗʰ birthday. Now living a couple states away, I hadn't heard from her in about fifteen years. Growing up I remember little of Sharon. Almost 14 years older than I, Sharon was out of the house before I can remember her living there. Family lore has it that she was a great lover of argument and confrontation. One story has it that she was praising Chairman Mao and Communist China one day when my father scolded her saying, "I'd be happy to buy a ticket so you can go there and live." Accurate or not, it sounds like dad. My own memories of Sharon are from later family get-togethers like Thanksgiving and such. All my memories are fond. I mostly remember her quick wit and laughter. It wasn't until mom and dad died I learned that she was my half sister. Since then she has told me several things about my family that I never knew.

On *Facebook* she offered up a challenge to me which is met in the pages that follow:

> Happy Birthday Paul! I was glad to find you on *Facebook* and it looks like we might have some interesting debates. I sparred with liberals on

the Tribune – as odd man out – until they banned me for being politically incorrect.

Thanks for the birthday wishes. I've seldom been much of a debater but I find nothing wrong with being politically correct. And I seem to get more liberal as I get older. Winston Churchill is quoted to have said, "If you're not a liberal when you're 25, you have no heart. If you're not a conservative by the time you're 35, you have no brain." But there is no record of anyone hearing Churchill say this. Paul Addison of Edinburgh University makes this comment: "Surely Churchill can't have used the words attributed to him. He'd been a Conservative at 15 and a Liberal at 35!" So perhaps it's me, Churchill and, later, Goldwater.

Many of our conversations were public insofar as anybody could read and follow our threads because most were linked to her, my own, or someone else's post. Sharon has never been shy about posting her opinions publicly. And the anonymity of the Internet removes any reservation that some people might otherwise have about voicing their opinions in reply. In answering my sister's assertions about race and culture, I had to do some studying-up as her intellect can be challenging. I was surprised as well as disappointed to learn that some of her ideas are still prevalent among certain intellectuals. I then brought up these discussions with co-workers only to confirm how prevalent some of these beliefs still are today.

Keeping track of our threads, however, could sometimes be problematic because our conversations sometimes became disconnected from the original post. So sometimes we would end up messaging each other through *Facebook's* "chat" feature. There was usually a day or two gap between comment and reply. Sometimes, however, our conversation would stall. I'm not sure if Sharon became disinterested or distracted. Sometimes I would try to jump start our conversation with questions of a personal note, or a change of subject. I insert notes herein with italics so as to provide context for certain references that might not otherwise be clear.

I was a bit hesitant to enter into this conversation for two main reasons. First of all I had a brief e-mail exchange with Sharon's husband about 20 years earlier in which he berated me for accusing him of, I can't recall now, sounding racist perhaps? I responded by reminding him that I was simply responding to the words of an article he had forwarded along to me, our siblings, and cousins. I did, however, tell him that if he shared this author's views then we could certainly address these issues together. I never heard another word from him. The second reason is that, not long before our mother died, our mother relayed a conversation (an argument) she previously had with Sharon and her husband which had left her in tears. She felt crushed. Regardless of these issues, or perhaps because of them, I decided to carry on.

The chat style of conversation can be a problem with such a small window and little opportunity for desired punctuation and spell checking, so I would copy and paste her email notifications into a word processor document for convenience. I would then write my reply within that same document and copy and paste the results into the chat window. Once in a while another friend of mine might comment (these people shall often remain nameless but I provide them with initials and a font) upon something that leads the thread in another direction and then back again. Sometimes Sharon's comments were, or seemed to be, in reply to the other party so I include some of these threads within our discussion. Please forgive any grammatical errors. Evidently Sharon wrote live within her browser, but to my eye she is an excellent editor for herself. Although I removed some family details, I didn't want to edit words that weren't my own and so I've mostly left the correspondence as it came out of our respective keyboards, warts and all.

THE DEBATE

Here is the comment I posted to Facebook *on June 26ᵗʰ 2015 that prompted my sister's challenge. My comment is about the recent Supreme Court ruling regarding gay marriage. 99% of the arguments I had heard against gay marriage were identical to the arguments proffered against interracial marriage up through the 1960's. The United States Supreme Court finally deemed anti-miscegenation laws unconstitutional in 1967.*

PAUL: Many people offer up the word *tradition* in defense of what they deem to be their long held values. They seem to claim right-eous monopoly on their values while ignoring the defects within their tradition as well as ignoring the value within others.

Historically, most of us realize that slavery, Jim Crow, and denying women the right to vote etc, were also long suffering tra-ditions. But in hoping to learn from history so as not to repeat the mistakes from our past, the greatest part of our American tradition has always been our society's ability to look beyond the limits of our current points of view in order to realize the greater values that exist beyond these limits. Why? Because tradition, by itself, is not a reliable foundation for morality.

Although many of us are uncomfortable with change at its onset, our ability to redefine our values has always been more than traditional, the results have often been nothing less than historic. So it is that we struggle with the same process today as we did then. Interested in ourselves and those closest to us, many of us cry for *freedom from*, but relatively few are interested in those further removed from us that will cry out in favor of *liberty for*.

The claim of tradition is linked with the multitudes who have followed its precepts through the ages. In this way tradition is linked with its history and our democratic value of majority rule. But we should never forget that a lynch mob is majority rule and that mob rule is neither valuable nor just. Over time, many of us have learned that *having always done it this way* does not necessarily translate into *something should still be done this way*.

Consider the time honored tradition of rioting as defended by Thomas Jefferson when he told James Madison, "I hold it that a little rebellion now and then is a good thing." Today I hear folks from the right and the left look from the Baltimore to Ferguson Missouri* and question the tradition that Jefferson so righteously defends. Yet others might well understand these riots by pondering the words of Martin Luther King Jr. who said that ". . . a riot is the language of the unheard." The traditional value of equal rights for all people under the law is certainly of value, and today we find many people still desiring recognition of this value as is demonstrated by the Baltimore riots as well as recent Supreme Court cases.

*And I could just hear Madison thinking, That's easy for you to say Mr. Jefferson, living way over there in Paris, but here the government is in crisis!

The next reference is to protests and riots that had been occurring due to local police killing unarmed black men within these as well as other American cities.

SHARON: Slavery in the U.S. was not a tradition, but rather an economic program of a relatively small minority of traders, and owners of large agricultural properties. By the same token, one wouldn't call indentured servitude or child labor traditions. Jim Crow laws were not traditional, but rather a codified, defensive reaction to the imposition of emancipated Blacks on the defeated and disenfranchised people of the South. Segregation might qualify as tradition because it describes a natural/biological tendency to separate along racial and ethnic lines. It was not a tradition to deny women the vote, but was a political institution that gave a single vote to be cast by the male in the interests of his family. Women's suffrage implies that women have interests of their own that are separate from the interests of their families. The practical effect of women's suffrage is to dilute or cancel the family vote. A better example of a Western tradition is the nuclear family – a tradition that is rooted in our biology and has evolved over thousands of years among European peoples. Morality develops as support for the social forms that have evolved to enhance reproductive success and survival; that is to say, much of what we consider immoral is judged to be so because it is destructive to the nuclear family, reproductive success, and healthy children. Marriage is the social form that defines acceptable sexual behavior and the vast majority of Western peoples implicitly understand that rape, pedophilia, incest, sodomy, premarital sex, pornography, prostitution, infidelity, abortion, sadomasochism, bestiality, voyeurism, and exhibitionism are wrong and even if they hedge with the idea of "consenting adults" they still balk at having their children exposed to any of it. Are these people just afraid of "change" or isn't it the case that they can already see the results of disrupting a tradition that has made us who we are?

PAUL: Well I guess I could say, nuh-uh.

According to the *Urban Dictionary* nuh-uh is, "A cool word used by cool people who are excellent at winning everything they do." Of course, the Urban Dictionary isn't exactly *Webster's Dictionary* or the *Oxford English Dictionary* but nevertheless, my bet is that we could parse words, compare semantics, propose definitions and etymologies all day long and it will only delay in our getting to what really concerns you.

I could say that I'm fine if all adults in a family can vote for their interests (as they can do nowadays) instead of the men voting for their interests or what *they* deem to be everybody's interest. But I could also ask, what the heck is a "family vote"?

But when it all comes down to it we simply disagree, and disagreement isn't a problem. I don't see some issues as matters of right *v* wrong. I see them as matters of value. So, we simply have different values. We can discuss such things rather than getting bogged down in right *v* wrong.

I'm also not much interested in whether people are born one way or another. I think it's okay for people to choose their religion as well as they way they want to identify sexually. Their choice (if that's what it sometimes is) is not about me. Their behavior doesn't harm my family . . . such as it is (or is not). It has been going on forever even if it is currently topical in today's news.

Also, there are vast differences between "**rape, pedophilia, incest, sodomy, premarital sex, pornography, prostitution, infidelity, abortion, sadomasochism, bestiality, voyeurism, and exhibitionism.**" I don't see these instances as being close to equal to each other. Premarital sex is a far cry from incest; voyeurism is not to be equated with bestiality. But perhaps you think it's a matter of perspective or semantics, in much the same way you don't consider women's inability to vote as not being a matter of tradition.

Traditions have indeed in many ways made us who we are. Traditions such as segregation also once made people who they were and kept them that way. My crystal ball is on the fritz but we might have chosen, and we might yet choose, better traditions than others. Some traditions might serve us better. We may never know. Why? because I suspect that if you and I were to live forever, we will still see the same things from different points of view and, if we value perspective above all else, we will likely conclude differently forever. The only way past this is to understand the limits of ours perspectives and to try our hardest to see and relative value within other points of view, but few people value this reality.

SHARON: Thanks for the thoughtful response, especially, the familiar "on the fritz" which sounds like something Mom or Dad would have said. Also, "Nuh uh" in our family dictionary is a variant of what pigs say when you pull their tails I think the points of disagreement are worth exploring especially since you suggest that those differences are differences in "values". That seems unlikely to me since we were raised in the same family at roughly the same time, in the same community, among the same people, same education, etc. But, Paul, I don't want to annoy, bore, or alienate you, so I will wait for your okay before answering.

PAUL: You don't bore or annoy me. I doubt you'd alienate me. I don't take myself so seriously. The world is big and I am small. I'm not *right*, I just like to consider questions and ideas that interest me. Some ideas have too many negatives for me whereas some seem more positive, and I tend to embrace the positive.

It seems to me that many people judge things in a dualistic sense such as right *v* wrong or good *v* evil, but I view them on a sliding scale of value. That's mainly what I mean by value.

I've changed my religious and political views several times over the years. I view both from a much broader viewpoint now than I used to. And this is okay. Many people begin arguments from a place of trying to prove their righteousness (i.e. how correct they believe they are) but I'm more interested in looking at where ideas are the same, where they diverge and the implications of this divergence. It seems more productive. I sometimes learn more from asking questions than from stating my own viewpoint. But then again, trying to explain myself sometimes causes me to realize stuff about myself. I benefit either way, so carry on.

SHARON: You may not take yourself seriously, but you are definitely - serious. It is rare to find someone on *Facebook* who thinks and writes with deliberation. That quality makes you a good partner in serious conversation. Criticism of women's suffrage always evokes disbelief as if it is unthinkable, like foot-binding. In other words we have come to accept it without examination – without thinking. But isn't that what you deplore about those who cite "tradition" as a reason for doing something? If the absence of the female franchise was a "mistake from our past" then shouldn't we see in the last hundred years the good results from correcting that mistake? Shouldn't there be an improvement in our society, our morality, our governance, and at the very least an improvement in the lives of women? It might help to look at the Suffragettes of the early twentieth century to understand what they expected to accomplish with the vote. How do those issues of 1915 compare with women's issues of 2015? Why do you suppose there are not any specifically men's issues?

PAUL: Good morning Sharon!

First of all, I'm not against tradition or convention in all its forms. Language, for example is generally a convention, and language can be a helpful convention even if we do have to constantly revisit, rethink and reapply terms. Some are irritated by this process, calling it a form of *political correctness*. But the process of rectifying names is so foundational to language that the term political correctness seems silly (or huge) at the linguistic level. In the greater scheme of things it occurs within all languages at all times; it always has and always will.

I am a thoughtful person so I do value a process of rethinking above and beyond adhering to many sorts of *tradition*, even when my thoughts go up against convention. And convention sometimes varies from room to room let alone over broader geography and spans of time. I am also sure I have never even thought of some things, and when I do, I'm as sure to be surprised as I was the last time I regarded something in a new light.

Generally speaking I wouldn't judge the value of a decision such as suffrage based upon supposed results. I'm not much of a consequentialist when it comes to civil or human rights. This is partially because of a skepticism I have about our more common process of judgment. When I face south (perhaps I prefer the view), I tend to be ignorant of that which is north. Although this is natural, we ignore or deny its implications for our thought processes.

East and west are only peripheral but I can always, from time to time, turn my head and even turn all the way around and look. This not only happens with my sensual (a word used seemingly out of place, yet fitting; causing one to look twice:) perspective, the process occurs within my rational perspective too. My mental perspective seems to grow out of my sensual perspective but it is often more rigid. I surely prefer some viewpoints to others, in much the same way many people go so far as to call their preferences *true*. (Or perhaps my rational perspective grows out of language, but that may be an Eastern story rather than a Western one. Sorry, I've been studying ancient Chinese.) But there also exists a similar problem to both physical and rational viewpoint with regard to time. I will likely attempt to view any past and any future from my current perspective. My hope is that history will enlighten me, or that the future may benefit from any enlightenment, but too often these hopes are dashed from the outset due to a lack of regard for the value within other perspectives. Our ability to step outside of ourselves is so far outside of convention that the ability or attempt lacks any real regard for its value. So, without being able to rewind and replay through history, given different realities, we can't really *know* how things might be different for us now, we can only project. (And then we still only project our outlook from within our current and preferred viewpoints.) I call this the process of *belief* and our resulting preferences are a part of these beliefs. (Although my definition here is perhaps more conventional than the standard philosophical definition.) So even though I refer to likelihood, it seems that most of our regard for the past and projection into the future is so stuck within our preferred perspective that we become or remain ignorant, for the most part, of the value of these other perspectives.

Recently I got in touch with a libertarian friend of mine that I haven't seen in 25 years. He still views himself in a libertarian light but he is decidedly right-wing. I entered libertarian politics on the right-wing and exited more toward the left. Ironically, I happened to become interested in the idea of liberty whereas few others were. Recently I discussed this circumstance with him and he admitted that he saw, and still sees, our country as on the wrong path. I admitted that I saw the country on the wrong path 25 years ago but that I now see things (or paths) more optimistically (or at least differently). So not only do the *same things* seem to change when viewed from different angles, our attitudes seem to *cause* similar changes. Yet we mix up the *change* with the *view* with the *values* with the, blah, blah, blah.

I'm not well versed in the suffrage movement but I'm sure that women's particular issues have changed quite a bit while the basic issues remain. As far as men's issues are concerned, I can only tell you what I hear and how I hear it. I hear complaints from certain men about "men's issues" all the time. Men are concerned that their rights are being infringed upon by women and minorities from all directions. These men feel put upon. They have to watch their language. They have to watch their gaze. They believe they are supposed to be color blind. First they have to regard (or disregard) not only gender but then they have to regard how one *identifies*! They feel put out. Everything is so complicated for them. All of their feelings come about because they seem to have started having feelings similar to the real, legitimate feelings that women and minorities have had to live with for a long time. Yet these men do not seem close to the point of saying, "Oh, I see how you feel. I should watch myself and become enlightened." Instead, many double-down on their disdain for this political correctness. They do this while those others simply consider it to be common courtesy within society. But when you have the power, you can *impose*. When you feel powerless, you have to *deal with*. Right now these men seem to be saying that the tables are turning and it is not fair. They feel this way without realizing it they are just barely tasting the unfairness that others have been fed all their lives.

But to be fair, this is not only a men's issue. It is an issue for anybody who views such changes from another (likely their own, but perhaps of one of tradition or something else) perspective. Still, I came out of my libertarian education with a new feeling for all those who lacked the liberties that belong to those in the majority (or at least those with majoritarian power). I also came away with a different view of democracy and a reevaluation of human and civil rights.

So, yes, there are men's issues, and they aren't limited to men. But I specifically hear some men whine about their *loss* almost everyday. But men still have most of the power, natural, political or otherwise. I say they whine because they are constantly whining about all the whiners that seem to force them to whine. Perhaps these men should should grow up into a broader more temporal view. It makes me laugh and it makes me cry. But, hey, I'm a sensitive cuss :)

By the length of my responses, you can see why I don't have a twitter account.

SHARON: Is the point of "turning the tables" to make men more compassionate or is it just a method of disempowering them and making them contrite? Do they really need to be taught a lesson? By "they" I mean you, your father, grandfathers, uncles, nephews, and cousins? By the same token do you think your sisters, mother, grandmothers, aunts, nieces, and cousins were or are being oppressed? Whatever the original justification for giving women the vote, a hundred years later it is impossible to see that women's lives have improved.

Motherhood has been devalued as the nuclear family is coming apart. When "women's issues" have been reduced to abortion and birth control – and women are being used as a voting block in the Democratic coalition of Blacks, homosexuals, feminists, and immigrants you know that women's real interests are not being served. Grievance groups are assigned grievances by those who manipulate them for political advantage. That's how gay marriage became an issue – and that is why the Supreme Court decision will not satisfy them.

The manipulation has been going on much longer with Blacks. Slavery was not the worst problem for Africans; their ruination came from being transported away from the evolutionary home, their culture, and their kin. If you had dropped them off here as free men the ruination would have been worse. Lincoln vowed to return them to their native clime, but the manipulators could see their usefulness as a political cat's paw. When Marcus Garvey founded the UNIA with the slogan, "Africa for Africans" and bought ocean liners to transport Blacks back to Africa, he accumulated five million members worldwide. But the Jewish-run NAACP, wishing to use Blacks, destroyed the Black Star Line and worked to exile Marcus Garvey. The NAACP never had a Black leader until the mid-seventies – sixty years after its founding. Blacks are still being used and their real interests are irrelevant.

PAUL: I don't think there is a "point" to the turning of the tables except that tables do turn. Perhaps it just comes about when other people want the equal justice that comes from the desire of equal rights being enforced. Other than that, the pendulum probably just swings from one side to the other. And I don't know that anything like this is otherwise *managed* by any person or group. I don't see much evidence that these changes make men more or less compassionate. But it's hard to say from my limited perspective. But I don't think this is necessarily the point. Like I said before, I'm not interested in some specific results or micro-managing consequences. I'm more interested in the process rather than talking points. Some men might learn new ways to think and act but many people refuse to be taught; whether they are me, my father, grandfathers, uncles, nephews, and cousins.

But all of this admits that men with power have withheld rights. And since then they have begrudgingly bestowed them. And so, yes, our sisters, mother, grandmothers, aunts, nieces, and cousins were all being oppressed if they wanted to have the voice that a vote might provide, but I personally don't know how each felt. Like today, there will always be some who might prefer not having rights (perhaps because of the responsibility that comes along with them). But the fact is that white men have generally held the power that is now being dispersed.

"Whatever the original justification for giving women the vote, a hundred years later it is impossible to see that women's lives have improved."

Impossible? Some might call the ability to vote, to own property, and to have legal recourse for an abusive husband as improvement. Some people appear to gain while some appear to lose some quality of life. For some people, their perceived loss is more important to them than someone else's gain (of rights they had previously been denied). Had I for some reason (be it my sex, skin color, country of origin, or even native American origin, civil status, etc) not been allowed the right to vote, the fact that I might attain this right shouldn't be dependent upon how someone else might imagine the consequences for them that might or might not arise from a civil right.

I don't devalue motherhood. But I think it might be argued that men have long devalued motherhood more than women have. The talk about abortion and birth control is typically placed upon women. What about fatherhood? Men have notoriously refused responsibility for their part in this dance. Men not only have the physical power to refuse responsibility, they have the political power too. As it is, men even blame women when women want to take responsibility to take for these *women's issues* into their own hands.

Whether I am, or you are, being *manipulated* for political advantage, doesn't make any difference to me. Evidently I have no control over it. I may simply be a puppet. All I can say is *there it is* if it is there at all. The very idea that we can manipulate someone or some group presupposes that there is something lacking that can therefore be manipulated. What do *we* or *they* lack? brains? power? rights? At best, focusing on ideas such as manipulation distract us from the prior condition. When manipulation becomes the focus, we come to view manipulation as the real problem and so we tend to ignore the prior condition. But we know there was a prior condition because it is part of history. Isn't it possible that the desire for gay marriage became an issue because homosexuals wanted to have the right to marry so they could have and participate in all that goes along with that institution. Yes, this is a possibility regardless of distractions like manipulation.

"If you had dropped them [Blacks] off here as free men the ruination would have been worse."

???

Once again, your crystal ball works better than mine. Of course how would I know what *the blacks* are really interested in or even what their relevant issues are? But my guess is that black people, homosexuals, immigrants, and feminists are quite like me. Human. But perhaps I'm simply being manipulated and I have not really considered or reconsidered these ideas at all. But unless I am allowed to have my own thoughts instead of having them devalued as manipulations, I'm redundant in this discussion. This argument will keep going around in a circle with or without me even being involved. Or perhaps I am fine here but it is *they* who lack something. What is it they lack?

It is a problem to presume the answers before the fact. But it is worse to presume the questions. Such a stance disallows the real intentions of others. So this says more about the devaluer than the devaluee because the devaluee (I'm making up new words for you) hasn't been allowed a fair hearing. Their humanity has been denied at the outset.

JB chimes in: Good points all. I submit also that many modern riots and "protest movements" are the language of monkey-wrenchers. A quick search for George Soros yields a lot of information about this guy's involvements in trying to re-shape the American political and social landscape. The last two general elections, Occupy, Ferguson, Baltimore all have his confirmed fingerprints all over them, he's been very effective. Next understand the principles laid down in Saul Alinsky's "Rules For Radicals", one of which is that you cannot replace an existing political system with another until the old system has been destroyed and a void exists. He recommends crashing existing systems by overloading the very elements that it's comprised of (law-enforcement and courts, social welfare systems, etc), then letting chaos reign freely for a while. In the end, the sheeple will welcome literally any new system that brings order back to their lives, to include communism. It should be noted that our POTUS - as an adjunct professor taught Alinskian theory, was raised and mentored by communists and stocked his cabinet with communist appointees. Of course, who am I to say?

PAUL: Hi JB. I too will admit to and accept a certain amount of monkey-wrenching but something has to spark a situation before it can be wrenched. One might even be able to say that talk about Soros is the real conspiracy that detracts us from the reality of what's really happening behind the scenes. Many people seem to want us to ignore the facts (or distract us from the facts) of each case that may have sparked the protests. Can't we look at the deaths and circumstances behind each one without veiling them with real or imagined conspiracy? What might happen if we dared consider our police and our culture as having basic long standing problems that are much more difficult to address?

People protest the war in the 60's and things turn violent. There might have been a Soros back then but I think this would happen were there no Soros' in the world. People protested for their civil rights and were beaten. Sometimes people get tired of being beaten and finally fight back. There are some folks who believe that self-defense is not only a right but a responsibility (such as so named

Stand Your Ground laws), that is unless it's someone or group we want to identify as *bad* or as a terrorist (MalcolmX?). Then we are apt to say that it was *they* who really started the violence. If *they* had done nothing, some people might call them weak, or accuse them of simply being communists (Martin Luther King Jr.?). Or perhaps those other terrorists (KKK) or the white political majority (*Citizen's Councils*) who would not allow lawful integration. Terrorists all?

I read the Communist Manifesto. It didn't make me communist. I might come to understand it well enough to teach classes on the topic but this won't make me a communist or president. Yet if I were to teach it I would be considered a *left-wing agitator*. Yet in the teaching of communism, perhaps people will learn how ludicrous two thirds of the book is.

BTW, I disagree with Alinsky. We can tear down a system, but since we are the same people who built the first system, the same essential system (or a reaction to it) will replace it because we can't build something we don't know. And if we knew it, we might have changed it more thoughtfully and deliberately. Yet most of us may only know our own *systems* and our reactions. People theorize this is why Nixon was elected: law and order. Well, we got Nixon. But my look into Alinsky does not make me agree with him; just aware of him; as are you.

So how do we keep the electorate from voting in Communism? Education? As long as it is not public education? I know those pesky *communists* won't call Communism "communist". The term is too closely associated with atheism anyway. And people say they would vote for a felon (I think it was . . . I don't remember really :) before they would vote for an atheist. But these communists might simply masquerade as socialists; same thing really, according to the folks I talk with. In fact, Democrats are simply socialists. So, as i t *is*, Obama and his closest relations are all communists. Or, maybe labels are big problem. Us against them, black *v* white, right *v* left. It is easy to manipulate, easy to control, and it is enticing.

I guess it could also be that people concerned more about the well being of a culture or society or community, many churches for that matter, can be labeled communistic. Who does this leave us with? libertarians? anarchists? Rugged individualists like those who founded our country and made the Shay's Rebellion and the

Boston Tea party possible. Wait, those were terrorist actions; or were they riots?

This is getting complicated.

JB: LOL - yep, it is. You make your points nicely; you really should consider writing a book or two. ;) Wasn't it you that told me back in the day that "a communist is really just a socialist in a hurry"? I guess I'm to the point in life that I can no longer take "stuff" at face value so I look for cause and effect. When I see where something is headed, it's easy to look back on it and while recalling where #it# came from and who the players are, what they've stated, what their record of prior actions looks like and see what their basic ethos looks like, I can make a pretty accurate estimation of how it will end. I tend to look at things through the lens of vigilance more than anything else. Following things closely gives us the opportunity to stay a step ahead, when necessary. In light of the fact that the ideology I tend to dispise the most claimed roughly 100 million lives world-wide during the 20th century, I tend to watch people very closely, and trust very few. There's too many that walk and act like ducks these days, and too few among us that recognize them for being what they are.

PAUL: JB, you said, "Wasn't it you that told me back in the day that 'a communist is really just a socialist in a hurry'?"

I don't think I can claim that one, but it's funny :)

It seems to me that the practical problem with looking for cause and effect is that we all look from our own point of view, and we tend only to the direction in which we face. We want objectivity but we are subjects with viewpoints. Luckily there are ways around this practical problem. This involves devaluing your personal perspective so that you can learn to value others. There are so many ideologies besides communism (as bad as it *has* manifested itself over time) to concern ourselves with. I find many people more complicated that I once narrowed them down to be. Since I suspect this is not unique, it might be far reaching error. For example, I could think of you as a right-wing conspiratorialist. I could put you in that box. Would you fit? Sometimes, maybe, but I bet you're more complicated than such labels.

Like you, I watch people carefully but I tend to trust most. By far most. I've been let down so seldom that either my judgments have been better than yours on the outset or perhaps the viewpoints that led to my judgments have been more vast. (Of course there could be many other options, but these are a few that strike me at the moment).

It strikes me as ironic that I had to become a libertarian in order to learn to value concerns beyond my own freedom and/or the so-cial clique that supports me. As I began learning about liberty, somehow, naturally, I started to look toward potential and I slowly became more positive. My values began change and, to my surprise, I steadily became more liberal; more in the classical liberal tradition than our current version of liberalism in the US. While studying the liberalism that led to the birth of the United States, it began to strike me, as it still does today, how odd it was that I had once assumed the foundations for our American traditions were somehow conservative or even right-wing when many of our lib-eral founders fought against conservative British tradition. Now, our previous liberalism has generally given way to conservatism. Conservatives have a tendency to devalue human rights in favor of higher security, all the while quoting Jefferson and Franklin, in or-der to chide the right-wingers and liberals who might agree. Many people are still working to keep the union (through our value of it) despite our differences. This is a social thing, not an individual thing. We can keep looking for and stressing our differences or we can do the opposite. When we put our individualism (and the un-mistakable viewpoint that goes with it) before the diverse society we all share, we can't help lose sight of social value. We all see the same . . . but can I just see a better future than you?

JB: I guess you just see a better future, my friend. My point in addressing your original post was just that things aren't always what they appear to be. Is it a riot made up of people sick of being kicked around by the establishment? Or is it an opportunity for a fervent America-hater to play his games? Maybe both? No answer necessary, it was just food for thought. Your judgements are what they are - just like mine are what they are. They're conditioned responses based on the hands that life has dealt us, how we played those hands and the paths we've walked. Mine has been far from charmed. Life has put me up-close and personal with too many vampires and parasites for too long to have a view any different. If a person has my trust, it's because they earned it.

PAUL: I'd agree, JB, that things aren't always what or how they appear. We can look for cause and effect only to find something that isn't there. Appearances can be deceiving, and in fact they usually are; on both *sides*. But once we understand this, it doesn't mean things are *bad* because of this, they are just a bit problematic. We should then work on *how* we see. It seems to be part of my responsibility and perhaps morality.

"Is it a riot made up of people sick of being kicked around by the establishment? Or is it an opportunity for a fervent America-hater to play his games?"

Rhetorical or not, I'll respond anyway by saying I've heard these same claims made by those suspicious about civil rights and anti-war movements. As one who supports civil rights and wasn't a fan of the Vietnam war, perhaps some America hater is leading me around by the nose, or perhaps my concerns are genuine as are many others who share my concerns. But our choice of who to believe and how to look at these protests may say more about our selves than any broader or truer view. I for one prefer a broader view to my own narrow view anyway. This is how I learn new stuff.

Perhaps my ideas might be dismissed as naively optimistic, but when I try to speak honestly of my own experiences within life, I might be considered by some to either be a flagrant liar or simply someone who you cannot imagine having such experiences. I would submit that either of these responses says more about the one observing than it does the one observed.

This is not to say that I think human beings are, by their nature, good. Humans are human. Some are humane, some devalue many tendencies toward humaneness and humanity. I do think that humans are, and human nature is, essentially social. Some introverts like me are much less sociable than others, yet even as an introvert, I can see what others value more than what I myself value, therefore I can value their value for what value it has. And since we are born into some sort of family and dependent upon some society for a very long time, the idea that individual freedom preceding social responsibility strikes be as odd if not backward. My conditioned responses are somewhat different. I've reconditioned them :)

JB:
"The line it is drawn
The curse it is cast
The slow one now
Will later be fast
As the present now
Will later be past
The order is rapidly fadin'
And the first one now
Will later be last
For the times they are a-changin'"
Bob Dylan

PAUL:
". . . All the people we used to know
They're an illusion to me now
Some are mathematicians
Some are carpenters' wives
Don't know how it all got started
I don't know what they're doin' with their lives
But me, I'm still on the road
Headin' for another joint
We always did feel the same
We just saw it from a different point
Of view
Tangled up in blue."
Bob Dylan

SHARON: Pendulums swing back and forth at regular intervals, but what you call "turning the tables" can't be seen as a role reversal that occurs periodically. As satisfying as it might be to anticipate a time when the "first shall be last and the last shall be first" it remains a fantasy of heavenly retribution. Nature is the critical element that is missing in political programs designed to remedy inequality. Male and female are biological complements whose quintessential function is successful reproduction. They are not the same; they are not equal; they are not antagonists or competitors. A political program that undercuts nature – as represented by successful reproduction, the stable nuclear family, and high investment child rearing – is dehumanizing. The evolution of the European peoples has given us the nuclear family, monogamy, and the high status of women. The last hundred years has seen a steady erosion of our most basic human values to the point that the fertility rate in every European country is below replacement level. Millions of healthy women have been denatured and have traded fulfillment for rather dubious "rights" of voting, abortion and birth control. I think this ruination has been imposed upon us because suicide in antithetical to survival.

Back to my reply to Sharon. I wasn't sure if she had been following along with JB's comments . . .
PAUL: By pointing to a pendulum swing, I simply meant a single motion. An idea might swing in one direction only to find it has exceeded its value and swings back. Not my best analogy but you didn't like "tables turning" either. Like a knife, analogies may cut both ways :) We can argue their value or we can accept what others intended by way of analogy and further explanation.

"As satisfying as it might be to anticipate a time when the 'first shall be last and the last shall be first' it remains a fantasy of heavenly retribution."

An acquaintance of mine recently quoted that Dylan lyric bit to me. I not sure he was talking about heaven; perhaps he was just noting how the pendulum swings back. Maybe that's why the analogy came to me. Either way, I'm not a necessarily a believer in heaven nor do I value retribution. I'm not a believer in equality (people are not equal) but I think government is charged with the task of trying to trying to be sure that all people have their rights protected equally. Since this is *all people*, it assumes an equality of protection; generally protection from those who have *natural* power as does the majority at a given time. The majority can bully and restrict the prospects of those weaker. Sometimes those weaker have less physical strength or some physical malady. Sometimes they have less mental capacity or a capacity (let's say artistic) that is different from a capacity required that might be employed in protecting themselves for those with more cunning attributes. A system of justice should give such natural concerns a fair hearing. If law didn't allow for difference, the value that those others might contribute might be suppressed or effectively taken away by the majority. This process may not be seen as natural to some unless you back up to a different definition of nature; *the nature of prior value*. (I just made-up that phrase; kinda sounds uppity European or something:) To recognize that our discriminations tend to be self serving and inherently ignorant of greater value is natural. The *greater value* is what naturally exists prior to our picking and choosing from it; our discriminations.

I, myself fail. I do not obtain biologically. I've been unsuccessful at reproduction. I've been chastised for it and held in contempt. Sometimes confusion or pity toward me seems to be the order of the day. Perhaps I'm inept, definitely unequal; not even equal to other men although I don't compete or claim my own righteousness. I've undercut nature – as represented by successful reproduction – I am less than human, less than natural, I'm dehumanized by others, though not by nature. Nature does not not speak; others merely speak or misspeak in its place. I've known others that have been beaten and killed; dehumanized by other humans perhaps in the name of nature. People like us require equal governmental consideration and protection. This should be a social and filial value not to be eroded, let alone dehumanized.

The evolution of all peoples, not just the Europeans, have given us families. And this evolution began long before the idea of codified marriage. Overall, world population has grown and still increases. Perhaps for Europeans, at the moment, growth has flattened or reversed but that may be because they see over population as a problem and have made natural, more responsible decisions. I know I've witnessed the problem and made my decisions, natural or not. Perhaps others don't see the problems. Perhaps they are the ones being most natural. Either way, replacement levels fluctuate from time to time and from region to region. It's okay.

I too, as a healthy man have been denatured; perhaps duped. (But I think I have reasonable arguments either way. I always invite more thoughts on these subjects.) As one who seems to have gone against nature, I'm immoral, if somehow *nature* equates to, or is somehow on par with, morality. Either way, my dubious rights have been exercised and government protects me. I still survive and it appears that other people, natural or not, are doing a fine job of procreating in my absence.

Weeks later
PAUL: Are you still out there Sharon?

SHARON: Yes, I am still here. I must apologize for not getting back to you sooner, but I have to do a lot of thinking before writing and I often get sidetracked with reading. Hank gave me a Kindle for Mother's Day and it makes reading a lot easier. I found a website that has a great many out-of-print books. I found a critique of women's suffrage in the U.S. that was written before 1920 and a book by Anthony Ludovici, Lysistrata. I read Ludovici's book, The Enemies of Women about 15 years ago and that has been important in my view of women and feminism. I have written an answer but it seems a little disjointed so I need a little more time to clean it up. Pearl onions are distracting, too. *(A reference to a* Facebook *post by our sister Jan.)*

What follows are my thoughts about a political quote that was superimposed over a picture of Albert Einstein that was attributed to Einstein but in fact couldn't be attributable to Einstein. I also comment on another post that stated assumptions and prejudices as truths.
PAUL: We find things to post. We seldom give a thought to whether they are accurate or not. Perhaps since we agree with them they might as well be true. We often pass them along without

thought, even though we have a powerful tool at our fingertips, at that moment, to research their supposed validity as well as the complications of the arguments. Yet without thought many of us repeat that which might be untrue. But the fact that we so strongly agree with its sentiments seems to overrule any search for, or value of, the accuracy. It is our choices that reveal our greater values. Rather than accuracy, we merely value our beliefs.

I recently saw a post showing a plane flying into the twin towers. The caption asked how we (Americans?) went from *this* to concerning ourselves with anything that might offend Muslims.

Is the presumption here that we can rightly (and should) offend people we deem guilty, regardless of obvious inaccuracy? Isn't this mindset at least partially what the terrorists may themselves had in mind while making their own decisions? Are we now somehow *right* in sharing these values with them?

How do I know that this post is obviously inaccurate? Since men did this, would we or should we then blame all men? Or should we narrow it to the country they were from? Their city, their family? Should we consider their genealogy and/or religious affiliation? For that matter, should we blame all Christians for the acts of a few fundamentalist Christian terrorists?

Perhaps we should simply hold certain terrorists responsible for their own acts of terror. But first, we should act upon what is clear: we should take responsibility for ourselves and our beliefs. We should take responsibility for what values our beliefs intend as well as imply. If not, we are simply passing along propaganda.

SHARON: Those who benefit from conflict and war rely on our gullibility to generate sufficient hatred and fear to justify everything from sanctions and invasion to torture and genocide. "Truth" is hard to come by when media propaganda is given the imprimatur of the President of the United States. Truth-seekers and skeptics are subjected to mockery and vilification so the desired conflict can escalate unimpeded. "Cui bono?" - "Who benefits?" is the first question to ask in our search for the truth.

PAUL: Who benefits from a society's belief in conspiracy theories?

SHARON: It depends on the particular theory. The theory that 19 Muslims armed with box cutters, directed from a cave in Afghanistan, simultaneously hijacked four commercial airliners flying them into the WTC, the Pentagon, and a field in Pennsylvania - because "They hate our freedom" - served to justify a conflict between the West and Islam - so the question is, "Who benefits from that contrived conflict?" The term "conspiracy theory" is used to discredit disbelief. independent inquiry. and investigation.

PAUL: So, a silly conspiracy theory served to justify the true conspiracy? The true conspiracy being that which was promulgated by a Bush/Halliburton alliance in order to insure the availability of oil (benefit) from the region?

SHARON: It was a "silly" theory that the Obama Administration, both parties, and both houses of Congress have accepted and promoted. The conspiracy is much wider than Bush/Haliburton and oil is a peripheral "benefit" if not merely a pretext for war.

PAUL: I'm trying to break this down.

1) Do you think that the theory of "19 Muslims armed with box cutters, directed from a cave in Afghanistan, simultaneously hijacked four commercial airliners flying them into the WTC, the Pentagon, and a field in Pennsylvania" because "They hate our freedom," is a silly theory?

2) Silly or not, is this "the theory that the Obama Administration, both parties, and both houses of Congress have accepted and promoted?"

SHARON: Yes. Have you heard any objections to any aspect of that theory coming from any government or party official?

PAUL: No. I think I'm tracking now.

So, setting aside peripheral pretexts, what is the overall benefit

of the war?
Who is the overall beneficiary?
Who is directing this conspiracy?
And just what is the much wider conspiracy?

SHARON: The "wider" conspiracy requires the acquiescence of both Bush and Obama and their respective administrations, both houses of Congress, and both political parties. It requires a controlled media, and an unquestioning posture among our allies. Accepting these propositions causes an abrupt halt to thought in most people, even among serious investigators. Why do you think that is?

PAUL: Why? Because I can't even get 7 people in our home owners association to agree upon or acquiesce on anything so it's terribly unlikely that more people, with such varied interests, would do so (as a matter of conspiracy anyway).

SHARON: As unlikely as it seems for so many with such varied interests to acquiesce to the official 9/11 tale – that is exactly what we have seen in the past 13+ years. It is that unlikelihood that must be explained. Is it merely coincidence? gullibility? belief? allegiance? fear? conspiracy? What drives 535 members of Congress to accept this preposterous tale and all its bloody consequences? The only time I have seen all the members of Congress agree on anything was in 2010 when they gave "His Excellency" Benjamin Netanyahu 29 standing ovations. That unanimity bears examination, as well.

PAUL: So, I'll ask again: What do you think?
Who is the overall beneficiary of these wars?
Who is the overall beneficiary of such acquiesce?
Who is directing this conspiracy?
Or, is the question, just who are we acquiescing to?

No reply.

After some time off, it seems Sharon is now on to a previous/an-

other topic . . .

SHARON: Government, law, and language are cultural products of unique peoples. There is no universal language, or law, or government. These cultural products are inextricably linked to racial character and have developed within the strictures of physical and social environments. Government and law are codifications of the practices and rules that have promoted group survival. That said, I think it is presumptuous for Westerners to assert the existence of a universal morality based on a common "humanity".

All that is to say that the world's people have followed different evolutionary paths. The concept of moral universalism is uniquely European probably because the salient character of European man is expansive, far-reaching, ever moving outward and working to overcome obstacles to that expansiveness. The Achilles' heel of this "Faustian" spirit is universalism which is inclusive and projects on others whose character and culture are not only exclusive and foreign, but are often fragile, confounded, and obdurate. When Jefferson wrote the Declaration of Independence asserting that "all men are created equal..." he may have been projecting a poetic sense of universal humanity, but either he did not really mean "all men" or he did not consider Negroes to be men. It could not be said that he meant to include women, other nationalities, sexual deviants, or the disabled. He used the language of universalism but his declaration was specific to the particular conflict.

For the last hundred fifty years an appeal to moral universalism has been used to pass judgment on the social and legal constructs of Western man – but only Western man. Racial/cultural homogeneity that is tolerated in Nepal, Japan, and Senegal is judged to be intolerable in all Western countries. The Japanese are not asked to provide a "better life" to Latin Americans, Syrians, or Somalis but the Swedes are. Japanese are not considered "uppity" when they express pride in their culture and wish to maintain racial/cultural homogeneity. It would be a grievous loss for the world for the Japanese to lose their racial and cultural character by flooding Japan with immigrants demanding citizenship, equal

rights, and even the right to maintain their own cultural integrity. (which requires effective segregation – another practice that is encouraged for others, but scorned when Europeans do it. You speak of "higher values" as if the traditions
of the West ignore or resist such values, but haven't the accomplishments of Western Civilization been fostered by the
traditions and values that you find lacking?

Charles Murray writes that 97% of the accomplishments in
the sciences occurred in Europe and North America from
800 B.C. to 1950. He also writes that, in the Arts, Europe
alone produced a far higher number of "significant figures"
than the rest of the world combined. In music, "the lack of a
tradition of named composers in non-Western civilization
means that the Western total of 522 significant figures has
no real competition at all". For the greater part of that time
period women did not vote, Africans lived in Africa, Asians in
Asia, and the nations of Europe were based on racial/ethnic
homogeneity rather than civic nationalism in which citizens
are identified by their rights. The Oaxacans, Mexicans, Fil-
ipinos, and Central Americans outnumber white people in
our town; they have large families and they have the right to
education, medical care, adequate food and shelter, and
many of them have the right to vote. Will this diversity bring
about some "higher value" – a better civilization than the one
we seem to have abandoned?

PAUL: It seems like much of this is water under the bridge. The
Europeans who expanded into the Americas should have known
better and stayed home and not come and mix with the cultures native to the Americans, but they did. For a couple hundred years the
US has been considered a melting pot. Has our culture ever been
one of, "these cultural products . . . inextricably linked to
racial character . . . within the strictures of physical and social environments?" If so, which race? Which stricture? Which
social environment? The peoples of the Americas been intermingling for hundreds of years. And those whose peoples which
haven't desired to intermingle have certainly been "obstacles" to
"overcome" by European "expansiveness". But if group survival is
the aim then the United States is surviving quite well; even as

mixed as it is.

Though our laws are generally European based, it is "presumptuous for Westerners to assert the existence of a universal morality based on a common 'humanity'." Perhaps the thought was handy and they appropriated this idea " 仁 " (humanity) from the ancient Chinese as well as concepts from many other cultures, before *European* was a word. And we might go back further but prehistory gets sketchy. We might go back 50,000 years and regret the Homo sapien intermingling with the Neanderthal. Perhaps they should have known better. More water under the bridge.

It is true that our "different evolutionary paths" have certainly crossed a lot over many thousands of years. And I'm not sure people are all that different although people's cultures often make it seem so. But various cultures tend to blend quite quickly given a healthy environment to do so. Still, with all these errors of thought, perhaps it is the European (Western) spirit that is fragile, confounded, and obdurate. Or perhaps "spirit" has nothing to do with it. Perhaps it is human viewpoint that is fragile, confounded, and obdurate. Perhaps inferiors such as Jefferson are inferior due to their lack of "universalism". Perhaps they are too cloistered within what they view to be *their own* culture. After all, biology not culture, tells us that Negroes are men as well as human; as are "women, other nationalities, sexual deviants, and the disabled." Perhaps *others* who assimilate into culture teach culture something important. Or perhaps we should follow the example of the Chinese: build a wall like the wall dividing Germany; the Israeli wall; the Hungarian fences being built. Perhaps Americans should build a wall between us and Canada and we can follow their cultural lead. Perhaps the idea of "racial/cultural homogeneity" should not be tolerated by any culture. It has been said that evolution requires diversity. Perhaps a lack of diversity is what is dumbing (European) cultures down. I don't think I speak of "higher values", I speak of broader values. Perhaps the accomplishments of Western Civilization has indeed been fostered by the values that I find expanding.

Like Charles Murray, I too can quote statistics from the European viewpoint while those in Eastern cultures can speak of their great art, most of which that I've never heard of within my culture.

Perhaps their artistic contributions are as perspectival for them as ours are to us. It sounds very likely. Perhaps rather than "civic nationalism in which citizens are identified by their rights," we can move toward a more inclusive civil society identified by broader human rights. Perhaps immigrants cloister themselves together not only due to commonality but also in defense or fear of exclusive attitudes of those in the majority they come in contact with.

Soon all of us *whites,* no matter how mixed-up we might really be, will be in the minority and then we will have to learn what all the mixed folks had to learn. We may begin to grow up just as they have grown up.

So, here we are, "Will this diversity bring about some 'higher value' – a better civilization than the one we seem to have abandoned?"

This is a better question than the ones you've asked before. Since my crystal ball is still on the fritz, I think an even better *water under the bridge* question might be, *where do we go from here?* Should we, will we, preach our superiority while *they* take over? Will we admit that perhaps those other people have shown themselves to be superior to us by way of this *take over?* Or do we admit that we are superior yet have failed anyway? What do we do now? Do we build walls, deport, imprison, attempt genocide? Do we try to accept reality as it is and work together toward an even more inclusive common culture? One that is more embracing rather than exclusive? Even if this new culture too will fail like many other cultures and species have before us? Will we go down and take everybody *else* with us or try something new (or old perhaps)?

Some context for my remark about Jefferson: It is too easy to look at the founding fathers as hypocrites. It is also too easy to give them a pass for being men of their times. They were very educated, well versed in freedom and liberty yet they were slave owners. Either way, they seem to have set up a government that allows government as well as its citizens to grow past itself/themselves/ourselves; assuming we tend to regard the idea of equal rights and equal justice more broadly than they did during their own times.

A few weeks later:

SHARON: If you subscribe to the out-of-Africa theory then the entire world outside Africa is peopled by immigrants. So-called "Native Americans" are said to be from Asia, though there is a body of research that supports an even earlier settlement of the Atlantic seaboard by European/Middle Eastern migration. The concept of the United States as a "melting pot" was first promoted by Israel Zangwill whose 1913 play by that name was concerned primarily with Jewish/Gentile intermarriage that was anathema to traditional Jews. It wasn't until the mid- nineteenth century that immigrants from Eastern Europe began to arrive in the U.S. For the previous 250 years European immigration had been largely Northern European led by the British, Scots-Irish, Dutch, Scandinavians, Germans, and to a lesser extent, France, Italy, Spain, Portugal and Greece. An amalgam of Europeans doesn't qualify as a racial melting pot and their cultural differences were negligible compared to the racial/cultural differences between Europeans, Asians, Africans, and the Native tribes of Australia, New Zealand, and the Americas. There was very little mixing of English settlers with Natives, probably because they came as families, unlike the Spanish and Portuguese who were conquistadors – without their women.

In 1950 the U.S. was 89.5% white. It was an amalgam of European cultures – all of which had developed on the European continent over thousands of years. It is significant that Northern Europeans tended to settle in environments that were very much like the ones they left – undoubtedly because they had a long history of physical and cultural adaptation to the North.

The races of mankind represent the fact that for many thousands of years people have practiced a high degree of racial exclusivity. Some of that exclusivity is reinforced by isolation, but much of it is not. For example, the San people, or Bushmen of Africa have lived side by side with the Congoid race and yet they are racially distinct. I doubt either group has laws against miscegenation but the natural tendency for in-group breeding is demonstrably strong.

You put high value on learning from other cultures, but

38

isn't that because you are a European? Who else in the world thinks they might learn something from the Inuit, the Bantu, the Chinese, or the Tibetans? Who have been the explorers, the anthropologists, archeologists and paleontologists? And who else on earth thinks in terms of moral universalism?

A people depends for its survival upon racial/cultural integrity. We have seen the result of assaults on that integrity, often by well-meaning people from outside who have little understanding of what's at stake.

Do you really believe that when non-whites take over Germany and Germans stop reproducing that the Turks, Syrians, and Africans will have any appreciation or understanding of the high culture of that people? Is musical genius evenly distributed throughout the human race and poverty the only thing impeding its expression? I worry more about Europe than its far-flung extensions, and while guilt over slavery is used to make Americans contrite and accepting of being invaded by Africans, Mexicans, Asians, and Middle Easterners one has to wonder what the Swedes, Norwegians, Danes, and Irish have to feel guilty about. Is it just that they are white? Do you feel guilty about being a mix of Scots, English, German, Swedish, Danish, and Icelandic?

PAUL: I don't mind being a mix of Scots, English, German, Swedish, Danish, and Icelandic people. If there is some African, Mexican and Chinese thrown into the mix that's still okay with me. Neither of us has taken a DNA test so we don't know; we only know what we've gleaned from others of what their kin claim about their own history. I tend to assume that many people within the Scots, English, German, Swedish, Danish, and Icelandic groups didn't like the idea of mixing with the other groups when it occurred (except maybe the mixers, although mixing also occurs out of the rapes of war and triumph). Over time, some people have seen that this mixing has been beneficial to the larger group. Generally, however, our dislike of mixing has probably always been with us as well. There are always reasons, but the reasons we prefer are always based upon our concept of good *v* bad. Our ability to focus upon the value of exclusivity (good?) is to mis-focus because *good* can never be exclusive of *bad*. These terms can only be realized in relation to each other. Dreams of cultural purity, even within similar cultures (Scots, English, German, Swedish, Danish, and Icelandic) is a fantasy but our exclusive views tend to keep us ignorant of this. Our ability to dislike *others* is as natural (and negative) as our distinctions of right from wrong; we invent these distinctions in accord with other things we value. Exclusivity is a prevalent desire for many people, whiteness, blackness, cultural, etc. So I simply think exclusivity is at least as harmful as it is valuable.

I don't feel guilty about slavery but it was wrong and everybody should recognize why. I generally don't mind people clanning up into their clans as long as laws protect all people equally. But there are practical problems that come of clan discrimination. Some groups my see incest (the closer held the family, or culture, the more likely it is practiced and accepted), rape (including statutory) or genital mutilation (male as well as female) as allowable under their culture/religion/race (or under the guise of each). Other groups may see wars, proxy or not, as acceptable. Others may regard democracy as survival of the fittest as best. Others may see overall human rights as more proper. Various cultures will disagree about any such rule. We don't even have to change cultures to find all of these conflicts within *our white culture*; or conflicts of religion to religion, state to state, time period to time period.

So the problem still is, what do we do? I tend to prefer rock & roll, blues, soul and jazz, whereas you prefer European classical music. I see influences crossing back and forth, and I see these crossovers as nice. I don't think the *idea of race* is the point at all. I don't see cultural issues as a greater problem for us than every other human distinction. All distinction arises from the same source and so distinctions can be helpful as well as harmful.

I regard human moral development to be in its infancy. If we can keep it going long enough, maybe we will be able to develop it, but I doubt tighter segregation can ever solve our ills. I think we have to go the other way. You and I disagree on very basic issues. You and I see the same things differently. We value different things while trying to achieve something better. Yet we are of the same family, state, nation, culture, race. So *race* is not the real issue when it comes to harmonious culture. I don't think there is a devil

40

here, nor am I brainwashed any more than you are. I don't think we have an inability to reason, yet here we are.

PAUL: Oh, I almost forgot to reply to this: "Do you really believe that when non-whites take over Germany and Germans stop reproducing that the Turks, Syrians, and Africans will have any appreciation or understanding of the high culture of that people?"

As far as non-whites *taking over* Germany, this will not happen anytime soon. Unless you consider the non-majority status of other groups growing into a majority as being equivalent with that of being *taken over*. Countries do change majorities from time to time. They also take over each other from time to time and genocide often ensues. I would hope that countries will learn to *assimilate* better.

And I do think the Turks, Syrians, and Africans likely have less appreciation and understanding of the "high culture" of the German people than do the Germans themselves. Just like you and me, Turks, Syrians, and Africans are likely be more appreciative of their own cultural contributions. Diverse peoples are remarkably similar in this sense.

Sharon writes to tell me that while she gathers her thoughts for a reply, here is a link to an article entitled Thoughts on the German Dispossession *via* TheOccidentalObserver.net
PAUL: Sorry, I can read an article by someone else but it doesn't tell me what you think in your own words. Does your interest in whiteness and its culture assume your value of a standard that you wish to return to, create or recreate? Was there once a standard bearing culture that was pure, or somehow became pure-ish enough over thousands of years that, in this process, the culture was able to attain great heights, somehow without much interference? Would this be correct? If so, I am interested in how the *somehows* of all of this that keep getting glossed over.

SHARON: I suggested the article because it describes what is happening in Germany – something that you believe "will not happen anytime soon": Native Germans have the lowest birth rate in the world having dropped behind Japan to earn that distinction and indigenous Germans are expected to be a minority in Germany within the next thirty-five years, if not sooner – the estimate was made 15 years ago. As recently as 1970 California was 80% white and in the 2010 census it had fallen to 39%. It can happen very fast. We moved here in 1977. The grade school a half a block away was at least 80% white and that same school today is 90% non-white and I wouldn't send my children there. That said, I will return to my reply and include your latest questions.

Before I could reply:

SHARON: Race-mixing has been most commonly associated with rape, slavery, war, conquest, and colonialism - all socially destructive activities and it is clear from the long-term homogeneity of racial groups that the protection of the fertile female has been paramount in maintaining homogeneity. The criminalization of rape, the codification of marriage, the punishment of female infidelity, and the ostracism against mixed offspring are probably universal methods of ensuring homogeneity. There are passive methods as well in which cultural differences create barriers – language, education, religion, class, concern for offspring, and negative genetic consequences.

The latest socially destructive program is massive Third World immigration into Europe, the U.S., Canada, Australia, and New Zealand. It is totally artificial and is harmful to both the settled European cultures and to the newcomers. To view positively this tumultuous invasion of people "looking for a better life", one must discount the value of the settled, homogeneous cultures that immigrants are leaving behind. That oversight alludes to what I was saying about the presumptuousness of moral universalism. The concept of universal human rights is European – not African, not Middle Eastern, not Chinese. Even the understanding of the geography of the world and the discovery of remote human types is European. Most of the world's people have no word for "freedom", and only Europe had the philosophical and political development that produced what we call universal human rights. Even though we might judge moral universalism to be altruistic and therefore noble, it remains a Western imposition on other peoples who have no basis for understanding it. It isn't theirs and at best it is translated into material goods that they can understand, use, and/or consume. Paradoxically, our altruism is the cause of poverty and maldevelopment in the Third World because the West upsets the balance that primitive cultures have achieved – a balance that has allowed them to survive unchanged for thousands of years. Primitive people are not poor – they are primitive, but when we replace their self-sustaining systems with that which is extraneous and foreign they become poor. They have food and Western clothing, cell phones and recreational drugs but their population grows quickly and they forget how to sustain themselves. Their streets are open sewers and the people are idle – they simply do not know what to do. Africans are currently flooding European nations and there is no chance that will do anything for them, but it is certain to create havoc in white countries. Blacks in the U.S. have had a hundred fifty years to assimilate but rather than recognize the folly of assimilation and the ruination caused by losing their evolutionary homes – white racism is blamed for the mess that is Detroit, Chicago, Los Angeles, Baltimore, and Saint Louis etc. and it is nothing short of bizarre that Africans continue to jump from the fire into the frying pan by invading nations that are filled with those same white racists. Something is wrong with this picture. To be continued.

PAUL: While I understand your point, I don't share your fears. Although I don't forget that North America was taken over once already by Europeans, I don't think America has been or will be *taken over* anytime soon anymore than will be Germany. Yes, Asians are the fastest growing minority group here. And when you add their numbers with those of Hispanic and African backgrounds, yes, they will soon out number "whites". Native Germans can still have as many children as they want. There is no law that forces them to have fewer. Majorities shift from time to time. And I think there are many Germans as well as Americans who consider themselves to be German or American or German/American even when they aren't as pure-bred as the term *white* or *native* presumes.

The baby boomers didn't takeover America although their numbers were majoritarian as a segment. Or if they (we) did, I missed
it. Women have outnumbered men but they haven't taken over. Or
is the *majority* only of concern when it is divided into racial categories? The majorities within political power often shift too but
they don't take over. Soon enough, as a block, whites will be in the
minority in the U.S. as compared with other minorities (considered
non-white) combined as a block. I understand that you feel like a
minority. I've felt like a minority most my life in many areas of my
life but that's okay. I tend to walk a road less traveled. I think it is
telling; I think it is educational to know how it feels to lack power
(if it is power you're concerned with). This should enlighten us to
how *others* must have felt for a long time. At least that's how I've
chosen to look at things; to learn and adjust, rather than to fear.
And I don't disregard the fact that I may be okay with all of this
because I am have enjoyed my white male status in America.

For clarity and to make it easier to follow, let me take most of
the second half of your reply line by line:

**"Race-mixing has been most commonly associated with
rape, slavery, war, conquest, and colonialism - all socially destructive activities . . ."**

If I were to pick, I would say that the most socially destructive
of all these example is rape, slavery, war, conquest, and colonialism, rather than and any "race-mixing" that more naturally occurs
between races. The problems of consensual race mixing pales (or
darkens :) in comparison to the others because those who commit
these atrocities think they are *better than* and so wish to conquer
and degrade those who are *different than*.

**". . . and it is clear from the long-term homogeneity of
racial groups that the protection of the fertile female has
been paramount in maintaining homogeneity."**

Or maybe races tend look down upon others, the *outsiders*, and
much prefer to keep their women away from those *others*, no matter the color. This explanation seems to be far more likely than any
forward looking anthropology between potential lovers. I know
that anthropology has never been a concern of most people I've
ever met, especially when it comes to sex.

"The criminalization of rape, the codification of marriage,

the punishment of female infidelity, and the ostracism against mixed offspring are probably universal methods of ensuring homogeneity."

The criminalization of rape has also been quite useful for a majority in convicting those who are out of favor and out of power. Just an accusation is enough to cause ruin or death for the powerless minority. Speaking of power, the men (of any color) who have it, will certainly not submit to themselves being punished for any infidelity. They will not be forced to carry a child and then care for it for many years. They are certainly not ostracized by society (it often seems the opposite has occurred) in any meaningful way when it's their offspring (mixed or not) in question. Men are given *a pass* so they seldom have to acknowledge, let alone care for, unwanted offspring. And often there is no law (most commonly written by males) that will come to the woman's, the child's, or society's defense. This has shown itself to be quite universal and it is a huge moral failing among many cultures.

"There are passive methods as well in which cultural differences create barriers – language, education, religion, class, concern for offspring, and negative genetic consequences."

Yes, religion and class have always been convenient for shaming women. Neither religion nor class shames men so. Men with little education can have a lot of power in areas such as religion. And as far as genetic consequences are concerned, my understanding is that inbreeding eventually has more negative genetic consequences than does outbreeding. Perhaps inbreeding is one reason it has taken evolution so long to reach the point that it has so far. This is to say that perhaps outbreeding has caused humanity to grow-up.

As I look around, I witness selfish (multicolored) male concerns that avoid concern for offspring. There is little concern for this state of events even in today's world. Women are denied (by religion and society) better control over their reproduction while being saddled with full responsibility of reproduction while the latter groups refuse any responsibility for the result that they help promote. Men are allowed (and sometimes defended and even cheered-on) to resist any responsibility. We then make use of our language to shame and maim and put down others for lacking proper education while we, all the while, put up barriers to *their* education.

"The latest socially destructive program is massive Third World immigration into Europe, the U.S., Canada, Australia, and New Zealand. It is totally artificial and is harmful to both the settled European cultures and to the newcomers. To view positively this tumultuous invasion of people 'looking for a better life', one must discount the value of the settled, homogeneous cultures that immigrants are leaving behind."

Program? Who puts this program in place? "Artificial"? "Invasion"? Who conducts this invasion? I can't group all of this (and these peoples) together as you do. Currently many people migrate to flee war, real war. They flee their "settled, homogeneous cultures". Their cultures are neither settled nor homogeneous or they wouldn't have to flee. People don't leave only for a better life but so what if they do? Sometimes people flee for life itself. It's totally "artificial"? I guess you'll have to define for me, "artificial", "invasion" and tell me who conducts this program.

"The concept of universal human rights is European – not African, not Middle Eastern, not Chinese. . . Even the understanding of the geography of the world and the discovery of remote human types is European. . . . Most of the world's people have no word for 'freedom', and only Europe had the philosophical and political development that produced what we call universal human rights."

Once again, all of this is simply looking back to another time that never existed. There was a time when even the Europeans didn't have these concepts either. Much of their ignorance continues to this day. If some of these unthinking Europeans attempted to spread theses ideas to those who couldn't appreciate them, they have only themselves to blame. Perhaps more importantly, they spread their value of non-responsibility among others too. These non or irresponsible ideas include their infamous and inherently conflicting ideas about individual freedom. Perhaps these dubious ideas arose from these same irresponsible values. My reading of history shows enough turmoil from within Europe for me to value it as any unquestionable or virtuous standard. I do think that if European peoples want to take credit for all that is good that they should then take responsibility for the bad; that part of their thinking and culture. And even if all of these examples you mention are accurate, do you think this reflects a difference in intelligence, priorities, conventions?

"Even though we might judge moral universalism to be altruistic and therefore noble, it remains a Western imposition on other peoples who have no basis for understanding it. It isn't theirs and at best it is translated into material goods that they can understand, use, and/or consume."

I do think there is something to moral universalism. And even the Europeans misunderstand it. It isn't *theirs*, it isn't *ours* or anybody else's to try to usurp although I'm sure that all those who think they are right will certainly try.

You and I accept, as a given, that all peoples develop conventions like "government, law, and language". Does the fact that all peoples have this tendency point toward some precedence? Is this tendency innate? Does this seemingly innate tendency toward some precedence point to some universal? That universals seem to precede race and culture seems to point toward some value more foundational than race and culture. Yet, as we've seen, these universals seem quite indifferent to race and culture, so to speak. Should we continue to hack at the branches if there is something even more rooted than race and culture to concern us? I'd love to talk about this.

So anyway, regardless of priority, we as humans implement our own priorities, via our social tendencies, and they differ from others only insofar as our viewpoint of the foundational values that we care to admit, let alone value. So it is that essentially everybody begins with the *same differences* and then continue to divide up this prior *unity* by stressing how we view secondary (less majoritarian) considerations. These may include everything from red headedness to left handedness to racial considerations.

The idea that "government and law are codifications of the practices and rules that have promoted group survival", points to humanity's desire to implement rules via the preferences (values) of their specific group. But many groups we will happily annihilate other groups if they "perceive" a threat to their own group's survival. Once again, we are all the same this way. There is a precedence (our sameness) that remains yet we often focus upon our differences and maintain that these differences are the real problem. So it is that the rules of each group is likely decided upon by the force of numbers (democracy) and/or the strength of a possibly arm bearing few etc. Still, there is a precedence that remains the same for any group. The fact that other people my be *like us* or *with us* is seldom valued as highly as those who are *of us*. Once again, our greatest enemies are exactly like us in this regard. And so this circle of value continues. And just what *is* the value we are preferring? The value of post foundational considerations that oppose other groupings? Yet all these groups make up their values while calling themselves, different or better than (certainly separate from) the other groups. They/we are all the same in these ways too.

Our first sense of culture is familial. In this sense family is both cultural and pre-cultural. We are often reminded of this fact both within the family and from without. We are constantly preached to about the importance of family and "family values". From time to time it is even in vogue to tell us how important we are as individuals, and how much we matter as free autonomous human beings. These values are preached to us as if we need reminding how much we must value our selves. Yet I'm always interested in what people think they mean by this. Are our greatest values to be known by their reduction to the smallest unit of personal exclusivity? In reaction we are told NO! Many people then revert back the greatest value being the family. And never forget that this immediate family has a lineage. Many people hold the belief that this lineage is, or should be, traced back further and further to our "roots"; far enough at least to realize where we came from; where we grew from. We are branches supported by a much larger tree of life. (Let's just ignore, once again, the fact that *their family* is exactly the same as *our family* in this manner. Instead, we are told to focus upon our perceived differences *branches* rather than our foundational value of the entire process.)

Given the current state of our values, no wonder we fight. It should be no wonder we have problems right from the beginning. We need to look no further than the family unit to find something as simple as being born left handed (if people really are born this way), or maybe one finds oneself to be that red-headed step child. There are so many problems that come from within, it's a wonder we can find the time to worry about those outside our immediate family. And God forbid that a member of our own family might be fraternizing with one of *them*.

Our desire to think we are *better than*, in whatever sense, is quite primal, almost universal and almost pre-cultural. I mean, few of us strive at being *worse than*. But for as much as we strive, there is always some way, a tendency in fact, to insist upon narrowing our points of view further so as to ensure our own exclusivity. Yes, *they* do this just the same as *we* do. Them and us share this. So there is a clue here that we keep coming across and devaluing because we don't know what to do with it. The clue that keeps rearing its ugly head is pre-cultural. We would do well to examine it. Yet we all travel down this same road of recognizing and defining the differences that can be observed and determined only to find we can never define them all. Infinity will always exist. Or we could consider the road less traveled; the one that begins prior to these other branches and consider it freshly from there.

So if there is a shared (same) root that precedes culture and race then I am apt to look back upon that root as foundational and start there. When we start elsewhere, we are essentially deciding that some offshoot is more essential than the tree that gave rise to the branches in the first place.

"Paradoxically, our altruism is the cause of poverty and maldevelopment in the Third World because the West upsets the balance that primitive cultures have achieved – a balance that has allowed them to survive unchanged for thousands of years."

Until the Europeans invaded them and upset this balance. Now we blame the invaded instead of blaming the wiser invader who should have known better.

"Primitive people are not poor—they are primitive . . ."

And non primitive people are simply less primitive in some ways than they are in others. But in other ways, all humans have been around for the same length of time. And those that were around earlier (longer?) seem to have assimilated. So, what do you mean by primitive? Age? The time a culture long dead spent on earth? Intelligence?

". . . but when we replace their self-sustaining systems with that which is extraneous and foreign they become poor."

We? The Europeans? Those of European descent? Those who

preceded the Europeans? We, of European descent, sound a bit too idiotic and destructive to be terribly virtuous. It sounds like "they forget how to sustain themselves" and the *they* are *us*.

"Africans are currently flooding European nations and there is no chance that will do anything for them, but it is certain to create havoc in white countries."

Did the African create this situation or did the Europeans? I don't really mean to agree with your premises or take them as seriously as you surely do, but if any of it is true then Europeans must take the lions share of responsibility because the others perhaps *know not what they do*. Europeans must stop avoiding responsibility for the world *they* created.

"Blacks in the U.S. have had a hundred fifty years to assimilate but rather than recognize the folly of assimilation and the ruination caused by losing their evolutionary homes – white racism is blamed for the mess that is Detroit, Chicago, Los Angeles, Baltimore, and Saint Louis etc. and it is nothing short of bizarre that Africans continue to jump from the fire into the frying pan by invading nations that are filled with those same white racists. Something is wrong with this picture."

I will agree that there is something wrong with this picture. You've painted locales in shades of black that are so far removed from the time and place of the inhabitants. Nobody has an "evolutionary home" anymore. Maybe *we* had one two hundred thousand years ago in Africa but we can now ignore that one. My guess is that you have an alternative theory to the *out of Africa* one.

After a few years of living in the U.S., everybody was born here. They can't remember some home that isn't theirs. I know I don't remember my evolutionary home. Do you? People don't really think this way except to try to make up a story after the fact that might possibly fit their choice of the evidence to consider. An evolutionary home? It doesn't matter to most anybody now. Like you've said, all of humans have moved far away from their source, even if their source was several different locales. Europeans seem to praise reason yet the talk of an evolutionary home implies that we react more from some ancient instinct than reason. Even if that is true, we will never grow beyond it if we don't practice and value reason.

SHARON: Paul, I have gotten so far behind in this conversation that I may have lost my place. I started to write something before you sent your last long note and so what follows is disjointed and doesn't seem very responsive. I will have to give it another try – but here are a few points in answer to somethings you wrote. You are certainly productive!

I haven't used the words, "pure" or "purity" in regard to either race or culture. My point is that the races of mankind have evolved over hundreds of thousands of years in relative isolation from one another, in varied locations that have required different physical, mental, and social adaptations. That evolution has produced substantial differences in the races and most of those differences have served survival/reproductive purposes. Just because the taxonomy and genome of Homo sapiens is identified as human doesn't negate the importance of our evolutionary adaptations and differences. Given the fact that all extant human groups carry the same human genome it would be fair to say that every group has been evolving from a common ancestor for the same length of time and has produced very different results in that time frame. The results are not arbitrary. The evolution of Europeans has produced the nuclear family, monogamy, exogamy, the high status of women, science, and moral universalism. Our evolutionary home is Europe and both our physical and cultural attributes are manifestations of that home. We don't "remember" the home; we carry it with us in our genes. For example, your mitochondrial DNA is designated U and has been passed from mother to child in Europe for at least the past forty-five thousand years. It is the oldest of the European mtDNA groups. That group is not found among Australoids, Mongoloids, Congoids, or Bushmen. Genetic diversity is good up to a point – that is why the exogamy of the Europeans is preferable to the endogamy of the peoples of the Middle East, however mixing people from different races can negate certain adaptations, dilute certain desirable characteristics, and introduce traits that have no use in a different environment, and are detrimental to the organism. An Inuit from the Canadian Pine Barrens could be transported to the Kalahari to live with Bushmen and those Bushmen might be very accommodating and friendly, but the Inuit has thousands of years of adaptation and reproduction in the cold north. Even so, he might fall in love with a Bushwoman, marry, and produce children. Will the Bushman's gene pool be improved by introduction of Inuit genes? In what way? By the same token would a hybrid of a 4' tall Oaxacan man and 6'8" Estonian woman be superior to either group?

Even though our "evolutionary home" is carried in our genes that is not sufficient to allow healthy development of the individual in a foreign environment because it lacks the adaptations to the physical environment and the socio-cultural elements that support that development. The Inuit in the Kalahari, like the African in the U.S. reaches a point in his development at which he requires a model of Inuit or African masculinity and social behavior, plus the cultural props that support the social forms. I think that is why Africans, Mexicans, Vietnamese, Tongans, and other minority groups form the ad hoc cultural form known as the gang. The notion that white racism is the central problem for minorities is an inadequate explanation and is, at bottom, unsympathetic to the people who are struggling to recreate the products of thousands of years of evolution that they have left behind.

The so-called minorities in the U.S. were all part of a majority of their racial kinsmen in the places from whence they came. Only slaves were uprooted and transported against their wills, that is to say, most have chosen to be a minority in a foreign land. Europeans were a tiny minority in North America and no one expected the Native Americans to take them in, feed them, give them medical care, subsidized housing, education, citizenship, and civil rights. People can go wherever they wish (within the limits of their invention of transport) but people also have the right to resist all incursions on their claimed and developed lands.

PAUL: Although you "haven't used the words, 'pure' or 'purity' in regard to either race or culture", you have recommended (by noting what you see as problems with cultures mixing) that races and cultures keep themselves separate. Even if this separateness isn't for purity's sake, you have explicitly said that Europeans have excelled in many areas beyond *others* and so I am left to assume that this separateness is to protect that *excellence*. Correct me if I'm wrong.

I am want to put the term "race" in quotes because the *idea of race* and racism also seems to have grown up alongside each other in Europe, but we've long known that there is no biology (science) that supports the idea of race within humans today. Race is a cultural construct, just as culture is a social construct. What you speak of as "memory" in our DNA is what I'd call a *marker*. Science can't tell us this marker has any memory. All they know is that it is a designation. We don't know what it marked then nor do we know what it represents today. Regardless, my ability to adapt to a foreign environment has much less to do with my DNA than a multitude of exterior things. And if my actions are so tied to DNA then my European bound reason is pretty much worthless. Free will seems overridden by the strength of our DNA. If a minor DNA marker can somehow over rule reason, then reason finds little value within any of us.

It appears that none of these markers are greater than anyone else's, they are merely local. Many people have birthmarks and belly buttons yet none of these contain memory either even if some people do believe in the *mark of Cain*. But I would submit that if these differences are so important, maybe we should find a way to hurry and mix all these markers up until there are no distinguishing differences to be recognized. Maybe such purposeful dilution might make race considerations a thing of the past. But I suggest we already do have, and still all we do is look for differences to put others down. We will likely never run out of ways to try to make ourselves distinct, read *better than* so we can *look down upon*. And here we are; the world is growing more crowded, more mobile, and communications have made the world so small that any idea of keeping us separate is long gone (except in the righteousness of our minds); and we are getting closer, moving faster everyday.

You mention that varied locations have required different physical, mental, and social adaptations. This may be true (even Europe alone has such varied climates, deserts, coastal lands, mountains, valleys, just like every other place on Earth where people have cultured up) so this *nature* issue is at least as much a *nurture* issue within Europe just as it is elsewhere.

"Given the fact that all extant human groups carry the same human genome it would be fair to say that every group has been evolving from a common ancestor for the same length of time and has produced very different results in that time frame. The results are not arbitrary."

My crystal ball says the results are often quite arbitrary. This is something we probably can't know; we can only assume; and we regularly assume too much. We are, however, pretty sure that nurture makes differences. We do know that natural disasters and climate make for differences in how similar people have lived and died. Not only may God indeed *play dice with the universe*, there may be no God at all that is micromanaging events. Perhaps God doesn't have time for dice. And we can be pretty sure that a specific DNA marker isn't managing these events either.

Once again, I doubt our ancestors gave much thought as to how to promote their survival, race or culture through mating so much as they just wanted to have sex. I'll bet they weren't so different from most folks today. The biology of sex seems to aim toward it being pleasurable rather than reasonable. And when you speak of the high status of women, many ancient cultures in China and the Americas as well as other places had developed matriarchal cultures from time to time. And many European individuals have abused women just like individuals of others cultures have.

You sometimes praise moral universalism and at other times you condemn it. I tend to agree that the practice of moral universalism is somewhat arbitrary. I think humans have a lot of moral issues to overcome and to promote. I think we are probably in the Neanderthal stages of morality, and that our claims to superiority are relatively childlike assumptions.

"Will the Bushman's gene pool be improved by introduction of Inuit genes? In what way?"

The Bushman nor most everybody else knows or cares about some *gene pool*. It seems the only ones who do care are those who want the keep these lovers separate. How will they effect the pool? My guess is incredibly little (in the greater scheme of things).

Hardly even a trace of a genetic marker's worth. I don't most people anywhere concern themselves with improvement of their gene pool and neither do their genes. They may only want to have a peaceful family and existence.

"By the same token would a hybrid of a 4' tall Oaxacan man and 6'8" Estonian woman be superior to either group?"

Perhaps neither need to feel superior. Perhaps they too just love and want to be loved. Or perhaps they just wanted to have sex. Perhaps they don't think in terms of the group so much as doing their best for each other.

"I think that is why Africans, Mexicans, Vietnamese, Tongans, and other minority groups form the ad hoc cultural form known as the gang."

Like the Italians, Irish, Germans etc? I think I could go on all day naming white European gangs. They are easier to point to when we call them mobs, Mafia, jack booted thugs, KKK, "citizen's councils" etc. Rather than racial concerns, gangs might often form due to their feelings about cultural marginalization, or perhaps due to a multitude or other possibilities.

"The so-called minorities in the U.S. were all part of a majority of their racial kinsmen in the places from whence they came. Only slaves were uprooted and transported against their wills, that is to say, most have chosen to be a minority in a foreign land."

You too have said that you feel like a minority in your community. Rather than moving, you seem to have chosen to be a minority within your *foreign* community. So, like those minorities that have become the majority, should you complain if you too have the freedom to simply move?

"Europeans were a tiny minority in North America and no one expected the Native Americans to take them in, feed them, give them medical care, subsidized housing, education, citizenship, and civil rights."

I will agree with the idea of civil rights being pretty much founded in European ideas. Good for them. And I agree that much of the value we now place upon civil rights probably grows out of issues of race and racism. Now, in a broader sense, human rights (those rights existing prior to the civil rights promoted by government) *may* have had European roots for us, but other cultures had ideas of human rights independent of Europe. I can cite chapter and verse from individuals in ancient China that also had the concept. I, for one, agree that human rights exist prior to government and government is only charged with their protection.

Europeans that came to this continent may not have "expected" help but they didn't refuse help when they needed it. In fact, when it was provided, the Europeans called it "civilized" behavior. But I also don't presume or rely upon groupthink that defines all people within a group as *them*. And I don't presume to know just how many people "expect" anything, rather, many probably just want to make a living. But on the other hand, I don't think that wanting *food, medical care, housing, education, citizenship, and civil rights* are undesirable things. These are civilized things that civilized people value and should not only promote but share if they think they are of such civil value.

I will also not forget that borders are make-believe lines, and that I might be born 2" one way or the other of this line and end up being grouped with the others instead of being considered an individual as Americans are wont to be valued. Perhaps our view and treatment of others has more to do with ideas and beliefs than it has to do with DNA. Or perhaps not. Perhaps the European DNA is lacking in this respect, and nature is finding ways to due away with this aspect of it. Or perhaps people are individuals as much as they are parts of families and extended families, and should be considered as such.

So, what are we to do about it? Perhaps now it's all DNA under the bridge. The question remains: What do we do now? Our genes are all mixed up and we can't easily separate us from ourselves.

SHARON: The term "race" is used to describe physical, physiological, genetic, and psychological traits characteristic of a particular people. All of those traits are biological and evolutionary. Humans are capable of distinguishing between the major racial groups and that ability has been observed in babies as young as fifteen months-old. Unlike the word "race", the words "racism" and "racist" are very recent inventions used as pejoratives against people who admit to perceiving racial differences. (The toddlers in the study were already racists at 15 months!). Race is a product of evolution and the evolution of living things is biological. So what we have seen in the past forty years is a program to delegitimize people's perceptions, that is to say, to tell us that we aren't really seeing what we see. It's the Emperor's New Clothes all over again. The words "pure" and "purity" are inappropriately applied to the things I have written. We can talk about purebred animals because that "purity" is an artificial manipulation of nature to get a desired result. But humans are not passively bred by others – at least not yet. I have to say that your idea that we should hurry and find a way to mix up human DNA to get rid of all distinctions produces a nightmarish dystopia that is just as revolting as a dystopia in which humans are bred for "purity." And though I suspect you meant it ironically, it does seem to be a last resort for those who wish to deny racial differences, that is to say, it might be easier to get rid of differences altogether than to prevent us from seeing those differences and acting on that knowledge. Getting rid of "race" by replacing it with "ethnicity" is another dumb idea that was recently exposed by Rachel Dolezal, an ethnically black woman who was ousted from the NAACP and lost her position as a college instructor because her "race" trumped her chosen ethnicity. Value judgments invoked by words like "superior", "inferior", and "supremacy" are used to negatively characterize race realists. The existence of a race of people is evidence of adaptation and compatibility with a particular environment, community health and sustainability. Whatever the racial characteristics of such a group they have evolved to enhance reproduction and survival. or at least they do not impair the same. The fundamental error in race-mixing is not an abstract "impurity", but a failure to appreciate what has evolved and why. I recently heard a pitch for race-mixing that said, "Race-mixing will make us taller and smarter." I can't imagine who they were addressing – certainly not the 6'4" white man who is thinking of mating with a Oaxacan woman. Their offspring will not be taller or smarter than the white man. This diversity ad brings up the question of how people choose mates. You say that sex is for pleasure, suggesting that any willing human will suffice as a sex partner because sexual pleasure is not dependent upon love, age, health, height, weight, deformity, fertility, odor, race, ethnicity, or social status. But we are not really that all-embracing in our tastes. Because sex is reproductive it is moderated by conscious and unconscious considerations for offspring – even when there is no possibility of offspring. Because sex is reproductive all human cultures have rules, proscriptions, and/or civil laws regulating sexual behavior which often include restrictions on one's choice of sex partner. Such restrictions are very common among primitive people who have erected bars to mixing between tribes that inhabit the same lands. You have your work cut out for you to get the races of mankind to mix so we are all one, big, happy, human family. Pygmies, at least can look forward to getting taller and smarter.

PAUL: I think most of us know what *race* refers to now, and although racism is perhaps a more recent term, racism itself has been a part of us probably even before the term *race* was coined. Once we define a term like "good" the idea of "not good" is nearly auto matic even if we have yet to create a special term for it like "bad". Even before the first distinction has been thought through, the sec ond distinction is just as nearly deep seated because they are related rather than distinct. So few things are as black and white as we attempt to separate them by definition. I suspect that you and I are more complex than most others might first presume.

You say that, ". . . 'racism' and 'racist' are very recent inventions used as pejoratives against people who admit to perceiving racial differences."

At what age do these terms have to reach before they are mature enough to accept their value? What follows is an example of where I might disagree, but I think you'll agree with me anyway:). I do not think that my ability to recognize race makes me racist any more than my ability to tell the difference between the sexes makes me sexist. Also, I might not regard these differences as race based at all. But since this may seem to be merely a semantic difference to many people, I'll speak more to the point. Even if I were so inclined to perceive certain differences as race-centric, my perception is not racist. I would say that racism exists when an ethnic group or some other collective tries to dominate and prefers to exclude other people or groups due to differences that it believes are hereditary and unchangeable. This definition need not be pejorative, the definition it is simply stating a fact of how people see, think, feel and react. I would say it describes you yet it doesn't describe me. But I don't see any reason to demonize someone by branding them as "racist" any more than I see any value in disparaging someone of a different race. Neither position seems useful, and both positions share very similar values; unbeknownst to the other.

"So what we have seen in the past forty years is a program to delegitimize people's perceptions, that is to say, to tell us that we aren't really seeing what we see."

I don't know what you refer to when you refer to "forty years", but I will agree with your concern about perception. We tend to see only through our own eyes. The Mormons believe they are right. The Catholics believe they are right. We see through our own eyes, and often our own culture. Rather than founding our values in personal perception, I endeavor to see more broadly. But this is anathema for those who believe that their belief itself is to be valued and defended. I'm not afraid of regarding your views, I have no belief to fight for or to maintain. But there is a current reality and perhaps a direction that it is heading. But it seems to me that we must accept this reality and its likely direction, regardless of our belief, if we are to move forward. More on this as we go along.

"I have to say that your idea that we should hurry and find a way to mix up human DNA to get rid of all distinctions produces a nightmarish dystopia that is just as revolting as a dystopia in which humans are bred for 'purity'."

I did mean my words ironically to some degree but not necessarily ironic in the way you might think. It's probably more ironic than that :) What I generally mean is that, in many ways, this is the direction humankind is heading and has been heading since the beginning of time. We will find neither Utopia nor dystopia here or there. Perhaps more on this as we go along.

And you probably have seen that I don't use the terms like "superior", "inferior", and "supremacy" as pejoratives. Like you say, ". . . the words "pure" and "purity" are inappropriately applied to the things I have written." Yet I think you will agree that your interest in this subject is for the "better". It seems to me that you think races are simply races and ought simply stick to their own because that's where their culture is and it's *best* for them. To aim at what is *best* for them is neither negative nor pejorative. Correct me if I've misunderstood you. I also think that you believe, generally speaking, that other races mixing is not for the best. Otherwise I don't think we would be having this discussion.

"Whatever the racial characteristics of such a group they have evolved to enhance reproduction and survival. or at least they do not impair the same."

Once again, I think I disagree. I think that if this is true, it has been happenstance. I don't think I'm much different than most people when I say that I've never considered *enhancing reproduction and survival* in my own process of mating. Perhaps some or many people do. I'm not a good spokesperson for reproduction anyway.

"You say that sex is for pleasure, suggesting that any willing human will suffice as a sex partner because sexual pleasure is not dependent upon love, age, health, height, weight, deformity, fertility, odor, race, ethnicity, or social status."

I don't think I claimed sex was for pleasure, I probably meant to say something like: *by it's nature, sex tends toward being more pleasurable than being a thoughtful experience*. Biology doesn't tend to regard love, age, health, height, weight, deformity, fertility, odor, race, ethnicity, or social status. But we, as discriminating people, might finally select a partner to settle down with for many of the reasons you mention. But once again, I don't think that many of these considerations necessarily have to do with passing on one's genes. But curiously it probably has more to do with how we discriminate. We all discriminate. We all judge. My interest is in how we judge and discriminate, not whether we all obviously do. Upon what do we base this? I, for one, don't think my genes have much to do with it. But perhaps this is some disguised envy I have in my wish to possess a free will that I don't. This could very well be (I'm not sure I've ever been able to observe myself too disinterestedly) but, depending upon just how far we wish to stretch the strength of our DNA, any discussion of reason and will might make our discussion pointless to some degree, or at some point.

"Because sex is reproductive all human cultures have rules, proscriptions, and/or civil laws regulating sexual behavior which often include restrictions on one's choice of sex partner."

This is true enough. And, once again, how we discriminate, *the* truth, reason or reality behind such discriminations (and the value they might have, intend, or result in), are all factors that modern cultures should be able to regard, with more information than we had in the past; we would hope. But, either way, I just don't see how biology is a major consideration given the world as it exists for us today.

"You have your work cut out for you to get the races of mankind to mix so we are all one, big, happy, human family. Pygmies, at least can look forward to getting taller and smarter."

Well actually I have no work to do here:) I'm not in charge. And I'm not interested in how we mix, nor am I interested in Utopia. I'm mainly interested in how we learn, why we don't, and in how we might get along. Races mix. Races coexist. Races fight and seg- regate. These things we know. I think you would prefer *they* value their own culture and remain separate from *us* for the most part. And I also understand why ethnic groups might want to culture-up. As a minority faced with a majority that thinks like this, I would too. And I think this is fine unless it causes too many problems for themselves or others. In a country that claims to value human rights as well as civil rights, we all should be careful that each of us don't claim to be above the other as a matter of our groupings. But, of course, we do it either way. Out of infancy, if not sooner, we begin grouping things together and separating them apart due to the ways we view these differences. We always tend to prefer our groupings no matter how random we have chosen to group them (economic class, height, skin color, weight, etc). Many of us will explain and defend our choices using creative methods. But given that we live together in a society, we should be very careful of our groupings and of our reasons. It has been said that my right to swing my fist stops at your nose. Not only is this is true enough, it never hurts to give others a bit of leeway in the case they we don't realize our own reach. Often our groupings don't serve us. Al- though we claim to value rights, we value other things more. Our valuing of rights is pretty far down on the list for most of us; well other people's rights anyway. We value rights when they protect *us* but not when they protect *them*. Most of us on either *side* are the same this way.

I don't much care who grows taller or smarter. I've never viewed height as a foundational value. I've never seen IQ tests as terribly useful. What is the correct height? Who is smart? Is the tall mathematician smarter or the short artist? Many discriminations we make are useless or at least not useful in slightly different situations than where and when they once seemed to have value. These discriminations, however useful, are simply discriminations. Many distinctions lose or have lost their utility just and many others gain value. I'm not much of a utilitarian but when we wish to regard utility, we shouldn't hold onto a distinction that is no longer helpful, or when its usefulness is so confused with non-usefulness that it has become de facto useless, no matter its perceived value.

You and I can discuss things because we resist unverified assumptions about each other. I don't tell you what you think, nor you me. We must check and verify. This results in a politeness because we seek to understand each other as we are rather than how we wish to cast each other. And I'm this way with everybody (not just you) because it seems to serve not only me but others. It serves communication and society. These things serve society as well as the society that values it, if wishes to survive long. It's always a pleasure reading and writing you.

The next comments are an aside about possibly visiting for vacation. Of course Sharon's comments had to include a political reference:)
PAUL: Maybe one day we'll take a vacation down around your way.

SHARON: That would be nice. We are betwixt and between all vacation destinations but our city is a popular sanctuary city.

PAUL: You never know. One day we might need sanctuary. Let's hope they offer it then. :)

SHARON: Not likely. The Chicano slogan is "Gringo exire Atzlan" Gringo out of Atlan!

PAUL: Well, like most groupings, I'll bet there are those within the groups who see things differently. You and I are proof. :)

Later:

SHARON: So, racism is a group program of dominance and exclusion? Does that mean a person who states or exhibits a preference for his own race is not a racist? Or does it mean that on the individual level we are all racists because racial exclusivity has been an essential factor in the evolution of races? The terms "racism" and "racist" are slippery because they were invented for political purposes. You can see how it works with another invented word – "homophobe". Even the term "homosexual" is of recent vintage, having been coined in the late nineteenth century by a Prussian pamphleteer who was agitating for the decriminalization of sodomy. There has been little resistance to laws regulating sexual behavior because those laws are seen as necessary for protection against sexual predators, public sex, and pornography. However, one of the previously prohibited sexual behaviors has been elevated to a separate human identity requiring civil rights in addition to the rights one has as a man or a woman. Ironically, while we are told to accept that race has no basis in biology we are told that "homosexuality" is both inborn and immutable. We are supposed to believe that our preference for our own race is learned while a preference for a same-sex partner is not. And while we are supposed to ignore, or at least not mention, objective, biological differences between races, there are no objective criteria by which a homosexual can be identified. In fact, the only way a homosexual can be identified is by his frank admission making discrimination impossible without that admission. Politically active homosexuals and their allies used "coming out" to create reaction among those who had been indifferent and that reaction was maligned as the homophobia of homophobes. In a relatively short time our society went from treating sodomy as a capital crime to treating sodomites as the victims of the malignant bias of ordinary people. And while one can make a case for the victimization of Africans in the slave trade, the vast majority of Americans and their ancestors had nothing to do with slavery but are now maligned as racists for reacting to the presence of a people with whom they do not wish to mix.

The Democratic Party having lost its base of working men has recreated itself as the party of the aggrieved – blacks, women, homosexuals, and immigrants, none of whom represent what is good about America. Perhaps Americans will wake up to see how they are being played. One can hope.

PAUL: You ask, "So, racism is a group program of dominance and exclusion?"

No. I infer from your word, "program" something being formally orchestrated. While there may be such programs, I do not refer to any such program. Individually or in groups, we tend to be exclusive quite naturally. Individuals can also view themselves or their group to be dominant and then desire to exclude others or keep themselves separate from members of the another group. Individuals simply have less power to do as much damage. But once we group, we then have groups that are "referred to as" and other groups that are *doing the referring*, until we've created groups that refer to each back and forth while dominating and excluding or become dominated and excluded.

"Does that mean a person who states or exhibits a preference for his own race is not a racist?"

No. See above. I think people can have a preference or a bias and not have it equate to racism. Everybody has preferences. I also think we have biases (implicit) that we are unaware of. Once in a while I notice a bias within my self that surprises me. So when I see it I consider it. What does it imply? I examine such things so I can be clear about myself. In the past I had a tendency to group people together much more than I do now. My biases, no matter how implicit, are more about me than others. Other people's biases are up to them. But, either way, a preference is not right or wrong but it might simply lack value for other intentions.

"Or does it mean that on the individual level we are all racists because racial exclusivity has been an essential factor in the evolution of races?"

I don't think any race is totally exclusive. Evolution continues when races mix; the races merely evolve differently, and then individuals of these races simply exclude differently.

"There has been little resistance to laws regulating sexual behavior because those laws are seen as necessary for protection against sexual predators, public sex, and pornography."

In the past, this may have been true but I don't think that consenting adults involved in sexual acts (that I might find distasteful) are sexual predators. My taste in such matters should not be of their concern nor my ability to overrule (if it's simply a matter of taste). We can have laws against predatory behavior that don't infringe upon the consensual sexual acts because there is a big difference between preference and predation.

As I've said before, I don't think it makes any difference whether people are *born this way* or *choose to be this way*. The reality could even be another option that we haven't discussed here. In this country we have tended to allow people to choose their own religions; we don't require people to be born into them. This seems to work. Liberty of conscience is accepted and beliefs are allowed. In order to be civil, others should accept this; nobody has to agree with the beliefs of others. In order to be civil we have accepted that bedroom behavior is private. I can defend other people's right to this without any dependence upon genetic judgments, just as I can other people's rights when they have different genes without referring to their genes. I don't have to accept the belief that homosexuality is genetic or not. It doesn't matter if either is true or not. It is either true or isn't. My belief or mis-belief doesn't change any facts of the matter. Beliefs become deep-seated and tend to sway people whether I am right or wrong. So I try to keep belief at bay. If there are genetics involved in either race or homosexuality, that need not influence civil law. We can write our own laws, and we do. We can make up our own words and we do. These are conventions. We may respond to genetics but we should also respond to society with civility. We can learn things beyond our genes, and these can be helpful things.

"In fact, the only way a homosexual can be identified is by his frank admission making discrimination impossible without that admission."

Also, in fact, people can make assumptions and discriminate

against people they simply presume to be homosexual. And they can be wrong. We see this happen time and time again. The fact of what or who people are or how they identify has little to do with *the* truth of those they condemn. This is why we enact some laws; in an attempt to dissuade people from behaving in unlawful manners but also to promote respect for privacy etc. This is part of why society values the rights and privacy of others. To value such laws may serve to protect some people's religion let alone someone else's sexuality.

A Jew might well have to identify oneself as such to be recognized as such. A Jew might alter her name so as not to be grouped with others who share their religion or ethnicity. A Jew might do these things to escape persecution or even death. A black person might not have the option of *passing as*. In any of these cases, the persecution of others due to groupings, or due to our assumptions of *guilt* are not the point. Perhaps homosexuals are late to the game not due to some sheep following political bosses but because they have *passed* for far too long. And they have had to pass perhaps not because of behavior or guilt but because of how people might violate them. And violators might violate them simply due to their own attitudes about sexuality regardless of the facts of the matter. Homosexuals, even with law on their side, might keep facts hidden due to their fear of exclusion. Fears that people might equate or group them with predators is evidently a real fear. Group-ism can be a problem for others by no fault of the *others* themselves.

"In a relatively short time our society went from treating sodomy as a capital crime to treating sodomites as the victims of the malignant bias of ordinary people."

And this capital crime (a crime punishable by death) has previously been applied to a private participatory sexual act between two people. The word "sodomy" is biblical yet the United States is not theocracy. Nowadays we have decided that such definitions are not only archaic, we've seen how they can breed attitudes of discrimination and violence. We might call these attitudes **"the malignant bias of ordinary people"**. These actions attempt to foster a value that is too often immoral. Perhaps we have decided that personal belief should not direct morality; that a more encompassing reality should prevail instead.

When you say that there, ". . . is a program to delegitimize people's perceptions, that is to say, to tell us that we aren't really seeing what we see. It's the Emperor's New Clothes all over again."

This seems to address a clue for us. We are too often confusing *what* we see with *how* we see.

People visually perceiving things is seldom the issue. But just as alternative points of view of the same thing can seem incomprehensible if not irreconcilable, if one refuses the value within any other viewpoint, more importantly this same condition (what we view) can easily be extended from physical viewpoint to rational (or mental) viewpoint of *how* we see. Like everything else in life, there are helpful ways of considering things and less helpful ways. The facts of the matter are often too narrow to fairly encompass any given topic, yet there is just so much to view that we have to pick and choose what we view. So there is a danger here. The *way* we view is probably much more important than *what* we view. This is why a sort of *infinite realism* seems preferable to me. To look at things narrower seems self-defeating and possibly negative in comparison. Defining another person too narrowly is unfair to them as well as to us. This is why I don't mean to be unfair when I seem to be defining you. I don't intend to be putting you into a group or into a box. Just as I, for one, am not being played by a political party or any other belief or ideology.

PAUL: *Some Labor Day thoughts:*
Since we seem to keep going over the same material yet still seem to talk past each other, I thought I'd offer up a summary of your points and my thoughts about them. I'll also pose more questions.

From looking at the past up till today, I find it easy to imagine that some families often grouped together, and that the value of all sorts of clans existed long before the idea of race arose several hundred years ago. I submit that racism existed long before anybody knew about genetic markers (they are not *racial* markers, they are only vaguely *continental* markers). Back then it was skin color and other physical features (eyes, nose, lips, foreheads, height?) that came to designate another human's race. So to attempt to buttress racial distinctions by relying upon a genetic marker might only demonstrate how these racial beliefs were prejudged. All of our ideas about race are simply human constructs, and all too often they have resulted in inhumane deconstructs.

In the *best* genetic test today for ancestry, we sample the Y chromosome inherited from my father, and the mitochondrial DNA from our mother. These two represent less than 1 percent of my DNA and each can only tell me about 1 ancestor per generation. If my math is correct, such a test can pick out only 1 of the 1,024 possible ancestors from only 10 generations back. (If we figure a generation to be about 25 years, 10 generations amounts to only 250 years.) So not only are we ignoring 1023 of my ancestors within only 250 years, when it comes to thousands of years of human change, we can't we learn much about ancestry that has any accuracy or value that can't be simply guessed at right now. Current genetic testing can't tell me anything about my *race*, and it can tell me next to nothing about my ethnicity. Even the *genetic patterns* we find today that might point *toward* the continental *home* of this one single ancestor, it may not even represent the genetic patterns that existed in the more distant past. Given the ancestry that is excluded in such tests, there is simply no reason for me to place value upon any of the generalizations assumed from the results. These generalizations are not science, they too are human constructs. As it is, the bias we impose during our interpretation of such tests not only exhibits the current limits of today's science but it surely points toward our preference for beliefs that intend to disregard science and math. Why? To prove a previous judgment; a prejudice?

Even if we could determine some more ancient *residence* via genetics, what would it do for us? In a very real sense it will only give us one more way to make vague distinctions about others we view different than ourselves. These others are different from us due to *one* possible continent of origin? Without this basis we still have a limitless supply of ways to judge others without needing to blame each son for the *sins* of the father. Besides, mathematically, this process makes devils of us all in very short order. We humans have never been lacking in our abilities or our confidence with our discriminations. Our general desire to prove ourselves *better than* is constant. In this way most of us are the same. We can take a look at the world and while considering the continents, we can subdivide these into nations, states, cities, all the way down to which side is which on which side of the tracks. Due to battles and/or ever changing discriminations (class, race, etc) we then redivide and re-subdivide again and again. Have these distinctions helped us or them? Do you see an end to this process? In the end will we be better for this process? Will they? And since we don't live in beginnings or ends, won't the process (all of that which happens in between) be better if the process is focused upon rather than the ends?

We all discriminate. We will always discriminate. We can and we must. We are all the same this way. Maybe we can do it better. Maybe we should place at least as much value upon all the ways we are the same; that 99.9 percent. Perhaps we can begin by discriminating about how and why we discriminate. What foundation do we choose? Belief? No matter which foundation we choose, will this foundation even be of value once we determine the results? We will judge the results. Humans will use their judgment during this process. We must. So what categories do we use? Will these categories be of value? Should our foundation be race, eye color, birthmarks etc? What is our goal? Is it realistic? Can we get there? where? from here? From there? In the past? What is wrong with starting here? Should we impose a goal or simply a direction? What method should we back? Should it be science, religion, belief, reason, feeling, preferred continent of origin, music style? What is our method of weeding out violators? Expulsion? Expulsion from the continent, nation, state, city, block, family? Should the penalty be death (like what used to be the crime for sodomy)? How should we keep *others* out? Walls? Death?

Group-ism has precious little to do with genetics, and people who have been denied rights and power by those around them may simply want rights and power. There is no need to look for some greater conspiracy. The desire for rights and/or power is so universal that the thought that it being more complicated seems very unlikely.

Many of those who have gained rights and power have fought for them for a very long time against oppressors. If they didn't or couldn't fight as hard or for so long, they had to put up with a lack of power and rights. I, myself, have supported struggles for such rights. I don't think the pie is one size or that I will lose rights because of their struggles or victories. Capitalist society values competition so why do we fear other values? The worst that can happen for me is that I might simply have to afford others some common courtesy and perhaps compete with them just as I might have to compete with others. But I also hope that extending rights (thinking fairly of others) will result in others thinking fairly of me. But even if this isn't the result, I think others (other than the current majority) should have rights and powers also.

Beliefs in conspiracies can be like beliefs in God; each work in mysterious ways. When arguing for them we are often met with the same problem as arguing for the existence of God. To win or lose doesn't prove much and seldom changes another's mind. Belief is too strong. And it doesn't matter whether the belief is *right* or *wrong*; the belief stands either way. We are all the same this way. I might voice some alternative explanation to God or a conspiracy only to be shot down by someone asking, "Are you blind? Can't you see *the* truth?" Yes, I'm probably blind much of the time and this fact indeed makes it difficult to see well but we all share the same tendencies toward mental blindness. And even when little can ever be proven, we will decide if it matters. Let's assume that there is a vast conspiracy and a few have noticed it. How does this knowledge help us? Let's assume that there is no conspiracy and therefore the few who have noticed it have merely been mistaken; perhaps only seen what they are predisposed to see given their viewpoint. How does this knowledge help us? It can't because we will judge in our own favor. We can't judge fairly because we insist upon judging from our own viewpoint rather than another. We simply don't value the *other*.

So, why do we want to be better than other people? Why do we want to condemn others rather than ourselves? They are also condemning; they say *they* are better. We are the all same this way. We want to blame others for the problems we see around us. We are all the same this way. We want to hold others responsible. We are the same this way. And as you've read my thoughts about any claimed superiority, one thing should have been clear; I have repeated it over and over again: We are the same this way. If we are all the same in these ways regardless of DNA or culture; the moral high ground is lost. We all have the same responsibility to work toward common ends. When it comes to common ground or common sense, what seems to be more common than, *we are all the same this way*? *This* is a very real foundation for our values.

But since we do have different abilities (the distinction here between better or worse does not serve us here), we have to work together on the same issues we all face. Rather than claiming to be better, we should realize we are all the same. We have this much in common. You can look at my life and point out where I've been hypocritical. And I can do the same for you because we're all the same this way. We are imperfect. Perhaps the most valuable difference between right and wrong is the value of how these opposites complement each other. These opposites are born out of the idea of the other. One can not exist without the other.

I would suggest that the difference lies in our sameness in wanting to be right while demonstrating where the other is wrong. We are all the same this way, and the sooner we accept this fact and work together on that which we have most in common, the *better*. I dare say that these words are embedded within language and that differing languages are embedded within everybody's *different* cultures and that these distinctions become ingrained *similarly* within our attitudes. We are all the same this way.

SHARON: Paul, Because I am so far behind, I have decided to send you shorter thoughts so you don't have to wait for days or weeks for any answer. All our "ideas" about physics or chemistry "are simply human constructs". Does that limit their value in understanding our world? Genetics is being used to understand the evolution of Homo sapiens and a major part of that evolution is the development of races, their history and geography. Tracing the Y chromosome or the mtDNA isn't really an exercise in an individual's genealogy, but rather is a significant repository of information about the peoples inhabiting certain areas of the globe. It is truly bizarre to watch the contortions of geneticists who study race markers like SNPs (single nucleotide polymorphisms) as they try to avoid using racial designations like black, white, or Chinese by euphemistically calling blacks=African-American, whites =European-American, and Chinese =Han Chinese-American. With that formulation Theresa Heinz Kerry is, as she claimed, an African-American. Scientists should have more backbone.

On the heels of the previous note:

SHARON: The trouble with the "consenting adults" formula is that rather than sex being a private matter between "consenting adults" it has been made public through political activism. That activism has made what "consenting adults" used to keep to themselves, the basis of lessons for public school children. Such lessons can only be termed pornographic. Sex is trivialized when it is disengaged from its reproductive moorings and children who are taught that sex has nothing to do with love, marriage, or commitment are vulnerable to predators and can become predators themselves. Sodomy in legal parlance (Black's Law Dictionary, 1967) is a crime against nature and refers to anal intercourse as well as bestiality. Normalizing anal intercourse has had the effect of obscuring its dangers and while young women might be "consenting adults", theirs is not informed consent. You object to the word, 'sodomy' because it is Biblical and implies sin, but the health risks are enough to argue that it should not be promoted. How soon we forget AIDS (originally labeled GRID- Gay-related Immune Deficiency).

PAUL: A reply to both your notes.

Yes, I do think that many human constructs serve to limit our understanding of our world. There are even constructs that are part of human nature that limit our ability to construct well. In these cases I think we should point them out and challenge ourselves to recognize them as to better ourselves and our world. So, we turn our attention back to human constructs.

Reality exists independently of our thoughts about it. Yet we apply our own constructs upon external reality. Yes, we construct the words for the study of chemistry and physics, but what we study is real and not a construct of our own. Since we tend to value ourselves, our viewpoints and our reason above our objects (or subjects), we impose ourselves upon that which we study. We attempt to study chemistry but too often we practice alchemy. Because we overvalue our ideas, we miss our errors. So the real trick is to devalue belief and proof while valuing *process* instead. And this is always an ongoing process.

Our mental reconstruction of reality should try its hardest to co-incide while remembering how limited our knowledge is in comparison with reality. The history of human knowledge and science is so filled with our errors of judgment; many people have become scientific skeptics. But all of the errors of genetics are due to human error. Humans have always prided themselves upon their superiority (we have no problem with this) yet our errors are so long-standing we confuse them with reality. Like religion, too often we want to learn what we want to learn, thereby misleading ourselves while blaming anything but ourselves and our constructs.

When it comes to genetics and our desire for it to define *race*, will we forget to question why race is important to us? Too often we value race in order to prove our value in comparison to someone else's value. Isn't it convenient that the Europeans who developed ideas of race and genetics found themselves to be superior? If genetics could just be found to pin down race rather than area, will we immediately forget and/or devalue just who determines just what this means for us. Science often fails to be science at that moment we decide what we think this science means. It is at this point, that this *meaning* becomes sociology or some other such "ology". The real issue is not science but rather what humans will do with this information, regardless of what we say the science means. If science were the intent, our current determinations about it would keep it in that realm and out of culture where non scientists misuse it for their own purposes.

As you say, sexual affairs used to be private. They are generally made public through innuendo, gossip and public accusation by those who don't like what they assume to be someone's personal sexual behavior. Much of the innuendo, gossip and public accusation is made by religious people (or other narrow moralists) who want governmental power to spread and maintain their version of morality. When I speak of narrow moralists, I mean those people who view morality only through their own system. Narrow moralists have long succeeded in making private issues legal and public issues. And persecution is not limited to those *guilty* but also those presumed *guilty*. Perhaps the fight for rights is a reaction to the behavior of the narrow moralists. To blame homosexuals is entirely misplaced. The right to privacy is more broadly moral. The right to not being persecuted, beaten, imprisoned and killed is also more broadly moral. It is not uncommon for morals and rights to conflict. When they do, broader morality and civility should triumph. We should not rely upon a morality that disregards time since its antiquity. Neither should we overvalue the narrow value of a group who continues to believe in it without regard to the values of broader morality.

I never said that I ". . . **object to the word, 'sodomy' because it is Biblical and implies sin.**" Furthermore, allowing homosexuals to be homosexuals is far from my promoting their behavior. The fact that the word sodomy comes to most of us from the Judeo-Christian bible speaks to a certain religious moral context; as does the evil of mixing wool with linen, and the eating of pork. The meaning and scope of the term sodomy is more (or less) than that of Black's Law Dictionary. I very much doubt it is in vogue for lesbians to have anal intercourse and I've never known any homosexual to be sexually involved with an animal. But something upsets the narrow moralists among us about *these* people. I would guess much of people's concern is less about homosexuals than about their own imaginations of what their actual behavior might consist of. But I submit that the persecution and gossip that surrounds homosexual activity remains constant and is itself a constant moral problem that many people wish to ignore.

"**How soon we forget AIDS (originally labeled GRID- Gay-related Immune Deficiency).**"

And let us not forget the common term Americans used for blacks and black slaves. And let us not forget what many people still call blacks. How soon we forget and forgive our own ignorance. What we *first* call something is not in any way the best or most definitive terminology.

AIDS may have been called GRID by Americans who were ignorant of what it was, where it began, who it could infect, and how. My understanding is that the disease began in Africa and was most likely was transmitted to humans through the blood of the chimpanzees that were caught to be eaten. Once transmitted to humans it mutated into HIV. Sexually transmitted diseases have always been a problem for all sexes (innocent, guilty, adult and child). AIDS was unique in that the stigmas surrounding homosexuality kept it from being swiftly addressed by good and moral people who thought they were immune and that it was God's curse upon homosexuals. Since AIDS had never been restricted to the gay community, it finally became important enough to finally be controlled, and the entire world, including Africa has been the better for it.

SHARON: The objective "idea" of race is the result of the classification of humans by observation, measurement, and description of objective characteristics of members of the genus Homo – "we are all the same this way." It is an exercise begun in the eighteenth century as Europeans circumnavigated the globe and brought back exotica for study and classification. The subjective "idea" of race is that of personal perception of "the other" and that perception is an important item of our survival equipment. The subjective perception of "the other" is not a methodical classification, but to a large degree, is an unconscious evaluation of friend or foe and has to be seen as a protective instinct. The fact that distinct races developed from a common ancestor suggests a high degree of racial exclusivity over tens of thousands of years that occurred in spite of geographical proximity. You seem to take a political view of race rather than an evolutionary or anthropological view and you say, ". . . government is charged with the task of trying to trying to be sure that all people have their rights protected equally. Since this is *all people*, it assumes an equality of protection; generally protection from those who have *natural* power . . ." I assume you are referring only to the U.S. government and the people subject to its jurisdiction? Or do you think that there should be a world government that protects the rights of all people? If so, what would those "rights" be? Voting? Owning property? Safety from abuse? Gay marriage? Abortion? Contraception? Sexual freedom? Free speech, gun ownership, freedom of religion? How do Pygmies, Goldi, and Fuegians fit into this dispersal of power and rights?

You mention the concept of "natural power" and characterize it as something from which people without that power need to be protected. However, natural power is what the

75

males of our race have used to protect their people – starting with their families. That natural power is what distinguishes men from women and consequently only men have been required to serve in our military. That fact alone is an inequality that was entirely ignored by the women's suffrage movement.

PAUL: You say that, "The objective 'idea' of race is the result of the classification of humans by observation, measurement, and description of objective characteristics of members of the genus Homo . . ."

Yes, too often the drive for objectivity seems to devalue the fact that it is we, as subjects, that do all of the objectivizing of our subjects. We objectify these subjects while using the term *objective* which tends to hide behind the fact that our judgments are ultimately subjective. It has little to do with methodical classification. I will agree that we are all the same race and that our ability to observe, value and stress differences between us often causes difference to come between us. So I will also agree that ". . . the subjective perception of 'the other' is not a methodical classification, but to a large degree, is an unconscious evaluation of friend or foe and has to be seen as a protective instinct." And far too often it is a conscious decision to view others as *foe*, or *less than*, or as those *we wish to keep down*.

And, yes, I take a political view of race rather than preferring some evolutionary or anthropological view because this is how most people *apply* the term race. Anthropology and evolution is the study of the past; often a past that doesn't resemble or matter to our present political climate. We must govern in the present with an eye toward the future. Much of my approach is because there is no such thing as difference in race; there are only differences in how others appear to us and main area of ancestral origin. The value of race within today's society is not a belief I harbor. And beyond this fact, government is charged with the task of trying to trying to be sure all people have their rights protected. In our real world this means the protection of those who lack power from those who have natural, majoritarian or political power. I think that any society that wants to elect a government that has maximum value should opt for a government that expresses these values. A world government is not my concern and unnecessary.

I do characterize natural power as something from which people without that power need to be protected. Our nation was founded to rule by laws rather than strength. It has been known by some as civilization. Many of us pride ourselves upon protecting those without power, the poor, weak, disabled, women, children etc. It is meant to be civil law rather than the law of the jungle. Society and civilization have evolved :)

The fact that "only men have been required to serve in our military" is true. And now women can be part of the military. Women have proven themselves to surpass some males in some traditionally male areas. This fact alone demonstrates that inequality has often been forced rather than evolving naturally. Perhaps it was enforced so that no woman could demonstrate their superiority over some males. A reality entirely ignored by those who don't like the news.

Too often women are too busy giving birth, feeding and caring for children to fight off the beast of the wilderness. Men generally took care of that task. But many women can take on that fight, but I know of no men who have the power to give birth. Yet men still wish to control the process.

SHARON: All thought is subjective by virtue of the fact that the subject is doing the thinking and to take it one step further one could say that an "objective reality" doesn't exist outside the thoughts and perceptions of the subject. Seems like a tautology and that is not what I was talking about. You slipped in a different meaning of the word, 'subject', to indicate one who is being "objectified" or judged inferior and that wasn't what I was talking about either. By ignoring anthropology and evolution you are devaluing those who have been made to give up their racial identities to live within a totally foreign environment, among people unlike themselves. How is that humane? That's cultural hubris. You pride yourself in seeing no racial distinctions, but in doing so you are denying the uniqueness of other humans who have their own ways of life. To understand them one must know and appreciate their past, not just charge the government with insuring their "rights" in someone else's world. You don't value race but that doesn't mean others don't value their racial identities.

You wrote "Civil law rather than the law of the jungle." Who lives in the jungle and why don't they have civil law? :)

PAUL: The idea "that an 'objective reality' doesn't exist outside the thoughts and perceptions of the subject" seems to be the majority view of philosophers today. I, however, am in the minority by placing more value upon the greater reality outside our view (and the possibilities) than upon those specifics upon which we place our focus. But most of us just mix idealism and realism together without much thought.

I'm not sure I slipped in a different meaning of the word "subject". When we treat a subject (a person) as an object (let's say a race), that person, the subject, is dehumanized by now being seen as an object. I guess you'll have to explain to me how this isn't what we are talking about.

I don't ignore anthropology and evolution, I've spoken of it often with you. I simply don't overvalue it. Evolution, by definition is process (hopefully progress). So I can't pick some specific time frame within history and declare that this is who we are and where we are from. It is simply where some of our ancestors might have been from.

Nobody is forced (or shouldn't be) to give up the way they identify however limited their definition may be. But we should recognize the limits of their and our distinctions. I also don't believe that when they move they will necessarily live within a totally foreign environment, among people unlike themselves. Among my neighbors who look different from me, we have much more in common than we have differences. What they thought they knew of "us" before they moved here, and what I knew of *them* was purely speculative. When now we speak to each other so that we may clarify our assumptions.

All of the ideas I learned in school about the subject of evolution have made several major shifts since then. Back then we learned about debates about whether there were 3 races, 5, 7? The *science* wasn't settled then and it is not settled now. In the 50's, many proclaimed the idea of race to be dead; there was only the human race. Then in the idea of race resurfaced through the noting of genetic markers. Geneticists noted that these markers may at least point toward a continental origin, but many people again saw this as a way to categorize race. I learned that humans originated in one place. Then I learned there may have been several places of origin. Now it is back to one again to Africa. Some said we all started out black and so the black race was superior. Other people said we were all covered in fur and that underneath we were all white and so the white race is superior. Both these ideas assume that the oldest has evolved the longest and somehow must there-fore be superior. Now, I may be condensing this somewhat but if I broaden it out it doesn't help much. We love the idea that the first was best, but we also love the idea of evolution and progress.

Now, I could pick the theory I happen to like but this isn't sci-ence. My preference might only point toward an idealistic ten-dency or displays my bias. I devalue such distinctions especially since we don't know. Then the practical side of me causes me to devalue these distinctions too, because these ever changing distinc-tions have next to noting to do with today, or with how people within a multicultural society deal with each other; unless of course we claim racial superiority above others within society. This option too has consequences. I see no benefit in greeting my *black* brother by assuming much of anything about his roots. He has no benefit in assuming much about mine. I don't even know my own father's *roots* past just a generation in Scotland. And there is no reason whatsoever for me to think that or assumptions about each others roots (no matter how educated we are in the subjects) will be accurate, let alone helpful or valuable to me today. Your studied views on these subjects are different from mine yet we've studied the same subjects. This should tell us a lot. So many of our opin-ions are linked to how we view rather than what we view (or even choose to view). I haven't seen where my ignorance of my own an-cestry has harmed me. But maybe it has and I'm too ignorant to know it. Maybe you can tell me. What answers will my research into my father's unknown ancestry give me? I suggest that what I get out of it has much less to do with science (anthropology and evolution) than what it has to do with the personal feelings and thoughts I put into it.

It is in how we discriminate that matters to society today. I see all kinds of distinctions but they are not race based. I can see skin color. I can see blond hair, blue eyes, freckles. I have no reason to pride myself on seeing these distinctions or not priding myself upon seeing or not seeing them. They simply are there. The blond hair, blue eyed people don't seem to be that different enough from the red headed, freckled Korean woman next door. These distinctions do not help us get along. In fact, the lack of distinction seems to suit us all fine. It is humane. And we are unique far beyond skin tone, blemish or fairness of hair. And once we get past our specialties at work, we share much more in common in our ways of life than not.

So, you are right, I don't value the idea of race the way some others seem to overvalue it. I'm not into sports either. I would assume that jungle dwellers live in jungles and I assume they may have some sort of civil law that intends to protect others more evenly unless the civil law is overridden by the strong. But I am sorry for this example. I was just trying to imagine a time long long ago that only *might* have existed. The law of the jungle applying to animals as well as humans. Just as the *wild west* might in some ways look like the *law of the jungle*. But my example was perhaps so far out of date that its usefulness to our current conversation is dubious.

Is somebody making you give up your racial identity?

Before Sharon replied:
PAUL: We seem to be going around in circles. We sound like a Republican arguing with a Democrat, or an atheist arguing with a Christian. Why is this? Isn't this the more interesting question? Why do you suppose a discussion about race and culture shares this similarity?

In your first comment to me, you questioned how I thought we could have different values when "we were raised in the same family at roughly the same time, in the same community, among the same people, same education, etc." Would you now say we have different values? Or is it something else?

SHARON: I like to argue because it helps me think. It is especially good to have a thinking man as an "opponent" because your input is stimulating. You might tire of "going around in circles", but I don't think we are as far apart as Christians and atheists and not as superficial as Republicans and Democrats. One essential difference between us is gender and, to some degree, life experience or age. I was much closer to your viewpoint thirty years ago.

PAUL: I agree that argument makes me think and keeps me sharp. Like you, I was much closer to where you are now forty years ago, and I used to argue as such. But several things happened over the next ten years that turned my head around. From then on it has been a slow, deliberate turning. I've turned dramatically before but I found myself being too reactionary. I'm much more methodical now because reaction isn't a process, it's, well, reaction :) I prefer action that almost borders on a sort of non-action. I'm pretty conservative that way. How do you think gender has influenced you?

SHARON: The female is tightly bound to her biological role - and most of us are not conscious of that bond and the effect it has on our thoughts, feelings, behavior, and interests. Women operate in a narrow sphere - practically, intellectually, and morally. There is no fulfillment to be found in competition with men and while a woman may excel in some field there are always many ordinary men who do as well or better. Filling professions with women when there is no lack of qualified men is irrational. I have reexamined my own development with this basic insight in mind and I find that I can explain things about myself that I never really understood before. Women need the moral guidance of strong and honorable men and that is one of the things so lacking in today's society that as Yeats wrote: "Things fall apart. The center cannot hold. The falcon cannot hear the falconer".

PAUL: "The female"?
I thought I asked about you :)
I've noticed that you are much more likely to group people together by various characteristics than I. You can say that: *the female* this, *the male* that, *this race* that, *this sexual group* who. You also tend to group into blocks of time like when you say, ". . . to-

day's society that as Yeats wrote: . . ." when this quote is from 1919, and some of your references to an era of western tradition go back and include hundreds of years. You also place more value upon area groups like continents. Another area of grouping seems to go under headings I'll call *that time in history when things were better*. In example you have pointed toward a group called the nuclear family: ". . . Western tradition is the nuclear family – a tradition that is rooted in our biology and has evolved over thousands of years among European peoples . . ."

This block gathers groups of people into time, hemisphere, group of science, the science group of evolution (as a group over time), then back to a continental grouping. For you these groupings are primary whereas to me they are necessary footnotes.

In another example you say, ". . . while a woman may excel in some field there are always many ordinary men who do as well or better. Filling professions with women when there is no lack of qualified men is irrational."

Like other examples of grouping, this generalization assumes too much. If there existed a monoculture in which a society was populated only with nuclear families, and some female individual wanted to break with culture by wanting a job instead of filling her role within the society of nuclear families, and there was some male who shared her qualifications and would fail in his role within the nuclear family if he did not get this job, then I can see why such a society might discriminate against this woman in order for the man to have *his* job. But this is not the country in which we live nor is it a country that has ever existed and can't exist. This sentence simply confirms that a desire is a desire, and it is not real - ity.

Now, it does no good to ponder that this world did exist or even could exist. Why? Because there will never be an equal ratio of men to women. Even if there was, the man of the family could be - come disabled in such a way that the very existence of the family might depend upon the woman working (unless the society insures that this family is cared for – or there is some other way for her to pull herself up by her boot straps – which she doesn't own because it was never conceded that the position might be relevant, neces - sary or even good) in order to support the family. Here we have an -

other problem within the problem. This family is no longer the nuclear family as defined by the term (the male head of the family can no longer provide for it). So even the society that can't be (as a collective), isn't. So, I'm less interested in discussing things that never were and that can't ever be. And while I know you are speaking in generalizations, we don't live in general. We live as individuals in a specific present. Individuals comprise a generality (it can't the nuclear family because the man might become incapacitated) which is merely a generalization. I think this reality matters.

When I speak of reality as it exists, I am also talking about infinite reality as spanning infinite time. There is inequality in ratios between the sexes; inequality in health, ability, income and outcome. There have been many families that fit the definition of a nuclear family at one time but not at another. But the essential reality is that within reality, nothing is constant or more general than change and inconstancy.

In today's reality (Sunday, September 13, 2015), in these United States, we have nuclear families and non-nuclear families. Given the realities of today, I could die and my wife's family changes immediately. This is no fault or choice (I hope) of her own. She has no desire for me to die (I hope:) nor does she want to work two jobs (I'm sure), yet she may have to get another job to supplement her income no matter her value (or lack thereof) of a nuclear family. She may be forced to compete with an equally qualified male to get this job or she might have to rely upon some sort of assistance from others within collective society in order not to work but in order to survive. So when you say that, **"filling professions with women when there is no lack of qualified men is irrational"**, I will say that the conditions that make this sentence true only exist within the grouping tendencies of the individual sentence as you have written it. It has no truth to speak to with regard to reality as it exists today. There is no collective that is filling professions. My wife is not *women*, she is an individual in a her own circumstance within a society that will either recognize and value the reality of circumstance or not. She has to deal with her personal yet ever-present reality as it now exists rather than some ideal.

I, on the other hand, accept the fact that reality is complicated and not uniform. In many ways, I have no way of knowing what people deny within their personal realities. I also don't presume to know. I accept what individuals say (even if the thoughts expressed appear to me to be a matter of false belief) for several reasons. One is that individuals have the personal autonomy (not by some right of conscience but simply because they have a mind separate from my own or the collective) to think what they want (no matter how foolish their thoughts may seem to me), and also because even if my own belief might simply be my own personal belief or individual value. And perhaps I too am fooling myself in thinking they (or I) have any (or even a little) personal autonomy. Perhaps I am fooling myself into thinking I can know what I can't know and what they can't know. Perhaps I'm in error with my own thoughts or in assuming I can know the myriad of points of view I am always missing. Or perhaps I can and do know more than I give myself credit for. But, regardless, the larger problem always enters when I assume that general knowledge is so broad that it applies to others. I assume that they are the same as me and so they will act in a similar way that I would given the same circumstance.

I'm not a big believer in free will. I'm not a big believer in grouping people together. Though extremely independent, I'm not a fan of the idea of rugged individualism. I narrowly value the idea of individual freedom. My coming to all of my ideas about such things has been a very slow turning for me. The ideas of free will, rugged individualism and individual freedom are not only obvious to the vast majority of people I know, they seem to be God given and not to be questioned among real Americans. I've met with more vitriol trying to discuss the idea of free will than I've met with when trying to discuss both religion and politics put together. If I were an atheist I'd be forgiven first.

But this little interlude brings up an interesting thought: I regard *society* as much more foundational and primary than I regard the individual to be. (I assume I'm a lot like you this way.) Also, I tend to take a long view of the value of history (I assume I'm a lot like you this way) yet my focus is always upon today and with how an individual fits within society. So although society is foundational with the individual secondary, the individual is the focus. (So much for what may sound like my Communitarian ideas.) Your groupings are not realistic to me because they value the idea of the group exclusive of the individual. Your groupings are more like Utopian non-realities for me. My individuals are based *within* the divergent societies of today, and my interest in individual rights (apart from any grand social goals over time) must correspond to society as it exists today. The individual and society are part and parcel of each other. So, many rights may be aimed toward the individual but their necessity is toward how well the individual fits into society and visa versa. Your groups seem to represent a majoritarian power while my emphasis upon rights give smaller groups voice and power.

I've probably not thought of these ideas in quite this way before so they might sound a bit jumbled. I don't work from talking points. I'll work them out over time and try to express them better at another time.

You said, "Filling professions with women when there is no lack of qualified men is irrational. I have reexamined my own development with this basic insight in mind and I find that I can explain things about myself that I never really understood before." Tell me more about this.

SHARON: I started at the top, but didn't get very far.

Both men and women are identified and grouped on the basis of their biology. As human beings we are aware from infancy of the differences between the two sexes that comprise the essential complement of our human existence. When you recognize any person as a man or a woman you are assigning him/her to a group. We assign ourselves to the appropriate group. While racial distinctions may not be as clearly defined, they are also perceived instinctively and it is only a pretense that one can ignore race and respond to people as undefined members of the genus Homo. I see time as a continuum, evolution as a process, and civilization as a cycle. Humans, like all other creatures have limits on their mentation. We have great difficulty in conceiving of infinity, creation, eternity, nothingness, beginnings and ends. As far as we can tell cats don't think about such things, nor are they plagued with concepts like good and evil, or right and wrong, much less "rights" and "power." To ease the suffering as we confront our mental limitations the wise men of the past created allegory for themselves and for their posterity.

The nuclear family isn't a group; it is a social structure that, along with monogamy, exogamy, and the absence of large, extended family, evolved in Northern Europe, where, it is theorized, the harshness of the environment required male provisioning of the female and their children. In other words, the nuclear family provided a survival advantage and over thousands of years that advantage has resulted in a people that unconsciously view that structure as optimal. If you consider monogamy and the nuclear family arbitrary "footnotes" rather than primary, evolutionary social structures one wonders why you have practiced monogamy within a nuclear family. There must be something unconsciously compelling about that structure in our people since it is imitated by little children and even by homosexuals.

PAUL: I understand that because we can recognize groups, we do group. I understand why we might group. I also see the hazards. So I simply value the fact that individual people (or things) make up a group. Without the individuals, there can be no group. But individual things are *primary* and exist prior to a group. Perhaps I'm unique but I can seldom assign myself to many "appropriate" groups other than the most basic, like a human being. I find it difficult to fit into most groups, yet people constantly ask me where I fit in. They want me to fit in somewhere probably so they can assume more things about me. It should only be a shortcut on your way to actually knowing someone. I'm not sure why else would anybody would be so concerned with grouping? Therefore I place much more value upon the individual makings of a group while I devalue my assumptions or presumptions about how I perceive a group, or how others perceive any group. And while you say "while racial distinctions may not be as clearly defined, they are also perceived instinctively", I don't know this to be an instinct at all but I do know that people's perceptions are almost always intermixed with (and confused by) their non-instinctive preferences and biases.

"I see time as a continuum, evolution as a process, and civilization as a cycle."

Good line.

"We have great difficulty in conceiving of infinity, creation,

86

eternity, nothingness, beginnings and ends."

I will agree even though these are a few of my favorite things. Sing along :)

"If you consider monogamy and the nuclear family arbitrary "footnotes" rather than primary, evolutionary social structures one wonders why you have practiced monogamy within a nuclear family."

I wouldn't, and didn't call these footnotes "arbitrary", I simply call them footnotes. I don't value the nuclear family as a main part of the story of humanity so much as I regard it as a footnote to it.

So, either other cultures (besides the Northern Europeans) have had very similar family structures or these other cultures faired quite well without similar family structures. Either way, the Northern European nuclear family would merely be a footnote.

SHARON: Haven't we been talking about the most "basic" groups – genus, species, gender, reproductive role, marriage, family, race (evolutionary adaptations), language, demographics (majority, minority), and mental scope as it relates to morality and social justice? In your first note in this conversation you grouped yourself as an American whose tradition has the "...ability to look beyond the limits of our current points of view in order to realize the greater values that exist beyond these limits." Surely, this "American" ability is an example of what Spengler calls the "Faustian spirit" of Western man. The ability to "look beyond" is one of the things that makes Western Civilization unique and that is hardly a footnote to your sense of who you are as an individual.

PAUL: While we've often spoken of your ideas about basic groups, we've also spoken of my preference for persons and things independent of these groupings. I've gone so far as to speak toward infinity, beyond individuals, things and groups. When we limit our conversations to groupings, I have noted that I don't value your groupings. I don't value the division of people into colors or peoples by continent. There are many other groupings we could focus upon. And this shift in focus necessarily shifts our viewpoints. And so yes, I too can speak of groups but I think there are limits in doing so, and there are limits to the conclusions we draw from our groupings.

Yes, it is important for us to look beyond the value of our groupings as well as looking beyond the limits of our current individual points of view. When we fail to realize the limits of viewpoint and the limits of our groupings, we fail to realize the greater values that exist beyond all these limits. This is neither an American ability nor a uniquely American disability. It may be a problem for Americans and the problem is not limited to Western civilization or any other group; every individual everywhere has the same limits: East, West, North and South, black, white, and all shades and locales in between.

After several weeks with no response, I commented upon a Facebook *post to an article about something the 2016 primary presidential candidate Ben Carson said about not allowing a Muslim to be president.*

PAUL: In the early 1960's Catholicism was inconsistent with the presidency. Questions were raised about whether John Kennedy would place national interests above the wishes of the Catholic church. Now in the latest news from 1960, Ben Carson says he wouldn't support a Muslim for president because Islam is not consistent with the Constitution.

Now, it seems to me that neither Islam, Judaism nor Christianity are consistent with the Constitution because monotheism admonishes adherents not to place any other god before God. In this way of looking at things, nationalism, pledges of allegiance, flags and other forms of patriotism are inconsistent with all these faith traditions.

SHARON: The Constitution was written to protect the people from a government-imposed practice of religion, and to give the individual freedom to practice his religion. It does not protect us from the judgment of others. Carson may think that the beliefs of Muslims are unacceptable for a president of the U.S. just as some would judge Carson's Seventh Day Adventist beliefs, Romney's Mormonism, or Kennedy's Catholicism to be unacceptable.

JB comments: Remember that the political edicts that were assembled around islam are what's known as sharia, and sharia is #not# compatable with our Constitution. Actually, it's not compatable with any institution that places value on human life and dignity. It's about force, really, and not much more.

PAUL: My point exactly. But as it is, not all Muslims support sharia law above other law, just like not all Christians or Jews support *an eye for an eye* or *the ten commandments* above U.S. civil law. (Though it is in the Judeo-Christian bible, *an eye for an eye* wasn't some command put forth by God. It came from Babylon's first king, Hammurabi.)

We shouldn't group all Muslims together this way. In this country we have fundamentalist Christians, Jews and Muslims whose fundamentalism makes them seem more alike than their differing religions might first suggest. Fundamentalism tends to make people inflexible. Flexible people, however, tend to place far more value upon humility, moderation, tolerance, patience, understanding, compassion, charity, social responsibility and graciousness, human life and dignity.

JB: The koran requires muslims to continuously "rise" to sharia, or the "correct path". Neither the Torah nor the books that make up the old and new testaments of the Christian bible contain anything like the koran's instructions to the people of these times to commit these kinds of atrocities against others.

SHARON chimes in: Both quotes are from the Jewish Torah, not the Christian New Testament. The Jewish Talmud is more than a match for the Koran.

PAUL: You are reading a different Bible than I. But I don't have the time to quote each and every instance of religious bigotry within the Bible. But I can tell you that the majority of Muslims are not as you claim. Islam is the largest and fastest growing religion on earth and there is good reason why they haven't risen to conquer the rest of us: most Muslims simply do not believe the fundamentalist strains within their own books. I'm sorry if you don't believe me but one's belief never makes something so. I suggest you go out and meet many Muslims and see if any you meet share your vision of who they really are.

JB: We can save discussion on the bible for another day. I'm guessing though that we probably have a similar translation. I'll also guess that the way it's being read is totally different. I'm not a bigot or a fool, Paul. But I will call a spade a spade if a spade I see. You're right - not all muslims are hard liners that want to roll with ISIS. I will venture to say that whatever goodness or decency or dignity they possess is not a product of this sick religion, but rather of a society or family structure that has survived in spite of said religion. It's strange to me that the teachings of Jesus Christ have largely been relegated to the trash bin of political-incorrectness by American society while every effort is being made to accomodate this blood-thirsty belief system that advocates the beating and subjugating of women, the murdering of people who might be gay, stoning someone who committed adultry, ad nauseum. At some point, America's going to have to reconcile it's lack of a backbone in its dealings with islam the religion, regardless of how many nice muslims we know.

PAUL: JB, JB, JB, I don't think I would ever call you a bigot or a fool, and I didn't. We just disagree about facts and belief. Muslims share and value some of *our* bible and find Jesus to be an important prophet. But like you and I, individual Muslims will read the same religious books differently than each other, just as you and I read our books differently. You and I will often read the same Constitution differently and it make neither of us right or wrong. It's okay. This is what people do. But I also think it's fair to note when your words do seem to contradict themselves. You say, "not all muslims are hard liners", but then you call Islam "this sick religion . . . regardless of how many nice muslims we know." So although you attempt to distinguish some individuals apart from their professed religion, it merely sounds like lip service.

I see no value in demonizing individuals who have their own understanding of things by labeling their religion as sick. It sounds like you don't like it when people (not me by the way) put down "the teachings of Jesus Christ [that] have largely been relegated to the trash bin of political-incorrectness".

It's always too easy to blame *them* for doing this but we find it perfectly right for *us* to do it. I think we can do better than this. If we don't try to do better, it's too easy for our own ideas to become a "blood-thirsty belief system". And if we should want to call ourselves Christians (whether some people find it to be politically correct or not) there should be some sort of difference between *our* foundational values and *theirs*. If there is no difference then we are just groups blaming other groups for being groups. We go around and around while we all claim to be better than those who do the same thing. I think we need a to take a bit more care with our words and the way we group other individuals.

JB: The individual who happens to claim islam as "their" religion is different from the "religion" itself. The member is the individual, the religion is dogma. Belief in a particular religion means spiritual and intellectual submission (in varying degrees) to that dogma. Christianity and islam are polar opposites - one elevates and celebrates while the other threatens and destroys. One teaches hope and faith, the other teaches fear and subjugation. Yep - there's good and bad among the adherants of islam, but the religion itself - the dogma - is sick. It's a work of darkness. The actual practice of islam is a train wreck.

I tend to write the same way I speak, but even so - I don't believe I demonized anyone. If someone's decent with me, they can expect better than that in return from me and I wont even check to see what dogma they adhere to. If someone does me dirty, I'll probably return the favor. If someone's dogma of choice presents itself as a rallying point for thugs, then I wont hesitate to call it as it is.

PAUL: I was agreeing with you until you said, "Christianity and islam are polar opposites - one elevates and celebrates while the other threatens and destroys. One teaches hope and faith, the other teaches fear and subjugation."

You need to read more; more about the Christian crusades, the burning of witches, the KKK lynchings that many people walked past on their way to church the morning after burning crosses in lawns. Yes, they called themselves Christians too. Slavery was defended by words in the Bible. So, "[i]f someone's dogma of choice presents itself as a rallying point for thugs, then I wont hesitate to call it as it is." So, will you call Christianity what it is? No, you don't have to. But for some reason you have to when one speaks of Islam.

You can also read about Islam and its value of unity. Yes, people and their beliefs and interpretations are imperfect, at best, often much worse. Sure I can pick apart the bad things about Christianity just as you can Islam. We can match jab for jab, but I will not change your beliefs. *They* will not change their beliefs either.

I will call *belief* The problem. It is a deep psychological condition (or conditioning) that opposes faith. I can quote chapter and verse that shows how true faith can keep us from these errors. But you seem to favor your belief that one religion can be right while another is wrong. *Belief* (*dogma* if you will) is the train wreck regardless of which religion admonishes anyone to believe. Belief causes you to miss the fact that you can say, "I don't believe I demonized anyone", and follow this statement with "the dogma - is sick . . . a work of darkness", and not realize that demonization and darkness go hand in hand. Individuals are members of religion and so you demonize entire groups with your beliefs; and you don't have to.

You can have faith (the opposite of belief). You can have the reality of God. You can admire Jesus. You can do these things without being blinded by belief. The words of Jesus are some of the best: Turn the other cheek and forgive. But I missed it when Jesus admonished that, "If someone does you dirty, return the favor." :) You're better than this JB. I know you are.

JB: We seem to be talking past each other, and once again you missed my point(s). People - as in individuals - are #not# religions, they are not dogmas. They are a member or adherant or disciple or whatever of a particular belief system, however spot-on or misguided they may be. Did the Christian belief system cause the crusades? No. Individuals acting at the behest of a leader with no scriptural authority for the crusades did. Did islam "cause" the 20 some odd thousand atrocities committed worldwide by its members or adherants since 9-11? The argument can be made that it did, based on what is written in their holy book. Almost every act has scriptural authority. A glaring difference between the two systems is the stuff contained between the pages of their holy writings. One provides authority for barbaric acts and subjugation, the other does not. I think if you and I were talking face to face we'd be agreeing more often than not, Paul. *Facebook* is to thoughtful communication what a chainsaw is to surgical equipment.

PAUL: Once again I was with you for half of your reply until you said, "Did islam 'cause' the 20 some odd thousand atrocities committed worldwide by its members or adherants since 9-11? The argument can be made that it did, based on what is written in their holy book."

You and I know (or should know) that arguments can be and are made that the Judeo-Christian bible too often intends violence too. And I could go on but it makes little sense because it is *ourselves* who act, not the books. It is *we* who interpret our books, and *our* actions will demonstrate responsibility or irresponsibility. It is *our* beliefs that feed our actions and so we must be very critical of our own beliefs. These are moral issues that people must talk about and deal with instead of hiding behind our books while calling them righteous and true. I'm not afraid to make this argument against *our* holy books as well as *theirs*, but we should always first intend to take the log out of our own eye before trying to remove the speck from our neighbor's.

Books have only the authority we lend them, and I'm a stingy lender when it comes to the authority of belief. I hope our communication always provides food for thought. I'll forgive the *Facebook* chainsaw. :)

SHARON: The politics on this point are very confused. First, they want to criticize Trump for not correcting a person who called Obama a Muslim - with the clear implication that it is would be intolerable if he were a Muslim; then they take Ben Carson down because he thinks Islam is incompatible with our Constitution; then you have liberals running to the defense of Muslims, inviting them to MIT and the White House because their adolescent genius has been wronged. "Cool bomb, I mean, clock, Muhammed".*

The last line is in reference to a young American named Muhammed who made a clock and brought it to school, and the teacher called the police thinking it was a bomb.

PAUL: I agree, the *politics* get very confused. So often ideas get mixed up with the other ideas.

My first comments assumed the main topic to be religious law *v* civil law; religious *v* secular. But there are other assumptions made or to be made.

You mention "they". I'm sure *they* are a group or groups. Who are *they*? The so called news media? The Democrats? The liberals? Entire groups? An entire group called Muslims are accused when one radical (or group of radical fundamentalists) acts radically. Is it no surprise (or instruction) that we are more careful when a Christian bombs an abortion clinic? We make sure that *if* we include them within the group called Christianity that we call them Fundamentalist Christians, or Christian radicals. We are far less likely to give Muslims, as a group, that latitude. This is because there is, like you say, clear implications.

By the way, what exactly do you mean by, "a clear implication that it is would be intolerable if he were a Muslim?"

Am I correct to assume that the "it" in this sentence is *the fact that*? And am I correct to assume that the "he" in this sentence is

Barack Obama? Do we *accuse* him (this is the implication) of being Muslim in order to taint him with that radical portion of a much larger non-radical group's despicable actions?

My own comment about why I think Ben Carson is concerned that "Islam is incompatible with our Constitution", was verified today when he made his concern explicit. He said that he could support a Muslim candidate who renounced sharia law. Indeed, the contrast and distinction between religious law and civil law is the point. But as it is, not all Muslims support sharia law above other law, just like not all Christians or Jews support the *law*, the ten commandments, above U.S. civil law. And hopefully none of our religious groups (Christians included) will ever be so numerous that enough of us will vote for some religious law in America. We are all for democracy and the majority until we find ourselves in the minority. Should Christians and Jews running for president be forced to renounce the ten commandments?

We shouldn't group all Muslims together this way. In this country we have fundamentalist Christians, Jews and Muslims whose fundamentalism makes them seem more alike than their differing religions might first suggest. Fundamentalism tends to make people inflexible. Flexible people, however, tend to place far more value upon humility, moderation, tolerance, patience, understanding, compassion, charity, social responsibility and graciousness, human life and dignity.

To bring up Donald Trump and an "adolescent genius" into this issue is to confuse the politics even further.

SHARON: "They" are the ones who orchestrated the response to this non-event. I mean, really - every newspaper in the country chastised Trump, not for what he said, but what he didn't say to someone with an axe to grind. The whole thing is so preposterous that I suspect the questioner was a paid provocateur. "They" include Hillary Clinton and the White House spokesman. The "clear implication" is contained in the meaning of the phrase "The lady doth protest too much methinks" The overweening reaction makes Muslims look bad - so bad that Obama needs to be protected from such a charge and Ben Carson must be chastised. What is a Muslim who does not support Sharia law? If a

Catholic renounces Catholicism is he still a Catholic? Would you say that religious fundamentalism of any kind is incompatible with our constitution and would you oppose the candidacy of any fundamentalist for public office? Do you criticize all religious fundamentalists for lacking flexibility, humility, patience, understanding, graciousness, moderation, tolerance, compassion, social responsibility, charity, human life, and dignity?

PAUL: Okay, just checking. I didn't want to assume who "they" were and then misunderstand. But I still wouldn't say they "orchestrated" the "event". I also wouldn't "**suspect the questioner was a paid provocateur.**" I think there are far more simple explanations. People are rude and love to shout their beliefs from the rooftops. I seem to remember a similar thing happening to John McCain but McCain handled his explanation a bit better. Still, all in all, I would agree that what grew out of the interchange was preposterous. There are better arguments we and they could have.

"**What is a Muslim who does not support Sharia law? If a Catholic renounces Catholicism is he still a Catholic?**"

Well, I would say that the person might be a bad Catholic but might well be a fine Christian. Sects are sects. Fundamentalists are fundamental (by definition) but perhaps my definition is too narrow.

I wouldn't say that a fundamentalist should necessarily be exempt from running for office, in fact it should be expected to be a large part of the debate. And I'd be sad to see America get to the point where fundamentalism is an extreme national problem. So perhaps the debate had better be very public, and the sooner the better.

I have yet to observe any sort of religious fundamentalism that is flexible, humble, patient, understanding, gracious, moderate, tolerant, compassionate, socially responsible, charitable, humane. But I'd be happy to learn of some if you know of any. I'd love to have my simplistic statement challenged so that I might learn.

SHARON: I said the response was orchestrated, not the event, and my speculation that the questioner was a plant could explain why it became the top news story nationwide within hours. It makes sense, too, that the McCain comparison was ready to go because by itself it is unmemorable as well as being inapt. McCain didn't dispute the statement that "Obama is an Arab". He didn't correct the questioner; he let her assertion stand, so it is hard to see how he "handled it" better than Trump. There is no question that Obama is not an Arab, while there are many reasons that people may believe he is a Muslim. In fact, Colin Powell's assertion that he has "always been a Christian" doesn't comport with the facts. I think it likely that "Christian Fundamentalism" is like "Radical Islam" in used more as a political pejorative than a well-defined set of religious beliefs. You define it negatively: It is inflexible and its adherents lack all the positive qualities that we generally associate with Christianity. It is worth noting that Jews seem to escape the charge of rigidity and yet Jews behave as members of a cult.

PAUL: I don't see that the response was even likely orchestrated as you suspect. There are easier explanations than the press getting together as some sort of cabal in order to respond in the same way. Each individual in a crowd will often respond similarly to an event because we tend to react in similar ways to similar events, even if those watching the same event describe it much differently.

There are many reasons why people hold many curious beliefs. The way I see it, belief is an outgrowth of knowledge and belief is the state where it stagnates, congeals and becomes rigid. We have a psychological tendency toward knowledge ending in belief rather than continuing on. The narrower one's field of view, the narrower the beliefs. We become more likely to compartmentalize thoughts into smaller and smaller groups. Our beliefs are as narrow as our vision narrows. Whereas the wider our field of view and the resulting inputs, the broader our ideas. But, unfortunately, we want ends. We want completion so we can make judgments. If we don't have ends, we assume them in order to judge. Even when we have a wide view, we want to express ourselves without having to say, *Hold on, I have a lifetime of things to see and learn before I decide. Hmmmm, I can't decide.* But we have to decide, while not closing our minds for the rest of time. Unfortunately many of us want permanent closure even if it closes our minds to the changing of our minds. I find certainty irresponsible if we think we can keep learning past the point of belief.

"You define it negatively: It is inflexible and its adherents lack all the positive qualities that we generally associate with Christianity. It is worth noting that Jews seem to escape the charge of rigidity and yet Jews behave as members of a cult."

I would say that when it comes to belief, most believers act cultish. I define fundamentalism as negative because the views focus upon the negative in all others but themselves. We would do better to consider the value of ideas and to argue them out to see which positive ideas rise to the top rather than pitting our blind belief against theirs, in a race to the bottom of this dark pit.

You like to associate positive qualities with Christianity but you want to condemn, as a group, all Jews. There are many fine Christians, Jews and Muslims. I would venture to say that the less fundamental they are, the more you and I might like them.

SHARON: When ownership of the media is virtually monopolized by Jews and their editorial policies are in agreement on important questions it is very likely that the amplification of this non-event and the massive response to something Trump did not say was orchestrated. You don't have to call it a cabal or a conspiracy, it's just the bias of the media that are protecting their own interests and manipulating public perception in order to control the political process in the U.S. Trump is an enormous problem for those who are used to exercising control. He has his own money. That is a game changer and they are having to scramble to find something - anything to discredit him. They can't ignore him. They can't really pretend that his popularity is fragile or that Ben Carson, Hillalry Clinton, Carly Fiorina, or Bernie Sanders can draw his support away. That leaves them with cheating. Stay tuned.

Sharon is speaking of some of the US primary presidential candidates.

PAUL: Oh, I think I forgot to reply to this one . . .

The only thing worse than a cabal is a Jewish cabal :) I think your term "bias" here is more fitting. If politics were a mere spectator sport (and a sport it is to most people who comment) without reporters (Jewish or no), I doubt the tweets and talk on *Facebook* about politics would be any different than how the media portrays it. Now, perhaps this is because the "Jews" have fed us the news for so long that we, as a society are so conditioned by their way of reporting that this conditioning of our society explains their reporting :) But like I said, bias is as more fitting here. Trump speaks well and directly to our biases. But perhaps I am one who is apparently too heavily influenced by Jewish media culture to recognize this, and so I should be more concerned. But I want to support candidates who help me rise above my biases. It has been said that in the time it takes to win over just one person by reason, a thousand people can be won over by appealing to their biases. Political Advertising 101.

SHARON: I have never talked to a Christian fundamentalist, much less known one and it seems to me that the reality has been supplanted by a media stereotype - white, ignorant, bigoted, Bible believer. It is significant that black, uneducated Bible-believers are not called Christian Fundamentalists - why is that? Aren't they rigid in their beliefs? You must have some experience with people who claim to be Christians, but who exhibit none of the values we normally associate with Christianity. It's a little more difficult to see the hypocrisy of Muslim and Jewish fundamentalists because we are not as familiar with their values as we are with their rituals. What are the fundamental values of Islam or Judaism?

PAUL: I've known many Christian fundamentalists and their beliefs don't necessarily have as much to do with their level of education as with rigid literalism and their conservative intentions to remain apart secular society. I personally don't know any black "Bible-believers" (living here is SLC) but from those I've read, they seem more liberal than literal. (By "conservative" I mean those who prefer more *traditional* (perhaps) understandings of words, whereas *liberal* tends to be more *liberated from* more traditional interpretations.) None of this seems to have much to do with color or education. But I'm sure that if I lived elsewhere I'd have more opportunities to meet fundamentalist blacks.

Some people (even including some diligent bible readers and church goers) seem to be more interested in broader society than exclusive society. In my book this is good. For me, faith and belief represent opposite things. Beliefs are focused and narrow whereas faith is lengthy and broad. Narrow thoughts tend to end in a belief and refuse any advancement. Such sureness leads away from the humility that allows progress. Faith values the progress inherent within reality because reality moves far beyond our selves and our egos.

I would dare say that most fundamentalist Christians I personally know exhibit few of the values many others associate with Christianity. Sects talk a similar talk, share similar beliefs, worship together, but their groups are more exclusive than the broader ideas of Christianity in general. But I am personally aware of many Christians who attempt to follow the broader teachings of Jesus. And most of these Christians, curiously, are social without being exclusive. They are non-denominational, and/or "Emergent". After thinking about this, it makes sense to me.

Jewish and Muslim fundamentalists share all the same characteristics as Christian fundamentalists because they all see themselves as conservative (even though they may actually be radical), and they all value belief over faith. The psychology of belief is the same, and exclusive congregations much prefer followers and believers rather than questioners. This is why such different beliefs can seem so much alike at the fundamental level.

No reply.

After not hearing back for several weeks . . .
PAUL: Some misc thoughts on a Sunday Morning.

During any age, many people share the assumption that we are quite wise at this moment in history. I'm sure this was the case in thirteenth century Europe when a person's guilt or innocence was established by "ordeal". A person accused of murder was lowered into holy water. If he sank, he was innocent, and if he floated he was guilty. Or maybe a person was made to thrust a hand into boiling water and remain there for a given time. Or perhaps grab a piece of red-hot metal and walk for nine paces. And even after the idea and adoption of trial by jury became more popular, trial by ordeal persisted because it seemed concrete rather than abstract.

Today, in our wisdom, we look back upon such times with horror, all the while praising our own wisdom, often without question, as if we can't improve upon it. Today we tend to look at our values as absolute truths. In yesteryear it appears that we understood religion as myth; we valued myth then while today we call it true. In this way, myth loses its livelihood. Or maybe we look back to the past and simply see what we want to see. There are several reasons why I tend to think that myth was more common than truth when it came to religion. When looking back thousands of years at documents compiled, like the Judeo-Christian bible, there are many contradictions. I'm sure they saw the contradictions. I just think they looked at the ideas differently than we want to today.

Not all of us instinctively see groups in the same *ways* that others do. I may consider the world in its entirety and not divide it into color or continents. Europe, Africa and China seem to be important divisions for you. They seem obvious to you, but one could easily divide them into other groupings. One might consider other aspects of people and label people as warriors, religion peddlers, brothers, silk traders, spice experts, gold sellers, weavers, gem traders, disease bearers, artisans, friend, foe; regardless of race or continent. Many attributes many be found in people of many colors. Today every color of people have experts in each of many fields but, still, some distinction of color will regulate some people's thoughts.

I think many people overvalue their view of objectivity. When most people tell me that I'm not being objective, what they normally seem to mean is that I'm not seeing something from their point of view. But when we look at something from many points of view, we will be looking at things from myriad subjective viewpoints. So speaking about objectivity is tricky. We, as subjects, can only approach objectivity sideways if at all. We can only try to do this while honestly considering as many points of view as we can. To do this honestly we must regard every viewpoint as true. In doing so we find that *truth* has little to do with specific viewpoint. During the process we find that we must regard (or imagine) each view for what it is; it is convenient. So, what we end up with are various viewpoints that may be subjective but have been regarded in such a way as to be more equalized. What is interesting about this process of objectivity is that it relies upon our valuing many subjective viewpoints.

But wait, there's more. We also have to remember that the further removed we are from anything, the more general it becomes (or now seems as it becomes) from the distance of perspective. To remove ourselves in space is to remove ourselves in time. We become further away from its immediate condition. We remove ourselves from urgency. Once again, this is not the immediate world in which we live and probably shouldn't be. The further we back away, the more general things are. We must care right here in the right now about other people (subjects). Yet while backing away in an *objective* manner, soon within the process, we observe fewer details and can't see many specifics; we can only see groupings. Hence, the further the human is removed from humanity, the less humanity is involved. So, an objective view can be extremely enlightening but it also has its drawbacks and can ultimately become relatively unrealistic and inhumane. We have to have a balance because humans and human viewpoint are part of our view.

There's a militancy that goes hand in hand with group-ism that doesn't so often occur without it. Many of us proudly wave our flags and spout our beliefs within groups who agree with us but when alone, or in the minority, less anonymous, we are more likely to defer than to be persecuted for our beliefs. All people have biases and preferences. Some prefer their own race. Many are not aware of their biases, but I think that the vast majority of us are trying to do our best, biases and all. When it all comes down to it, I don't see how group-ism or a reductionism to individualism in another extreme can serve us well. The pie isn't one size, it seems to expand infinitely.

All this being said, I think that our ways of looking at things has much more to do with our own psychologies than with some sort of objectivity. I was born a white male into a society that values white males. Being decent looking is another thing society values. I am a thinker (tending toward the abstract) yet I grew up with feelings of inferiority; feeling out of place. People sometimes equate me with being geeky. I am introverted; not something society values. I was the youngest in our family. I was a boy with four older sisters. I'm not terribly competitive. If someone values winning, I'll likely allow them the space to win. And although I once tried, I can't follow the dominant religion. This fact is not generally valued. I have more tendency toward broad perception than narrow judgment. So, I can study and point to all the scholarly points of why my ideas may be reasonable yet I suspect all of this has much more to say about me than it has to say about scholarship, truth or anything else.

SHARON: You differentiate between faith and belief. I can understand belief as a sure sense that something is true or comports with reality, but what is faith and how does it relate to belief?

And before I could reply:
SHARON: In our lengthy conversation about categorizing and grouping individuals you have stated that you do not "value" groupings by race or by continent. At the same time you group people as victims, i.e. women, homosexuals, non-whites, immigrants and victims of colonialism. So what is the common cause of their victimization? Isn't it another "group" - namely, straight, white, males? Maybe it is the fact that you are inextricably identifiable as belonging to this group of oppressors that you do your best to decry and correct racism, sexism, homophobia, and xenophobia in yourself and apologize for your straight, white, male forebearers.

At the beginning of this discussion you indicated that a people's acceptance of tradition makes them uncritical of the defects in their own tradition while blinding them to the value of other traditions. Can you give me an example of another people's tradition with values that could correct the defects in our tradition of the nuclear family and monogamy?

PAUL: Today, faith is often spoken of like this: *We can't see God or even prove God's existence so we must have faith. Our hopes can only correspond with reality when we allow ourselves to have faith in what we can't ultimately have any proof of.* Curiously, we can swap the word faith for belief and the explanation still fits (as your question seems to recognize). So do the two words mean the same thing? I submit that when we confuse faith with belief, we leave the door open for anybody to claim truth in the name of faith. Cult members speak of belief as faith. Terrorists do the same. Political rhetoric confuses these words. But either belief and faith are the same or there is some difference. I suggest that they actually oppose each other. When we are speaking of faith, we must be speaking toward reality beyond our personal reality. For example when we speak of truth, we might be talking about *facts* as they relate to our current personal reality (situation). But we may instead try to speak toward truth that extends beyond our selves and our personal situation toward reality more common and general. (So, if we consider my opening quote to be about God to represent *infinity*, the quote is accurate enough.) When attempting to address more infinite reality (existing beyond our personal reality, situation, viewpoint) one cannot speak of specific beliefs without error because to *define* infinity down to specifics makes infinite *finite* and so becomes a contradiction. (As you see, any talk about faith need not be religious. It is a point of reason.) So whereas certain beliefs claim specific truths, faith reminds us that there is multitude of *truth* beyond our view that we don't and can't know. In fact, most everything remains outside our current or possible views. Unfortunately when most of us speak about faith, we seldom express ourselves clearly, perhaps because we misunderstand it's full value ourselves. We confuse faith with belief. And our confusion resounds.

So to tie in with my last reply, it is to the benefit of ourselves as well as reason that we back away from our specific beliefs while valuing a larger view. The larger view might be likened to objectivity, and this is fine so long as we don't also come to value some distant objective *view* as being true or best. The trick is to constantly value the greater reality that everyone has in common (before we stamp our divisive beliefs onto it) while not removing ourselves from the immediacy of our own present condition and relationships. We have to retain some balance here because our human viewpoints are tied to our humanity.

Belief can and does obscure much vaster unseen value because we stop at our beliefs. We stop looking for something once we believe we have found it. We call beliefs true and spend our time defending them instead of listening to and learning from broader reality. Most of us have no trouble accepting that what goes on behind our backs does indeed go on behind our backs, but what is lacking is how our conscious understanding of (and personal commitment to) the inherent value within our own ignorance can benefit our everyday thought process. This seems to have little to do with religion but much to do with our fundamental psychology and rationality. Valuing infinity tends to bring us to humility, moderation, tolerance, patience, understanding, compassion and charity whereas overvaluing our specific beliefs tend to bring us opposite values because we know that we are right, and therefore lack concern for what we might be missing. Too often we overvalue our thoughts and so our beliefs become immovable. Yet, too often we praise this condition. We say we are standing for something so that we don't fall for anything. But when we look toward those we vehemently disagree with, what would we say this same attitude does for them and the more general human condition?

Valuing reality in its infinite sense seems to be a good way to keep all this ordered. And it is constant work. So this is why I value realism over idealism (idealism meaning, in the philosophical sense, the belief that our perception *is* reality). Idealism is merely an unfortunate byproduct of perspective that we must constantly remind ourselves to overcome so that it doesn't have us think our thoughts somehow control reality.

Moving on to your second reply, as far as groupings go, I seldom group people in the ways you do except in giving or replying to conventional examples. I merely respond to how other people have grouped them and note that I disagree with the value of these groupings. For me, groupings are a tool rather than a truth. I can group myself in the ways I've previously stated because I've heard these groups applied to me by others. I'm not sure if, on my own, I'd quickly come up with these groupings as especially relevant on my own. I might only use the established groupings because society impinges upon me. So indeed I note that certain groups have been victims because of other people's groupings.

Perhaps if I lived in a bubble I'd still come up with similar groupings to those of others but I would hope that my own groupings (whether similar of vastly different) wouldn't be valued as truths. I would hope such groupings might simply help communication rather than box in people for some other purpose they can't move past. So, yes, certain people's victimization is caused by other people's need to contain them in certain groups. I simply have little need or desire for such certainty. Still I feel no need to apologize for the groupings of others. There are no constant *others* except those who constantly group themselves as opposed to others.

I have tended to resist groupings (imposed by myself or others) because of their necessary shortcomings and errors (there are always exceptions we necessarily ignore within our groupings). Lately, however, I have found one group that I tend to place myself in. I tend to call myself a realist. I do this although I constantly battle my own tendency to be too idealistic. But, since few people know what I mean by this, I give myself the chance to define myself a bit.

I don't identify myself as a white male (for example) except for purposes of illustration of how I've been grouped or might be grouped by others. Recently I've been grouped with atheists, the religious, capitalists, and communists. I wonder how these groupings serve those who group me into them. They definitely say much more about the people doing the grouping than these groupings say about me. None of this is to mention the past groups that people have identified me(?) with. The grouping, whether I pick it or another picks it, is merely is a tool for communication or, more likely, miscommunication unless the groupers can be less strident and more honest about listening to what I claim about myself. Now, they can say I'm deluding myself, but if they do then let's talk about this and not delude each other into the possibility that we are not.

"At the beginning of this discussion you indicated that a people's acceptance of tradition makes them uncritical of the defects in their own tradition while blinding them to the value of other traditions. Can you give me an example of another people's tradition with values that could correct the defects in our tradition of the nuclear family and monogamy?"

I don't know of another *people* who I can point to, but I can again point to ourselves and our own traditions. This is especially important since it is ourselves that are the only ones who might help us all improve. For example I have nothing against the "nuclear family" or monogamy. I think the concepts are just fine albeit unrealistic at times or even idealistic. Within marriage, for example, when a spouse dies the nuclear family doesn't become *less than* (in some moral sense), it has simply changed. The new situation is something that we now work at and try to help each other out with as best we can.

When I dated I wasn't necessarily monogamous but I generally was. I don't know that that was a moral problem. When I was married I was monogamous. I think that was as much a part of my own commitment as it was a part of what society expected of my commitment. Now, at one time I didn't think society had much to do with my personal commitments, but I later came to realize that my commitment was also a societal commitment to some degree. The civic duty of a social contract has some relevant social penalties and sanctions of its own even if they are not legal or necessarily moral. This is only one reason why I found it impossible to deny homosexuals the right to marry. We as a society have to correct our own defects and this decision is as much a part of our social contract as when we *allowed* interracial marriage. And this decision isn't simply a social or moral question, it is a legal one. When law grants advantage or disadvantage to a social institution, this becomes a sociopolitical moral issue that has to be met with something more than labeling people *sodomites*; especially when it is our own laws and mores that causes one group to tag another group with a label that we ourselves (our group) creates against them.

"Sodomy in legal parlance (Black's Law Dictionary, 1967) is a crime against nature and refers to anal intercourse as well as bestiality."

This is a good example of what I intend within my previous paragraph. We can point to a group that we call homosexuals but then we label this group *sodomites*. This extended definition no longer accurately applies to the group and definitely to all individuals within the group. I know few homosexual women who engage in anal intercourse yet I am aware that many heterosexual women and men do or have. I know of none, zero, homosexuals who engage in bestiality yet here it is in 1967 this was legal parlance; flawed as it was (is). Yet you desire to paint with such a broad brush presumably because you simply don't like certain individual acts. We as individuals and as a society must do better than this. I think monogamy and a two head of household family is great, but a death or divorce doesn't ruin it or make it immoral or socially inappropriate. Choosing a mate who is of the same sex doesn't ruin it. In fact, if we value a two head of household committed marriage, a homosexual arrangement might be said to support our greater more foundational values.

Let us not forget that it is *us* who apply stigmas rather than simple designations to *others*. A mother who gets divorced is stigmatized more than the man who may have prompted the divorce. The child of such a relationship (innocent as he or she is) is often stigmatized by necessary parental association. This is neither fair nor valuable. Yet these are common choices of individuals and societies. Promoting stigmas often aren't of as much value as they are of harm. None of these judgments are written by the hand of God. They are choices we can make and unmake at the stroke of a pen; even if that stroke won't change some individual's minds. Beyond morality and its values, none of this should be a question of religious liberty once it reaches the level of civil or criminal law. We all love to talk of religious liberty in a society where the majority is Christian, but let that majority change and watch people's minds and values change. We must learn to be more careful with our language, intent and values.

No reply.

After a week or so. . .
PAUL: By the way, would you consider yourself to be Christian? Atheist? Agnostic?

Do you remember your 1966 Chevy wagon? Did you learn how to drive in that car? What year did you get your license? When did dad leave? Around 1962? and for how long?

A PERSONAL NOTE: Our dad was having some psychological troubles and left home for a while when I was quite young. Our family got by with some LDS church assistance. (In her last years, our mother spent time volunteering with the church's welfare program; probably as repayment.) Before dad made it home again, he had checked into the VA hospital for treatment . . . perhaps for alcoholism and depression. He may have also had a gambling prob-

lem. Correctly or incorrectly, for some reason I'd associated this addictive behavior to his time in the military during WWII. Our mother took him back after his treatment but she went back to work full time as soon as she could; probably so she wouldn't feel vulnerable like that again. (I recall nothing about this from my own childhood, but after our mother died, I think it was Sharon who told me a bit about it.) Mom always stressed to me (probably to my sisters too) that a woman should always have her own money and bank account.

SHARON: You've hit on a way of breaking up the logjam in my mind - ask me some easy questions. Starting with our Chevy - Yes, I do remember it, but I thought it was a 1965. Matt bought it used from a professor at the U. and we kept it until the early 80's when we bought a later model station wagon. I did learn to drive in that car and as I recall I didn't get my license until 1973 and that was just before I started working. Matt had tried to teach me in his VW convertible when we first got married, but having only one car until 1975 and having four kids by 1973 limited my practice time and we gave it up. Grandpa used to let me drive his Cadillac to work at the Drive-In, even though it made him nervous to sit in the passenger seat (the parked cars seem so much closer from that seat) Mom drove for years without a license.

I believe Daddy left or disappeared twice. Once while I was still living at home and I am guessing that it was in 1960 or 61. I don't remember how long he was gone, but it seemed like a couple of months and then he turned up in a hospital somewhere. The next time was after I had left, possibly in 1964-65. I was told that he had checked himself into the VA, but Grandpa didn't believe that and told me that he had started drinking again and had been hospitalized. My childhood between the ages of 11 and 19 was dominated by their problems with alcohol. I have a lot of stories about that time and as you would expect they are not nice. I don't think I ever confided in any family members and I thought that the younger kids were oblivious to what was going on or at least satisfied with the explanations they were given.

I'll answer the harder question in the next message.

Easy questions???

These dates do seem to fit with what my sister Jan and I have discussed about this.

SHARON: @#$%^&* I just spent the last hour writing a thorough answer to your first questions and Firefox crashed and lost it all. It is now 3 am and I can't begin again. I'll have to try again tomorrow. It crashed just as I was listing the Seven Deadly Sins, one of which is anger - the one I most commonly forget, maybe because it is one of the most difficult for me to avoid.

PAUL: I feel for you. As someone who writes a lot, I've developed habits that have kept me from this anger. BTW, the eighth deadly sin is talking like a cartoon character . . . but since these sins haven't been updated for general publication, I forgive your @#$ %^&* situation :)

SHARON: For many young people college is an eye-opener and both the expanded social environment and the new educational opportunities make many young people question their religious upbringing. After Mom's divorce in 1946 my childhood was dominated by a definite rejection of Mormonism. I was too sensitive and imaginative to accommodate even tales of the Easter Bunny and Santa Claus, much less the Crucifixion – a story so unpleasant that I was consigned to bed to remedy my overreaction. I was six. My next "religious" experience was with my friend, Jimmy, at St. Paul's Episcopal Church on a beautiful Easter morning – replete with white robes, candles, crosses, singing, flowers, and stained glass. That experience gave me an aesthetic appreciation for Christianity that was absent in the Mormon Church as well as the Unitarian Church that Mom took me to when I was nine or ten.

When I was ten Grandma and Great-grandma gave me a present of an illustrated Book of Mormon for children. It disappeared soon after it arrived and I think Mom probably suppressed it.

I was never comfortable in the Mormon environment and when Grandpa pleaded with me to be baptized I agreed to prepare myself for that by studying and attending Sunday school. I started reading the Bible and after too many begats I gave up on the Old Testament before I could get to the Christian books of the New Testament. Sunday school didn't work because I sensed that I was the only one there for religious instruction – everyone else seemed to be there for socializing. I had to disappoint Grandpa and that was very hard to do because I loved him more than anyone.

The friends I picked in high school tended to be irreligious or Mormon dropouts and I thought we were the smart ones. At the same time I have had dear friends and relatives who are dedicated to their Mormon beliefs and that has never bothered me and I make no judgments about those beliefs because all these people are good. I don't feel so smart anymore.

I see things now from the perspective of the uniqueness of human life, that is to say, man seems to be the only living form endowed with conscience and the only creature that is troubled by questions of beginnings, ends, purpose, and design. I believe that these things have always puzzled man and the great minds of antiquity have created metaphor and allegory as a way of "seeing" what cannot be seen.

The story of the Garden of Eden has come to have a metaphorical meaning for me: When Adam and Eve were cast out of the Garden for partaking of the Tree of Knowledge of Good and Evil what is represented is being cast out of the natural existence that belongs to all other life forms.

The knowledge that man took for himself was self-knowledge or self-awareness, a knowledge that carries the burden of the sins of self. Life for man becomes a struggle to regain what he lost, that un-selfconscious, blessed state of the animal that does just what he is wound up to do.

It is a difficult struggle, partly because we do not understand why we should struggle against the sins of self. We are so covetous of our "awareness" and "freedom" that we cannot see for ourselves any value in the state of blessedness of the animal that simply fulfills his promise. For me the sins of the self are represented by the Seven Deadly Sins and while they have been seen as an integral part of Christianity, I think their source pre-dates Christianity – in the form of Aristotle's Nicomachean Ethics – the rules for living that Aristotle compiled for his son.

For my own part I believe that motherhood opened the door to that holy, selfless state of the creature who does just what she is wound up to do. The sins of the self are incompatible with being a mother so I was given a chance to fulfill my promise almost effortlessly. Loving, giving, sacrificing, sharing, toiling, protecting, overcoming, rejoicing, and gratitude all became part of my natural life as a mother. That is a most blessed state and a perfect representation of the Garden of Eden.

Genesis isn't Christian and the little I know about the New Testament and the teachings of Christ wouldn't qualify me as a Christian. Christianity was imposed upon the people of the North who already had a fully developed allegorical understanding of life. The only way Christianity could be imposed upon them was by modifying it to make it more compatible with their existing philosophy. In that process Christianity lost much of its Middle Eastern character and became Europeanized and Europe became known as Christendom.

Parsing out this complicated construct to get to the essentials is beyond my knowledge and abilities, but I believe that there have been very wise men since ancient times who can help us to understand, but they can't do our thinking for us.

As for God, I am not sure what to think. I don't believe that makes me an atheist or an agnostic. If I look at it allegorically I could say that conscience – the one thing that distinguishes us from all other living creatures – is easier to explain if it were given to us for a reason - a reason that has nothing to do with biology or survival. Such a gift requires a giver. Is that God? As I said, I am not sure what to think.

PAUL: Thanks for all the family info. I appreciate it. *(Some of it, family names etc redacted here.)*

Jan and I were *converted* to Mormonism as I turned 12. Most of our neighbors were in the Boy Scouts and I wanted to belong.

Also, the church's Mutual program went hand in hand with the scouting program (for the boys) so it seemed that to be in step I should join the church. I went headlong into it as a believer, but like some others, I started to have more serious questions. Oddly, my questions couldn't be answered; they were generally met with stock replies like, "have faith" or "God works in mysterious ways", "pray about it". It seems these comments were the lowest common denominator and couldn't be reduced further, or even expanded upon. As I questioned more, faith seemed no more than belief. I left after four years, the day I was ordained a priest and, as it turned out, and never went back. I never railed against it. It just wasn't for me. I needed understanding rather than platitudes.

I went on a quest to learn about all the major world religions. I was not interested in any of them for long except Taoism (Daoism) which intrigued me like nothing else I had looked into. I didn't understand it but it kept me revisiting it from time to time until I came to understand it in my own way. Before I really understood it much, however, I was looking for common threads in all the religions I studied. I would say that the search for common threads was the best technique about life I ever learned.

I liked your thoughts about the Adam and Eve story. I came up with my own. The story is about knowledge, and I take it just literally enough to find it to be about the psychology of knowledge. I'll restate the story. My restatement itself might tell you how I regard it:

Adam and Eve were without knowledge. Like children they were innocent yet aware of everything before their eyes; happy, naked and unashamed, just as God created them. God provided for them a Garden of Eden that contained everything needed to sustain their life and God told them to be fruitful and multiply. God's only caution to them was that "death" would surely result if they partook from the tree of knowledge of good and evil. Still, a "serpent" convinced them that rather than death, the knowledge of good and evil was valuable and would make them godlike. In spite of warnings provided by their Creator, Adam and Eve were tempted by this knowledge so they partook of the tree. And so it was that their eyes were opened. But their newfound knowledge of "good" in turn gave rise to the idea of "evil". It was by this that they determined they were naked. Calling this "bad", they became ashamed, and hid themselves from God. Now, separate from the Creator (theo-logically, sin is separation from God), God searched for them, found them and had them confess. When they admitted to the obvious, God explained the unavoidable consequences of their new-found circumstance. Separate from their Creator, theirs was a whole new world. Their Eden was essentially lost and this new world was one of enduring hardships caused by knowledge reign-ing untempered by greater reality (God).

As a psychological parable, I can take the story quite literally. Knowledge, of course, is natural and can't be avoided but once we become aware of its pitfalls we might be able to compensate for the errors in judgment we ourselves create through knowledge. Note that the story of Adam and Eve speaks to the specific dangers of a black and white sort of knowledge; the sort of thoughts that lead away from a common source and toward divisive belief. Be-lief overvalues dualism (good and evil) in our thought. There is plenty to lose and little to gain when we value our distinctions of right and wrong above the source (God/reality) that gave rise to the ideas in the first place. Once we take responsibility for our natural faults, we can forgive ourselves as well as others since we are all the same. Forgiveness is preferable to defending our limited view-points while blaming others for their lack of vision. Because we all share the same errors of perception, this blame game seems quite effective. There is plenty of blame to go around and around in a never-ending vicious cycle.

Unlike many people, I don't have much concern for beginnings, ends, supposed purpose or design, or even a Giver of such gifts. This is not to say there is none. To pretend that I can know that which I can't seems to put myself in the place of God. This seems to be against God and or reality. And I can value that which I'm unaware of without valuing that which is fantasy. I value reason and so I think it's most helpful to read such stories in the best pos-sible light of their reason. I can in no way be sure there is any de-sign geared toward ends, but I can see valuable patterns within the process. After all, we live during the means and not at beginnings or ends. While valuing common patterns, I've found that I have to be humble and take care. Patterns I once valued as common were later found to be too exclusive to be of common value beyond my own beliefs. I'm more careful now.

You say: "Christianity was imposed upon the people of the North who already had a fully developed allegorical understanding of life."

Who are the people of the North, where did they hail from, what were they called, what do we call them now, and what was their understanding of life before, at the time of, and/or in lieu of Jesus?

Why do so many people agree with you that they should *make no judgments about those beliefs*? Especially when most of clearly make these judgments in private. Do you suppose it is because none of us have any firm leg to stand on when it comes to belief? Do we fear entering into the discussion because our other leg might be chopped down as well?

No reply.

After about a month, I posted this on Facebook . . .
PAUL: Recently I watched a TV program about The *War of the Worlds* radio broadcast from 1938. It focused upon how many people believed this event was actually happening. Now there is an easy, time honored way to check this out: They could have simply changed the channel. Changing the channel provides you a quick reality check. It allows you to compare what you are hearing on this channel to a multitude of other media outlets available. They could have simply surfed up and down the radio dial and not finding this same *news* anywhere else, they might determine it is not real or true. If it were real, other outlets would likely be competing and clamoring to report on it independently. To believe news from a single source can't help but leave us vulnerable but we can compare it with a broader spectrum of sources.

This is, after all, how we check everything else in our lives. We hear a strange noise and we are afraid, but rather than thinking *ghost* we look for evidence only to find the wind making a branch tap on the window pane. Simply by broadening our perspective and valuing alternatives outside our current view we can find better reasons that may allay our fears better than the reasoning style or conclusions we first picked or usually depend upon.

After watching this docudrama, I watched a news broadcast about the recent Republican debate. Debaters and many of viewers alike seemed to agree that they couldn't trust the "liberal" or "mainstream news media". This same view is promoted on right-wing talk radio and Fox news to the very same segment of the population who have become single perspective *news* gatherers. Many people consider their switch to these channels to be *balance* and they come to find no problem with restricting their input to these outlets. But in restricting our input to certain outlets we are doing the same thing we may have chided others for doing, yet we claim righteousness. We say, "those *others* are ignorant of our viewpoints and therefore they just don't get it." We then must go so far as to accuse these other media outlets of narrowness, and in doing so we must form a sort of conspiracy theory so that our views can remain coherent rather than contradictory.

When it comes to our beliefs, few of us use reason in seeking truth or in reaching toward greater reality. Instead we use our own *reasons* to prop up and support our viewpoints and beliefs. Yet all of these methods, so prone to error and contradiction are easy to check and correct for: Simply change the channel of your mind. Don't look for media outlets that confirm your current view. This isn't getting news, it's pandering. If they aren't pandering to you, you are pandering to yourself. Challenge yourself to argue with yourself. Learn what you can about all kinds of views from their own viewpoint rather than trying to learn about a viewpoint from somebody biased against it. This is simply bias supporting bias but you will never be able to tell this way.

SHARON: What if every channel tells you the same story - does that make it true?

PAUL: No. But some alternate explanations, even if believed by many, don't make a story true either. And if our healthy skeptical search leads us to an alternate story that just happens to fit with our personal world view, we should be especially skeptical of both the view *and* our reasons.

SHARON: What if healthy skepticism leads one to the truth?

PAUL: How could one tell? All warring factions believe they have found truth. Each side believes it is right. So it seems neither can really tell. Or maybe they can tell they know *the* truth and so it seems that at least one is in error. So we have to be very suspicious of this method. Shouldn't *they* (the other side)?

Perhaps a clue is that *truth* isn't "the". How would we know what *the* "truth" is? How do we define truth? We seem to agree yet still disagree. Is this not *true*?

SHARON: How does fact and reality relate to truth? You are suggesting that there is no objective truth, but rather truth is a subjective perception or belief. In that system there is no use in changing the channel in the search for a more truthful or realistic story.

PAUL: *Facts* are details of a specific event. But broader *reality* in might be more valuable for us to consider as *truth*. This is seeing truth as a function, or as a process, rather than viewing *facts* as the answers: *the truth*. Unfortunately many people consider their perception *to be* reality because they do not value reality beyond their view (the few channels they tune in to).

Let us say we have a dozen witnesses to an accident and they all give different accounts of the same event. We have *facts* within these perspectival accounts. One point of view captures certain aspects (facts), while another viewpoint captures different aspects (facts). Who is lying? Eleven of twelve witnesses? Nobody is of course. Reason reveals that no point of view is absolute or correct. Viewpoint is merely convenient. Yet, in argument (about our points of view) we amazingly deny this. My view (or even my opinion about it) must be correct and the other view must be that of an idiot.

We all talk a good game when it comes to truth but few of us ever think about it much. Rather than truth, we value belief. Then we call our beliefs true while devaluing reality beyond belief. We settle upon belief for reasons of convenience, and then we fit additional (often conflicting) facts into our belief systems by using reasons that will support these preexisting beliefs rather than attempting to use reason to inform us the greater reality (truth?) that exists beyond our beliefs.

So, no, I don't suggest there is no objective truth, but unless we are going to understand the complexities and paradoxes of "objective truth", I do mean to admit that we are *subjects* who try to lay claim to *objectivity* within our beliefs because few of us will ever attempt to reach toward greater reality. In this way we hide behind the term "objective".

So, yes, within a system of belief, "there is no use in changing the channel in the search for a more truthful or realistic story." Since this is such a basic problem when it comes to human reason, I doubt I can demonstrate this personally to you, I can only demonstrate it when using other people as my examples. Let's look at someone we might consider to be our enemy. Why are they our enemy? Probably because they refuse to agree with us. They call us wrong; they may call us devils. Let's choose to look at a Muslim fundamentalist who has a fundamentalist view of sharia law and is involved in terror. Now, not all Muslims adhere to fundamentalist views because they have a larger world view; they look toward a bit larger reality. So, this already gives us some general (but not concrete) clues: The more narrow someone's reality (truth), the more extreme. The more narrow the beliefs, the less likely they will agree with others. The more narrow their beliefs in morality, the less tolerant they are of others. The more narrow their regard for others, the narrower their dress codes. The narrower their moral codes, the more leeway those in power (men) will have to subject women to men's narrow and self fulfilling beliefs. The more they value belief above broader reality, the more they will value destroying others with whom they disagree. They might go so far as to bomb themselves so as to take as many others with them that they can so they can get their reward in heaven.

I think we can all see a pattern here. I think we can all see how belief blinds others to greater reality beyond their viewpoint. I think we can all see the dangers. Without valuing the view outside their beliefs, they become the enemy of truth (a greater reality beyond rigid perspective) in the instant that they preach their value of truth.

What is more difficult to see is that each of us are, to some degree, the same as they are. Perhaps we are the same but to a lesser extent. Perhaps not. Perhaps we absolutely refuse to see ourselves in this example. Perhaps they do too. They see our faults clearly. We see their faults clearly. Neither we nor they can or will see our/their own faults, clearly. Rather than admit this, we prefer to defend ourselves while condemning others. They do the same yet we claim it is *their* responsibility to change. We are all too invested in our beliefs to keep looking for greater truth. We are damned.

These are all clues.

SHARON: Your description of the personal view of "truth" appears to be a surefire recipe for interminable conflict and a fruitless quest for truth. Perhaps if we bring it down to a search for the truth of a particular situation it might be easier to analyze. You began with an astonished criticism of people who were taken in by War of the Worlds and you wondered why they didn't simply change the channel. On 9/11 did you change the channel to verify that there was an attack on America? If you had changed the channel and found the same story would you keep on checking until all sources had been exhausted? And importantly, did you have any doubts that what you were being told was true? Were the government's statements and the news coverage convincing? Fourteen years later do you still feel confident that 19 Muslims armed with box cutters, hijacked four commercial airliners and flew them into three buildings and one field because "They hate our freedom"? Or do you believe they did it because they disagree with our view of reality and became the enemies of truth? Was the extreme nature of their method a result of the narrow scope of their religion? Is Obama's use of drones to kill philosophical enemies an example of extremism generated by narrowness? Or isn't it considered extreme when the perpetrator is out golfing? Perhaps it's the case that most people are not truth seekers or even skeptics until their personal comfort is threatened. Those who feel compelled to question and express doubts about 9/11 are maligned as "conspiracy theorists" while the majority never question and never doubt what they have been told. So who is narrow and rigid?

PAUL: You say, "Your description of the personal view of 'truth' appears to be a surefire recipe for interminable conflict and a fruitless quest for truth."

I would say that our quest for *the* truth is indeed "fruitless" and that it has indeed led to "interminable conflict" simply because we claim to have *the* truth; they claim to have *the* truth so we fight. Given the sureness of our perspectives we must fight and we do fight. And yet we agree; we are the same in this futile quest that makes so little sense to greater reason.

Simply because you can pick an incident like 9/11 that doesn't seem to fit with my *War of the Worlds* metaphor doesn't make my metaphor useless, it simply calls for enlargement.

With 9/11 we did get the same story on many channels, but not all, or how could you have your alternate information? You found alternate information. Isn't this correct? Or did you make it up? Is truth whatever we make up? I suspect you heard or read it from some other source. Did they make it up? Why do you believe it? Because it fits with the events? This is why most all of us believe the stories we believe. Now, just because you found different information doesn't make this information correct or incorrect. And since it happens to fit with your world view, this should make you question it. I've learned to question anything that conveniently fits with my preconceived notions because I know how prone I am to believe them without question. Do you doubt that your *enemies* prefer information that fits conveniently into their belief systems? We are all the same this way and we should be wary of it.

Like you, I found alternate information. I tended to devalue it because it fit too well with my own world view so I kept looking. Why? Because when it comes down to it, what I *believe* has little to what is true. What I believe has more to do with what I value and how I reason.

When I face south and you face north, each of us is absolutely positive of our viewpoints. You can prove yours, I can prove mine. This circumstance doesn't make each other's viewpoint wrong; it simply notes its relative convenience. But for me to reject, out of hand, your viewpoint simply because mine seems so absolute, leaves us in a state of endless conflict unless I am willing to turn around. At this point we not only have to accept each other's view, we have to find agreement with its value.

So, here's what I agree with you about:

"19 Muslims armed with box cutters, hijacked four commercial airliners and flew them into three buildings and one field because 'They hate our freedom'."

This story does sound unlikely. In fact, it is. It is a caricature of the story (even if I find the non caricaturized version suspicious). Just like north *v* south, truth is not simply a this *v* that proposition. Do I think the government told us *the* truth or that we have *the* truth from them now? No. But mainly because there is simply no such thing as *the* truth. At best, we always form a caricature of those we disagree with. At worst we demonize them so we can kill them with impunity. Right/wrong, good/evil, us against them.

"Or do you believe they did it because they disagree with our view of reality and became the enemies of truth?"

If we have a many witnesses to an accident and they all give different accounts of the event, who is lying? Is the difference between the accounts the result of some conspiracy? Do these citizens have a hidden agenda or simply a specific point of view that accounts for the value of their story? Or is this simply immature human nature? Shouldn't we mature?

"Was the extreme nature of their method a result of the narrow scope of their religion?"

No, it was do the rigidity of their individual beliefs, not an entire religion. Many others share the/a religion but not the narrowest reading of these beliefs.

"Is Obama's use of drones to kill philosophical enemies an example of extremism generated by narrowness?"

Yes, to some degree.

"Perhaps it's the case that most people are not truth seekers or even skeptics until their personal comfort is threatened. Those who feel compelled to question and express doubts about 9/11 are maligned as 'conspiracy theorists' while the majority never question and never doubt what they have been told. So who is narrow and rigid?"

Everybody in your scenario is being rigid. This is why we fight. To theorize a different possibility is not wrong. To theorize toward truth beyond your viewpoint is not wrong. To conveniently find agreement with the solution that happens to fit your world view should cause skepticism because it can't reveal truth for them or us.

There are conspiracies. Watergate involved a conspiracy. We should beware and be aware. There is a natural conspiracy of viewpoint and belief that we should be aware of and then seek to mediate. Our senses deceive us. We are prone to deception even though we possess reason. We tend to employ reason to support our beliefs rather than in support of reality/God. We have to get better at recognizing the limits and horrors of belief than we do currently.

No reply.

A few weeks later . . .
PAUL: You mentioned in a very early response to me that, "I think the points of disagreement are worth exploring especially since you suggest that those differences are differences in 'values'. That seems unlikely to me since we were raised in the same family at roughly the same time, in the same community, among the same people, same education, etc."

Regarding our discussions so far, would you still agree we share the same values? The examples you noted in this quote are essentially about family and time. Yet families evolve over time into communities of individuals that value different things. Over time we fail to recognize how we are related to others in our community. This happens even when we devalue those we disagree with. We might even come to think of them as *others*; simply outsiders on the fringes that are to be suspected because they are not like *us* in some way. Perhaps it's their flag or their *outsider* art.

You and I might desire the same *ideals* such as strong loving families, community, and responsible government, but for me, values are not ends. Values relate to a shared process over time because we don't live at ends or beginnings; we live along a continuum. To devalue this reality is to make errors of value. This is partially why I accord such ideals *belief* status; because they tend to be considered right or true rather than part of an ongoing conversation. Ideals, in order to be realized, must be realized at some fixed point in time. Yet families grow, change and evolve. The process spans many points in time.

As you've grouped yourself with Northern Europeans, you've noted a preference for a separation from of others. You've spoken of repatriation of others. Some people may want this for the benefit of all involved. You believe cultures should stick together and not integrate. Yet these ideals are fantasy in that they don't correspond with the greater part of reality in which we live. We do integrate. We have always integrated. We will always integrate. Males and females are different yet they integrate. This is how we carry on. It isn't always easy but people integrate through marriage. It is not always easy yet most people regard the commitment as a value that should be sustained, promoted, and not taken lightly.

Now, I guess we could get bogged down in semantics and say that *values* are really not that much different than *ideals*. But regardless of the terms we employ, the same issues exist. It seems to me that ends and means must correspond if ideals were ever to comport with reality. How would this happen? It appears as though there must be some integration during correspondence, or the process breaks back down into factions. This process, and the reason for breakdown, seems built into the world in which we live.

SHARON: You said that males and females are different, but they "integrate". "Integrate" doesn't seem like the right word – wouldn't "complement" be more apt? They are biological complements and represent a procreative unity. Racial and cultural integration, on the other hand, represent differences that can be antagonistic and destructive. Integrating a culturally primitive people into an advanced culture destroys what has taken thousands of years to evolve and stabilize. That is the root evil of advanced civilization's conquest, colonialism, and slave trade – the destruction of stable, primitive societies and/or the removal of primitive peoples from their native environments. In many places in Africa everyone has his cell phones, and plenty to eat, but they have nothing to do. They have lost what had sustained them for millennia, lost their identity, their self-sufficiency and have become dependent.

There is a difference between the very, very slow integration of peoples in the cultural periphery over thousands of years and the artificial integration that has occurred in the last two hundred years. What we are witnessing now in European countries isn't integration, but invasion. There has never been a people that did not resist invasion – not the tribes of North America – not the aborigines of Australia, not the tribes of Central and South America – not the Indians, Africans, or Asians. It is not natural – not biological to fail to protect one's people, one's lands, and one's livelihood, nor is it natural to integrate racial and cultural strangers into one's community, much less into one's family. The disintegration of the family, the atomization of society, and the anomic individual's taste for nihilism are classic signs of a civilization in decline.

This was just a response to your last note, but I have two previous notes that I haven't yet addressed. Stay tuned.

PAUL: You mention, "You said that males and females are different, but they 'integrate'. 'Integrate' doesn't seem like the right word – wouldn't 'complement' be more apt? They are biological complements and represent a procreative unity."

Like I say, we can get bogged down in semantics yet the issues remain. We can use the term "complement", but I've never viewed a woman as a procreative utility even if, together, some males and females might achieve those ends. I've also never viewed someone with different shade of skin or a different background as one who had to integrate with *me*. For me to view *others* that way seems "antagonistic and destructive". I will admit, however, that it can sometimes be the common majoritarian view of social relations. This is one of the aspects of libertarianism that attracted me. For me, the idea of human rights (and the inherent relations) preexisting government seemed to be an attitude leveling reality that seems more valuable than majorities *v* minorities. Majority itself has never equaled value or correctness except in the minds of the majority (many of whom already assume their righteousness).

"Integrating a culturally primitive people into an advanced culture destroys what has taken thousands of years to evolve and stabilize."

Let's look at some of the assumptions within this statement: The overall view is from that of an *advanced* majority that assimilates a primitive minority. (Now, the majority could be trying to assimilate a majority of refugees, and this can indeed be be a shock to a culture that values majoritarianism over human rights. I'll get back to this seemingly topical topic in a bit.) Now, not stated within this presumption is why the cultures are assimilating. This might be an important clue as to the problems that might be confronted. Secondly, we have the devaluation of the primitive culture's values. Hence a third assumption seems to be that the assimilating culture *is* advanced. A forth might be that the minority primitive culture can destroy the advanced culture through the act of assimilation. A fifth could be that the advanced culture evolved (perhaps assuming that the primitive culture didn't) and that the advanced culture is stable.

I'm not going to detail my response but I'll sketch out some ways of looking at this scenario that are likely ignored. Why do we call others primitive while calling ourselves advanced? Is ignorance a virtue here? Is ignorance an advance? Isn't the fact that larger groups of people prefer their majority status to human rights a clue here? We all know the larger pack of wolves have a natural advantage but an advanced society should know that the size of the pack doesn't make the pack *correct* in its behavior. Related here is that it is likely that the majority "advanced" culture is conquering the minority culture. There are so many problems with people getting along after such a defeat that advanced *v* primitive is the least of our problems to surmount. The very idea of advanced *v* primitive is the greatest factor to get over. The belief of the conquering culture that it is the advanced culture is likely not related so much to truth as to perspective. A truly advanced culture might well understand this and not conquer (as if *might makes right . . .* the embedded assumption of majoritarianism) until it knows how to behave toward and assimilate other cultures (hence slavery, colonialism etc). So if the primitive minority can bring down the advanced majority, perhaps the primitive is more advanced. Perhaps they possess values that the majority can't fathom. The majority simply doesn't have the necessary power by *virtue* of their numbers to make slavery or colonialism virtuous . . . because it isn't. Adherence to rigid point of view hides this fact from us of course. All of this may be "antagonistic and destructive", but it has little if nothing to do with primitive *v* advanced.

You say that, "That is the root evil of advanced civilization's conquest, colonialism, and slave trade . . ."

This much we can pretty much agree upon.

And then, "There is a difference between the very, very slow integration of peoples in the cultural periphery over thousands of years and the artificial integration that has occurred in the last two hundred years."

I disagree. My reading of history implies, if not shows, a different point of view. War and conquest has been going on for thousands of years and it has been, "artificial integration". It has been brutal, often to the point of genocide.

"[N]or is it natural to integrate racial and cultural strangers into one's community, much less into one's family. The disintegration of the family, the atomization of society, and the anomic individual's taste for nihilism are classic signs of a civilization in decline."

Once again I disagree. Thousands of years of history is packed full of racial and cultural integration. Integration within the community and especially into one's families. How do I know this is so rather than simply being MY reading of history? Because everybody belongs to a family. Everybody who integrates, integrates into a family. This is how families, from the beginning, have carried on. It hasn't always been easy, but when people have simply integrated without forced slavery or colonization, integration has been easier and quite natural.

"What we are witnessing now in European countries isn't integration, but invasion."

Sounds dramatic enough. Invasion is a negative term used in the way most people use the term racist. The reason why many people often use words like invasion and racist are not because they are right or wrong but because they seem to fit *those who* they think they apply to. Invasion is a term used from the point of view of these who might feel invaded. Just as fleeing might be a term used from the point of view of those who are leaving. From a distance we only see movement. Close-up the terms depend upon perspective and associated values.

Most of those who might be termed racist aren't generally speaking of race in some scientific like term, they tend to regard races as inferior. They generally have a political/majoritarian bent that takes their racism to levels that have so many assumptions built into them that they become untenable. These assumptions are sometimes full of other unseen or unvalued prejudices; full of half truths that are mistaken for, or disguised as, truth. Invasion is the wrong word. There are masses of people (often families) on the move. Taking many risks to leave their homes and most of their possessions behind. They are trying to enter someplace that seems hospitable. Most keep moving toward that goal. It is at this point that many people then begin to suspect and assume. Some say this mass migration is chocked full of terrorists. We can place all kinds of suspicions upon this migration especially when factions are at war. We can even find individuals or individual acts who/that will bear this fear out. But like most of our fears and prejudices, they are amplifications of a situation that seldom exists in a reality de-void our distinct points of view and our fears.

So, here we have a clue as to how to approach real life situa-tions. Since attitudes are so rooted in the definiteness of our per-spectives, we should try to use the most neutral terms so that we don't reinforce our views so as to believe and spread propaganda. We should employ this as a way to retain balance through less value laden terms. So as to be most honest with ourselves. It has been said that words and language are the root of propaganda; that we use words to conceal what we want to say rather than using words that intend what we mean. We should not paint with a broad brush because you hate it when others paint you into such a corner, and I know how sensitive you are to being labeled in a negative fashion.

Well hidden/revealed within all of this talk is the question of what is primitive and what is advanced. We have come back to this theme throughout our conversations. Unfortunately we only have about 5000 years of history we can look back upon. Before that are tens of thousands of years of prehistory remaining mostly hidden. Even with the history available, much is written by the winners, the powerful, the majority. Most minority view is repressed, sup-pressed, burned or otherwise destroyed. So what we *know* is often biased from the beginning. Luckily much of our most ancient works are in the form of fiction (if we assume Homer and scared scripture was often written this way rather than strictly as history). Unfortunately/fortunately we also have our own imaginations (no matter how much they may be maligned) to employ as a way to transcend and temper the strength of our perspectives (physical or mental). But, as it has been said, we too often use our imaginations much as a drunk uses a lamppost; more for support than for illumi-nation. It could be that what we consider to be either advanced or primitive is in error. Perhaps "primitive" humans did just fine for tens of thousands of years while our current advancements can ruin the entire planet within just a few thousand years of *progress*. The comparison may seem unlikely because of the myriad of factors beyond our knowledge. Perhaps we should be more skeptical, not of truth or morality but of the limits of our perspective. After all, perhaps it is the strength of perspective that keeps us embattled. But we will surely fight for these limits until they are ours; to proudly possess in our righteousness.

SHARON: Procreative unity, not utility.

The differences between male and female in any bimorphic species are rooted in biological fact - it doesn't matter how one "views" individual males or females. That you perceive the difference in humans speaks to your biology, not to an ideological point of view. Identification as a female does not depend upon fulfilling her procreative role.

PAUL: It does matter how we view individual males and females. We can view them as vehicles to procreation, sex objects, home-makers etc regardless of biology. I doubt my biology is what causes me to perceive differences between men and women. I can often perceive differences in everything else including gender regardless of biology; physiology often is my likely clue but not always. So, I will agree that "identification as a female does not depend upon fulfilling her procreative role", but some people seem to have an ideological need to identify males and females in a very specific way yet, for some reason, they don't call *this* need of identification *identity politics;* it seems to be *utilitarian* hence my use of the word *utility* rather than your word *unity*. (Procreative unity, not utility.) This utilitarian way of defining people apart from each other is divisive rather than unifying, regardless of biology.

SHARON: It is biology that underlies all perception. Perceptions that are critical for survival and reproduction are the most important in all living creatures. Much of what we perceive about others is unconscious - that is to say, out of our

128

control. In addition, there is tremendous redundancy in nature that functions to insure survival and reproduction and that means we perceive what we need to know in many different ways. The perception of sexual difference is multifaceted and so basic to life that an animal that lacked all the means of distinguishing between male and female would be defective and likely nonviable. All that is to say, that I don't think it possible to view males or females without reference to their biological complement which represents a procreative unity. The very fact that sexual identification is the most basic distinguishing factor in the human species speaks to its profound importance. Some might claim to be blind to the differences between male and female, but even willful blindness doesn't remove what nature has provided.

You say, "Majority has never equaled value or correctness except in the minds of the majority", but couldn't the same be said of a ruling minority? Is the majority never right? Does a minority always have the status of an underdog? Does a minority never assume their righteousness?

Then we come to a critical misunderstanding: When I wrote, "Integrating a culturally primitive people into an advanced culture destroys what has taken thousands of years to evolve and stabilize." I was referring to the primitive culture's destruction, not the demise of the advanced culture. Do you really mean to say that "primitive" and "advanced" cannot not be applied to human cultures? Our "advanced" culture is not the majority culture in the world and never has been. My criticism of slavery, conquest, and colonialism is based on my belief that all three have destroyed cultures that evolved over millennia to sustain their people in a culturally stable environment. Such cultures must be judged successful by evolutionary standards, but they did not evolve in the same way our culture did. Superimposing an advanced culture on a primitive one is ruinous and it is doubtful that it can be remedied. Artificial sustenance only allows artificial reproductive levels that cannot be sustained without the advanced culture's interference. What worked before has been lost. The residents of West Point Nigeria have cell phones, shelter, and food, but they have no sewage system and the beach is covered with human feces as far as the eye can see. There is nothing left of their evolutionary product, nothing to sustain them, nothing to do. Is the remedy to transport them into an advanced country with a sewage system? Take them from their majoritarian existence and make them a minority in a European or Asian country?

I have to stop here because I have to make dinner.

You rely too heavily on "majority vs. minority" scenarios while it has been the other way around in conquest, colonialism, and slavery. English, Dutch, French, and Belgian Colonists were always in the minority. The overwhelming majority of inhabitants of North America were racially and culturally distinct from the early white settlers from England, Holland, and France and it was only advanced technology that allowed the Europeans to survive the determined resistance of the natives. Europeans were a minority for at least the first 150 years and vast areas of the country were controlled by natives until the middle of the 19th century. Only the European colonies of Canada, the U.S., Australia, and New Zealand grew into majority populations while colonies in Central and South America, Africa, India, and Asia never came close to a European majority. The native inhabitants of the U.S. and Canada did not welcome immigrants, integrate them into their societies, guarantee them human rights, and help them make a better life. Is that because they were the majority? Or because the aboriginals were racists? Perhaps they felt they were being invaded by an incompatible, foreign people and worried for their lives, their families, their livelihood, and their culture? Why is their reaction understandable while the same concerns of Europeans are not allowed?

PAUL: I guess we can say that "it is biology that underlies all perception" because we have senses due to biology.

I will agree that our concept of free will is much more limited than many people would like us to think but I'm not sure it gets to the point you want it to get to either. Indeed "an animal that lacked all the means of distinguishing between male and female would be defective and likely nonviable" but as a human I have ways to distinguish sex that are beyond biology and not beyond my control. This control is evidenced by our choices. I chose not to have children. Many people choose different sorts of birth control that are not beyond their control. In the US, it is the liberty that exists beyond our biology that secures this.

"All that is to say, that I don't think it possible to view males or females without reference to their biological complement which represents a procreative unity." This we can't know if we accept your assumption, we can only accept or reject it. But either way, I don't think it addresses your point.

"The very fact that sexual identification is the most basic distinguishing factor in the human species speaks to its profound importance."

Evidently to any species.

"Some might claim to be blind to the differences between male and female, but even willful blindness doesn't remove what nature has provided."

I don't know who claims to be blind to it. I claim to have a greater awareness of it beyond simple biology.

You say that, "Majority has never equaled value or correctness except in the minds of the majority." I will agree but couldn't the same be said of a ruling minority? Is the majority never right? Does a minority always have the status of an underdog? Does a minority never assume their own righteousness?

All of us assume our right-hood or we wouldn't disagree. Yes, twenty men in a room have natural power over the one woman in the room. This isn't limited to male *v* female. A single person with a more powerful weapon often holds sway over a majority without such a weapon. So, majority represents power but doesn't always have the power. In a government that claims to be a constitutional government that follows the rule of law, law is supposed to become the power instead of majoritarian muscle. Without laws based upon values beyond other power, might simply makes right. Without some ability to enforce this rule of law, our rights don't help us. Our Constitution intends to give the people rights beyond majoritarian power. The practical problems are the citizenry's value or lack thereof of this constitutional reality, as well as the government's ability or will to enforce it. Often the majority enjoys their power to overlook the rights of the minority . . . until *they* are in the minority, they then suddenly value rights and the equal justice required to stop the new majority from overlooking their rights.

"Then we come to a critical misunderstanding: When I wrote, 'Integrating a culturally primitive people into an advanced culture destroys what has taken thousands of years to evolve and stabilize.' I was referring to the primitive culture's destruction, not the demise of the advanced culture."

Me too. The two often go hand in hand just as rights and power do.

"Do you really mean to say that "primitive" and "advanced" cannot not be applied to human cultures?"

No, like I said, they can be *applied*, just as laws are applied; sometimes unjustly. Modern humans can effectively destroy what has existed for tens of thousands of years. This ability is surely advanced but without the morals and values that might keep us from doing this, I'm not sure we are any more *advanced* than *primitive* humans. Our errors may surely destroy their cultures too. We have some responsibility to the past here. I think the *way* we apply our terms "primitive" to the past and "advanced" to our present is dubious at best. I may accept that you have great reverence for primitive cultures and that you don't mean *primitive* in a pejorative sense but the main thrust of your argument and politics is that current cultures should be separate. Perhaps the values and insights we lose when separating us culturally keeps us separate too. We are superimposing our cultures upon theirs. We always have done this and probably always will. Many people lack the value you have for them, and so they enslave, colonize and marginalize them. I'm not sure your alternative of separation is the best option even if it were a realistic one.

"Such cultures must be judged successful by evolutionary standards, but they did not evolve in the same way our culture did."

I agree, our own culture has often done quite poorly.

"Artificial sustenance only allows artificial reproductive levels that cannot be sustained without the advanced culture's interference."

We could let them starve and not have created this problem by feeding them, but even here in the US, many maintain their own values about birth control. Many are against sex education, birth control, abortion; and then some refuse to feed the offspring due to *moral hazard*. We don't want to provide education, health care or food and so we are back to the value of letting them starve. It's a curious morality we have; a curious sense of moral hazard.

"The residents of West Point Nigeria have cell phones, shelter, and food, but they have no sewage system and the beach is covered with human feces as far as the eye can see."

Rivers in America have caught fire as we dumped our waste into them. All sewage systems have been poor and they still are. We still don't know quite how to handle our garbage.

"Is the remedy to transport them into an advanced country with a sewage system? Take them from their majoritarian existence and make them a minority in a European or Asian country?"

This would be one way to approach it. What is your solution?

"You rely too heavily on "majority vs. minority" scenario . . ."

Perhaps. And you rely too heavily upon, **". . . it was only advanced technology that allowed the Europeans to survive the determined resistance of the natives"**, while *our* European technology is poised to destroy the world.

I'm saying that your advanced culture is apt to destroy the world while primitive cultures that were *just fine* prior to *European help* have turds in the ocean. Personally, I'll pick the turds (and help pick up the turds) before saying that the best our "advanced" culture can do is to let them starve. I'll bet that a truly advanced culture could do better than this if we were to consider advancement instead of valuing or settling upon Malthusian values.

"Europeans were a minority for at least the first 150 years and vast areas of the country were controlled by natives. . ."

I spoke of the minority/power, power/majority earlier. Here we're talking about aggression and colonialism that you at once deplore and yet embrace as a European value.

"Only the European colonies of Canada, the U.S., Australia, and New Zealand grew into majority populations while

colonies in Central and South America, Africa, India, and Asia never came close to a European majority."

Perhaps this is why I put such a heavy emphasis upon the "majority vs minority scenario". In a country ruled by laws; a supposedly valued constitutional government that restricts powers while valuing rights, hypocritical as it began and sometimes remains, it currently seems more moral than the forces of colonialism. European values have led to attempted colonization of all these places, "Central and South America, Africa, India, and Asia". I say *attempted* because the grand Europeans with their laws and morality, prefer hypocrisy and muscle to law and responsible morality. Many Europeans/ Americans find no problem with creating all sorts of problems with their morality and then suggesting that the best we elevated people can possibly do is withdraw all, "[a]rtificial sustenance [that] only allows artificial reproductive levels that cannot be sustained without the advanced culture's interference."

"Perhaps they felt they were being invaded by an incompatible, foreign people and worried for their lives, their families, their livelihood, and their culture? Why is their reaction understandable while the same concerns of Europeans are not allowed?"

Because it is wrong. Natives agreed to treaties with these European descendants before these same Europeans broke the treaties. Given this understanding the native reaction was right and just. Current history bears this out. The natives were right in every one of their fears. They tried to fight and we killed them. They were left to subsist on reservations that we relocated them, and relocated them and relocated them once we need the railways, found oil etc. The European/ American values that drive this is wrong. Morally wrong. Many people have had enough of hypocritical European values. What people want is law; law based upon human dignity and equal justice rather than excuses for why *their* dignity isn't *worth it* compared to other these European values. Europeans are the majority and they now want to get all high and mighty about how righteous they are. There is more than one point of view to consider here and these views are begging to be explored for their value rather than for a defense of irresponsibility.

All of this must be better than a morality based upon *might makes right* or *European makes right*.

SHARON: Describe how your extra-sensory perception works that allows you to distinguish between male and female and explain the function of such a distinction.

PAUL: I'm not sure what you mean. Would biology also apply to extra-sensory perception? When I look at people they appear male or female. It doesn't always work. I can't explain the function of such a thing, but I doubt my inability to properly describe it doesn't make it extra-sensory, or change the alarming accuracy with which I'm able to do it. Frankly I can't describe how I recognize a Chevy from a Volkswagen either. Visual clues are best but often other senses often provide clues too. So, it seems to be sensory rather than extra-sensory.

SHARON: So, if being able to distinguish between male and female doesn't depend upon the senses and you can't describe how you know the difference, wouldn't that suggest an unconscious process? You, like all other creatures, have a multiplicity of perceptions, some unconscious, for making such distinctions but the question remains - why are bimorphic creatures endowed with this ability?

PAUL: Perhaps I mistyped.

Let me restate myself to see if I can get it correct: When I look at people, they appear to be male or female. But this doesn't always work at first glance. Sometimes I need more clues. Sensory clues. I can't explain the function of such a thing, but I doubt my inability to properly describe it makes it extra-sensory. And being sensory doesn't change the alarming accuracy with which I'm able to do it. Frankly I can't describe how I recognize a Chevy from a Volkswagen either. Visual clues are often the best in these cases but often other senses provide clues too. So, it seems to be sensory rather than extra-sensory.

As to, "why are bimorphic creatures endowed with this ability?" I couldn't tell you. But I can tell you that my senses often mislead me. This is a problem with our senses. We then rationalize what we read or misread into all sorts of other nice things or even more mistakes. Perhaps you can tell me how the unconscious extra-sensory perception functions and why. And is it accurate, and how can we tell?

SHARON: We are endowed with the ability to distinguish male from female to facilitate reproduction.

PAUL: Sorry, the grand daughters are over today. I get distracted :)
I can normally tell the difference between male and female due to the same senses I use to tell the difference between a Chevy and a Volkswagen. There is no further biology to it other than using a few of my five senses. But maybe I'm missing something. I never had kids so perhaps I'm clueless somehow. Is this ability to distinguish between male and female a sensory ability? Or is it extra-sensory? If it is extra-sensory, is it accurate and how can we tell? Do we need an extra-sensory ability if we have our other senses, or is it akin to male nipples? I'm not even sure of such a thing as extra-sensory perception.

SHARON: It is a multi-faceted (redundancy) mix of conscious and unconscious sensory perceptions. There may be extra-sensory perceptions, but I don't know. People talk of "animal magnetism" and a "sixth sense", and I have always thought it was strange that we can tell when someone is looking at us, even though we cannot see their eyes. There may be things we perceive without any conscious awareness. One experiment was done in which people were asked to respond quickly to pictures shown in rapid succession of different racial types. What was revealed was an unconscious, first response, that was "corrected" by the subject apparently to cover the unconscious first response.

On the heels of her previous comment:
SHARON: All our perceptions, sensory and maybe extra-sensory, have evolved to serve a survival/reproductive purpose. The acuity of the sense of smell is closely linked to the environment in which a people evolved. Some people, apparently, can tolerate the smell of raw sewage better than

others. By the same token, the major races differ in the number, placement, and odor exuded of scent glands. On the face of it such differences impede race-mixing.

PAUL: And I always thought it was my deodorant and cologne that made me sexy:) So much for TV commercials.

An aside: Sharon comments on an OccidentalObserver.net *post about Roger Cuckierman:*
    "France's tradition of secularism (laïcité) should be abolished in order to finance 'moderate' Muslim clerics:..."
SHARON: Secularism was used to abolish Christianity, but he now suggests that secularism be dropped in favor of promoting Islam.

PAUL: Christianity is by far the largest religion in France.

SHARON: A 1905 French law institutionalized secularism. This man thinks that law should be abolished in order to support Islam and have the French government pay the imams. He only wants secularism for the Christian majority. As a Jew he fully supports the religious state of Israel in which people are judged to be citizens by bloodline in spite of their religious claims.

PAUL: It might be said that in 1789 the U.S. institutionalized secularism.
    This man your quote is simply a lobbyist. He is not president or a high ranking official. The job of a lobbyist is to think and say things that very narrowly support their narrow visions.

SHARON: What is the interest of the French Jewish Lobby in pressing for more Muslim immigration and a revocation of secularism for Islam? We have a similar lobby in the form of AIPAC and as lobbyists they support "their narrow vision", but the entire U.S. Congress supports those same narrow interests with such enthusiasm that when Netanyahu came to Washington in 2010 a joint session of Congress gave him 29 standing ovations. It would seem that our tradition of secularism is set aside when it comes to the Jewish state.

PAUL: Our tradition of secularism (if there is a real tradition here) is most often set aside for Christianity too; so much so that it is ex -tremely common for people to call this a *Christian nation*. And, yes, AIPAC, like all lobbies has narrow views too. As to your question, "What is the interest of the French Jewish Lobby in pressing for more Muslim immigration and a revocation of secularism for Islam?" This I haven't looked into. Perhaps to create a larger non-Christian voting bloc within a country that insists upon calling itself Christian? Is this reactionary? Backlash? Regardless, is this lobbyist a minority voice among most Jews in France, or are his words being misunderstood and/or misrepresented? Perhaps other media outlets report the same news yet draw different conclusions?

SHARON: Our secularism is constitutional, that is to say, it was meant to prevent the government from establishing a national religion; it was not meant to replace Christian belief and practice, but rather to afford religious freedom for the individual. Because the vast majority of settlers in the U.S. between 1620 and 1960 came from what was known as Christendom, it follows that the U.S. has been known as a Christian nation. Many, many people today consider themselves Christian on the basis of their personal philosophy rather than doctrinal adherence or religious training. In other words, much of what Americans consider virtue is understood to be "Christian virtue", e.g. love, selflessness, humility, honesty, chastity, generosity, loyalty, moderation, patience, understanding, compassion, charity, work, and social responsibility. Jews living in European countries have always been proponents of immigration from Third World countries and at least part of the reason is, as you suggested, a way to enhance their own minority status. As Jews have taken control of the Democrats they have created a coalition of minority and/or grievance groups: blacks, homosexuals, feminists, and immigrants while middle America migrates to the Republican Party, or rather, to Donald Trump. The other reason why Jews would see Muslim immigration into European countries as a good thing is its racial and socio-cultural destructiveness.

PAUL: This lobbyist is not changing, or is in any position to change, any French Constitution.

You say, "Many, many people today consider themselves Christian on the basis of their personal philosophy rather than doctrinal adherence or religious training. In other words, much of what Americans consider virtue is understood to be 'Christian virtue', e.g. love, selflessness, humility, honesty, chastity, generosity, loyalty, moderation, patience, understanding, compassion, charity, work, and social responsibility."

Let's see, you added *chastity* and *work* to my own list but left out *tolerance* among a couple others.

Aside from the fact that far too many Christians say they believe in these values, there are many who don't practice them. Unfortunately as beliefs get strident they get in the way of practice.

"As Jews have taken control of the Democrats they have created a coalition of minority and/or grievance groups: blacks, homosexuals, feminists, and immigrants while middle America migrates to the Republican Party, or rather, to Donald Trump."

Jesus was a Jew. He was called rabbi. He didn't set out to create a separate religion. He didn't renounce Judaism. Today, I hear many white males, complain that they are persecuted while sounding and acting like the victimized grievance groups you speak of . . . at least in the way you hear them.

"The other reason why Jews would see Muslim immigration into European countries as a good thing is its racial and socio-cultural destructiveness."

Are the Jews then working in concert with the Muslims to destroy the world? Or do I misread you?

Stay tuned, given the chance Trump will speak before AIPAC and give *them* his love too.

SHARON: I left out "tolerance" because it suggests one is simply holding one's nose - I thought "understanding" and "compassion" were more virtuous. I linked this article, written by a Frenchman because it presents an extraordinarily positive attitude of a Jewish organization toward Muslim immigration into Europe. Why? Since Frenchmen don't benefit from this program it must be that the Jewish Lobby sees such immigration as in their interest. What is that interest? Don't you think that is an important question since the program is damaging to European countries? It doesn't really matter that the speaker has no personal power to change the French constitution, the important thing is that he revealed unguarded, Jewish enthusiasm for immigration. Americans are identified as Christians as a way of criticizing them for what others judge to be un-Christian thoughts, speech, or behavior. Jews and Muslims are never called on their failure to demonstrate Jewish virtues or Muslim virtues while every white person is expected to practice Christian virtues. Jesus was a Galilean, not a Judean. The Jews of his time were called Pharisees and he mercilessly condemned them. For this condemnation he was crucified. Jews don't claim Jesus as their own and the Talmud is filled with hateful and mocking references to Jesus and his Mother. Was your assertion meant to elevate Jews or to criticize Christians for being un-Christian toward Jews? Jews. as a small minority, always pit their enemies against one another. Muslims are their enemies and Europeans are their enemies. Why else would Jews be agitating for Muslim immigration into European countries? They aren't humanitarians; they are not worried about the welfare of people forced from their lands by violence; after all, the Israelis forced 750,000 Palestinians from their lands in 1947.

PAUL: You say, "I left out 'tolerance' because it suggests one is simply holding one's nose - I thought 'understanding' and 'compassion' were more virtuous."

While it is true that the word tolerance implies someone or some group to be tolerated; and to tolerate them assumes you are better than them so they must be tolerated; and although tolerance is a lesser virtue than some others, sometimes it's the best some people can do. And it is better than most less virtuous options. We can do better than this if and when we accept that our thoughts of *them* probably have much more to say about us than it has to say about them. And *we* are all we can really work on anyway. We can't *fix* them.

Migration is people just moving around until and unless they immigrate. These are individuals unless we or they place them into a group. We have spoken about one Frenchman speaking. He isn't all French men. He is speaking for himself and whoever listens. I assume he is a Jew but he is not all Jews. Even though there is a mass migration going on from the middle East toward Europe, it doesn't serve us to look at this migration only or necessarily in religious terms. There are other terms that are just as, if not more, relevant. I also don't and won't look at this issue as an exclusively European issue. "**Don't you think that is an important question since the program is damaging to European countries?**" I don't see this migration as a program (who manages this program anyway?) or as damaging to all European countries.

I'm unclear as to your concerns. You say, "**the important thing is that he revealed unguarded, Jewish enthusiasm for immigration.**" These are the words of one man (perhaps that he is a Jew perhaps matters to you).

"**Americans are identified as Christians as a way of criticizing them for what others judge to be un-Christian thoughts, speech, or behavior.**"

I would say it is ignorant of *others* to regard me first and foremost as an American or as a Christian unless they know me and these classifications point directly toward an issue that we are discussing together. Their value of group-ism is in error when it comes to the individual, and therefore their judgments become faulty.

"**Jews and Muslims are never called on their failure to demonstrate Jewish virtues or Muslim virtues while every white person is expected to practice Christian virtues.**"

I think they are. This is part of why ISIS/ISIL (DAIISH) goes into areas that are not *fundamentally Muslim enough* for them and wish to force upon them sharia law. This is generally why there are fundamentalist Jews who fight with progressive Jews; *progressive Jews not Jewish enough* in their opinion. This is why we in the West look at fundamentalist Jews and/or Muslims and falsely try to group them together as terrorists. This is why fundamentalist Christians persecute other Christians that are *too modern* and *not Christian enough* for them. This is where what once may have been conservatism turns into extremism.

"Jesus was a Galilean, not a Judean."

Or Jesus was Nazarene, or from Bethlehem; it depends upon how you want to view it I suppose.

"The Jews of his time were called Pharisees and he mercilessly condemned them."

Not all Jews were called Pharisees. Pharisee is a Jewish sect. Jesus was a Jew; evidently not a Pharisidic Jew.

"For this condemnation he was crucified."

You'll find a lot of disagreement about this reading too. It isn't this simple.

"Jews don't claim Jesus as their own and the Talmud is filled with hateful and mocking references to Jesus and his Mother."

Some Jews did claim Jesus as their own. Some people claim or disclaim lots of people or groups of people.

"Was your assertion meant to elevate Jews or to criticize Christians for being un-Christian toward Jews?"

I don't know what assertion you speak of. I don't intend to elevate or criticize Jews, Christians or Muslims.

"Jews, as a small minority, always pit their enemies against one another. Muslims are their enemies and Europeans are their enemies."

I know Jews, Muslims and Europeans who don't do this belief so your broad assertion is false.

"Why else would Jews be agitating for Muslim immigration into European countries? They aren't humanitarians; they are not worried about the welfare of people forced from their lands by violence; after all, the Israelis forced 750,000 Palestinians from their lands in 1947."

None of the Jews I personally know do this; and I don't know who "they" are. I only know individuals. Many individuals fight over things. Some will fight over things that happened in 1947. Some will continue fights from 6000 BCE.

". . . they are not worried about the welfare of people forced from their lands by violence. . ."

And many of the people we have been speaking of are people forced from their lands by violence. Can I quote you on this? :)

No reply.

After several weeks . . .
PAUL: I hope you and yours had a pleasant Thanksgiving. I was thinking about something you said in a recent reply and thought I'd reply to it.

It might be easy to get the impression that I might see *truth* as relative, but this wouldn't be quite correct. Even absolutists agree that we have different points of view, and that we even have different viewpoints of the absolute. And so absolutists are *functional relativists* in this way because there is no way around this/their predicament. Absolutists love to say they are right and relativists wrong. Relativists love to say they are right and absolutists are wrong. We can't help but fight over an absolute. Both sides can, however, stop regarding truth or God as an *it* or as *an absolute* or as *The Absolute*. Instead we can regard the indefinable infinitude of reality as an ongoing process. Aware that there is so much reality beyond our comprehension, and that therefore any comprehension partial, any attempt at making infinite definite, should keep us from fighting for some definitive that is only a matter of perspective. As it is, this attitude does not devalue truth/infinity/God, but instead places truth/infinity/God where truth/infinity/God beyond our grasp because it *is* beyond our grasp. We are just not that great.

To simply recognize and value this circumstance should guide our understanding. It should keep us from fighting for something we can't possess. We should (but we don't) clearly realize how our viewpoints mislead us due to our viewpoint's ability to be so certain yet limited. Since viewpoint must fall short, our views are simply definitions of facts, and facts of perspective are transitory.

Hence it's easier to talk about what is wrong with our ideas of truth than it is to talk about what truth is. This is the nature of things. Morality is much the same way. Many people have ideas about what is moral and what is immoral and we fight about these things just as we do truth. Although I see the problems with how people view morality, I'm not a moral skeptic. There is a constant pattern that morality fits into, which can guide us just as patterns within reality might guide us if we would let them. But it can be as difficult to value abstract thought as it can be to value abstract art. Yet our mis-evaluations says less about art, morality and truth than it does about the critics of these things.

Since the idea of an absolute can't help but give rise to the idea of right *v* wrong, I don't buy into the idea and implications of good *v* evil. We can't even know evil unless we define something else as good. The terms are complementary and dependent rather than opposing. Furthermore, hardly anything or anybody is good or evil. Things and beings are more complex than this. The dualities that follow from absolutes setup a situation where dualities almost become absolutes themselves and thereby guarantee our inability to reason our way toward a common understanding of morality. And this conglomeration seems best to describe the confusion of the world in which we live. Without a common foundation, the idea of good *v* evil tends to demonize some people while putting them in a group that is essentially *given up on* or *persecuted for*. But once we give up this false dichotomy, not only is redemption possible, we ourselves can no longer seek refuge in the solace of duality.

For a while I also didn't really have a philosophical foundation for my politics; my values were merely conventional. I found no real foundation within the Republican or Democratic parties. When I looked into the Libertarian party I thought I'd found a foundation until I saw how most everybody seemed to look at freedom in a negative light; *freedom from*, instead of *liberty for*. Finally freedom seemed to be such a narrow foundation. We aren't born into freedom; we are born many years dependent. From family we learn (or probably should) a responsibility that tempers our freedoms into what I understand to be liberty. And civil society, at its best, probably should reflect this; and we should treat those in greater civil society with the same kind hands as we do our family members. So I looked back into the classical liberal traditions from whence libertarianism came and found that there is a wider, more positive basis there than I suspected, although modern libertarianism has constructed/reconstructed it so narrowly. Still, I had to find a way to broaden these assumptions before I could be comfortable with Locke and company. (I had to broaden/revise some all too certain natural law ideas.) I suppose my understanding of pre-Socratic and ancient Chinese philosophy helped alter my way of looking at things.

After about a month with no replies, I had followed Sharon's Face-book *posts and here I make general comment about a few of her most recent comments upon the posts of others.*
PAUL: *False flags* and *psyops*. These are the new popular terms bandied about nowadays.

The grouping and generalization of others tends to minimize not only the arguments of an entire group, it minimizes the arguments of an individual because individuals make up a group. This situation essentially creates the framework for psyops and false flags.

It is all too easy to take something that may be an extreme view of a single Democrat, or several Democrats and then say Democratic views and/or Democrats themselves are idiotic. This can be said about conservative, right-wing, libertarian, Christian, Muslim views as well as any other group. Curiously we speak this way knowing full well that we don't really understand their views or perhaps we would find agreement with them. How do we know this? How can I make such an absurd statement? For the simple reason we that we call others idiots because they don't understand our views; they in turn call us idiots for not understanding their views. I would say nobody is an idiot; we all share in the ignorance. To purposefully ignore this reality while calling others idiotic is ignorant. I once held views opposite from the views I held at other times and, surprisingly, they both make sense. Yet there are all kinds of ideas that I can't support because they insist upon ignorance of so many points of view. Some views are naturally exclusive of each other yet they can and must play in concert with each other. They can complement and harmonize, but too many of us have either lost sight of this greater reality by refusing to look beyond our preferred views, or we have never looked in the first place.

Then I read posts where people call others "liars" because they define mass shootings differently. One group says it's a lie to call shootings involving more than 4 people a mass shooting. Another group agrees that this definition might fit as long the shooters/shootees are not *gang members*. I assume gangs don't count as people. Their terror isn't terror? Their lives don't matter? Innocent lives in the crossfire don't count? I assume we must consider the possible guilt or innocence of all parties involved before we make this determination? *Bullshit!* is the reply I receive to my questions. Or: *the point is that the 'media' is lying by using statistics this way so as to serve their purpose*. Yet those who manipulate the *same* statistics so as to exclude gang shootings are also manipulating statistics to serve their purposes. If they weren't doing this, they wouldn't comment upon the *misuse* of the same statistics. So am I left to suppose that both *sides* are *liars*. Statistics are just numbers. Each side *uses* these numbers as they see fit. I see little sense in calling both side liars or truth tellers. To devalue this fact is to devalue something closer to truth and, as such, to value something more akin to lying. It seems to me that the worst kind of psyops are those that are embedded within ourselves that we refuse to see. They mislead us while we argue for our righteousness while suspecting and blaming others for what we view as their wrongness. This is the original false flag. Our original sin.

False flag and psyops are terms generally used by those on the *right* only because they have been popularized by those who tune into the same right-wing channels. For everybody else to get their news from the many of the similar, more vetted, sources leaves them vulnerable to being misled? Isn't this what false flag and psyop purveyors always claim? This could be accurate but there are ways to check, but like most false flag wavers and those preaching about psyops, these methods are minimized, scoffed at or denied. But isn't this also the purpose of psyops: *to influence people's emotions, motives, objective reasoning, and ultimately their behavior*? The psyops that result from our insistence upon our own point of view are the best because they never fail to work; they can't. Every psyop purveyor should know this in order to be aware of the dangers of themselves becoming trapped. Otherwise we are playing a blame game rather than claiming responsibility for our own lack of view. (The premier psychological false flag.) When we refuse to take responsibility for the narrowness of our views, we will regard views as true those that simply masquerade as such while appealing to, and fitting in with, our preconceived notions.

SHARON: The President of the United States does not count gun violence among blacks in Chicago when he talks about mass shootings and gun control. In other words he doesn't appear at funerals, candlelight vigils, nor does he make appearances at the scene of such shootings in Chicago. He defines terrorism and mass shooting as Sandy Hook, Charleston, Roseburg, and San Bernardino. I don't recall that he had anything to say about Isla Vista – maybe because three of the victims were said to have been stabbed to death. He even excludes Charlie Hebdo and the recent Paris attacks when he said, while in Paris, that mass shootings only occur in the United States. So, would you say that Obama is manipulating the statistics for his own purposes?

I think current events give us a very similar view of how people believe what they want to believe, that is to say, they believe what fits their political view. This is what I wrote on one of the *Facebook* articles on the San Bernardino "mass shooting":

"False flag 'mass shootings' are used to divide Americans into two camps - the left that wants gun control and loves Third World immigration and the right that opposes immigration and loves the 2nd Amendment. No one, not even the President, waits for an investigation before putting the psyop to use. We have been conditioned since 9/11 to believe the most preposterous tales, replete with glaring contradictions and impossibilities. All in positions of authority express their belief and the skeptic then becomes everyone's enemy. That is how mind control works."

This contrived division between Right and Left is beautifully illustrated in the San Bernardino event. Obama was Johnny-on-the-spot with his gun control speech, but the Right was positively ebullient when that message was drowned by the fact that the putative shooters were Muslims. In the end people believe what they want to believe and it doesn't matter that the event was staged, that no one died, or that it doesn't make sense on any level. Because all authorities both left and right express belief in these false "realities" everyone must signal their belief, if only to send a teddy bear or to cover one's profile picture with the French flag.

So all that is left are a few skeptics who think an impartial investigation is necessary; skeptics who will be vilified by believers - both Left and Right. Did you ever see the movie "The Body Snatchers"?

PAUL: An interesting reply Sharon.

"So, would you say that Obama is manipulating the statistics for his own purposes?"

Yes. Everybody does. Numbers are value neutral; they need context. So everybody chooses their context and the context they choose generally represents their interpretation of what they think the numbers might mean or should mean. Like you say, "I think current events give us a very similar view of how people believe what they want to believe, that is to say, they believe what fits their political view."

For example, you say: "False flag 'mass shootings' are used to divide Americans into two camps - the left that wants gun control and loves . . ."

I don't think you are using the term "false flag" correctly here, but regardless, people often assume how I must think about gun control but they are likely wrong with their assumption. They might think they know what I currently think about the second amendment but are likely wrong there also.

"No one, not even the President, waits for an investigation before putting the psyop to use."

The term "no one" is too limiting here but I would agree that many people tend to post their points of view (Teddy bears and all) o n *Facebook* immediately, regardless of their preferred perspective. I wonder how many of these people realize how much they are led by their own perspectives let alone by the perspectives and propaganda of others.

"This contrived division between Right and Left . . ."

I will agree that the division is too often contrived but it is also a *conventional* reality. If it wasn't, you and I couldn't employ these terms so readily.

"In the end people believe what they want to believe and it doesn't matter that the event was staged . . ."

If this "event" was "staged", who would stage such an event when it, "doesn't make sense on any level"? If impartial investigations were constantly performed for the benefit of skeptics, it seems to me that the skeptics would be skeptical of the results. They would likely be condemned as impartial; at least by some sides. Some skeptics seem to enjoy skepticism simply for the sake of being contrary. Perhaps they are quite aware that skepticism is difficult to rebut. Much skepticism tends to be negative and it is hard to disprove this negative without being negative let alone be- ing heard. Regardless of possible intentions, skeptics often feel vil- ified from all sides simply for being skeptical. They also know that people believe what they want to believe and so will be unlikely listen to any results or even listen to their skepticism. Do you have any suggestions?

No reply.

Off on a different post from Facebook *that began with the com- ment:* "Is there something to making love 'official' that actually strengthens it? Want a long lasting marriage, avoid cohabitation."
SHARON comments: The traditional view of marriage is based on our reproductive biology, that is to say, the primary purpose of marriage has been to bind the couple and assign responsibility for offspring to them.. Contraception and abor- tion have allowed people to engage in sexual intercourse without love, responsibility, commitment, and respect for one another's reproductive role. Cohabitation and premarital in- tercourse circumvent the woman's ability to choose a partner who is committed to fulfilling his role as protector and provider of his wife and their children. The result is that young women today settle for the "relationship" in which they fool themselves into believing that their feeling of love is re- ciprocated and has the same weight as the marital bond. Even after a series of these "relationships" the woman often fails to see that interfering with nature has unhappy conse- quences.

JH replied: I am married, I live with my wife in a house that we own, and we use contraception because we do not feel that we are ready to have children yet.

SHARON: Don't wait too long. Divorce is most common in those who have no children and the rate decreases steadily as the number of children grows. Women have a built in timetable that is connected to their reproductive cycle (a cycle that begins with ovulation and ends with the weaning of a child - roughly two years.) The inability to complete her cycle often results in a subconscious dissatisfaction that is transferred to her mate. While this scenario is more common in unmarried relationships, being married doesn't change female biology.

I poked my nose in:
PAUL: Golly, I thought I married my wife because I love her. We have never and will never reproduce. She'll be off put to hear that our loving commitment was just a matter of "nature". But I guess if our love and commitment is true and of value, homosexuals could, and should participate in it too. But, alas, if what you claim is true, I guess we can look forward to our pending divorce. I just hope it is as happy as our marriage :)

SHARON: If love for one's biological mate is not a matter of nature, what is it? Supernatural? The male/female complement is the essential paradigm of our human existence. Love between a procreative couple is the emotional affirmation of reproductive choice - even if there are no children. We don't fall in love with our grandparents, though we do love them. And the love we have for our siblings is very different from the love we have for our own children. These differences derive from our biology. Because marital love is the expression of reproductive choice one would expect that the feelings accompanying divorce would also have their root in biology - and for many women those feelings arise from biology thwarted.

PAUL: Your use of the term "nature" makes it sound destined and not a matter of choice. But I doubt that's how you think about homosexuality. Homosexuality to you is unnatural, perhaps supernatural because it isn't supposed to be as defined by Nature (capitalized) or biology? But if the King of nature didn't command it then all behaviors are natural, and some behaviors you just don't like. Homosexual behavior is a common minority behavior found throughout nature in many species. In at least one species the outward behavior is prevalent. The species has been around for a long time. The species is natural and has perhaps been paradigm to their existence. It might be more accurate to call most of the species bisexual I suppose.

Now, love is more complicated. It is natural but the word is complex and so implies a complex, perhaps uniquely human understanding or determination. The complexities of love are, and never have been limited by biology. Like you say, love is much more broad than *falling in love*. So there are many levels and complexities to it. Some are so powerful that we don't seem to choose them but they are real. They are natural, of nature and of our natures, whether heterosexual, homosexual, bisexual or asexual in action. Biological? Yes. Psychological? Yes. Derived from our being? Yes. So how is one, two, or a third option wrong? I'd say the options are different rather than right or wrong. Reproduction isn't a part of my marriage. It doesn't have to be for my wife and I to be *natural*. The same goes for a homosexual, bisexual or asexual couple. There is nothing wrong with their biology or choice (if these are our only options here). It's just different. And our pending divorce or lack thereof for not having children to keep us together will not be based in or upon biology. Somehow we simply love each other while biology is thwarted every step of the way; without the *expression* of our love biologically :)

I was curious to see if Sharon would inquire as to which species I am referring to. I was referring to Bonobos.
But back to false flags and psyops . . .
SHARON: A false flag is an event contrived to look as though perpetrated by another or others. It is a form of propaganda that has a dramatic and instantaneous effect on public opinion. Questions that arise later do not penetrate the consciousness of most people who have internalized the meme - especially when it appears that those in authority have accepted the original story. Having Obama pretend to wipe a tear away while talking about the "victims" at Sandy Hook is a powerful thing because most people cannot accept

the idea that a president would participate in a cheap psyop designed to propagandize them. It is enough for most people to ask, "Why would he do that?" as a way of answering the question negatively - "He wouldn't do that"; therefore, the event in question should not be questioned. It's one thing to think that 19 Muslims armed with box cutters, directed from a cave in Afghanistan, hijacked four passenger planes, evaded all air defenses, crashed the planes into three buildings and a field, because they "hate our freedom" -- than it is to think that Obama would participate in a false flag operation - lying to the American people. In another post you referred to my description of 9/11 as a caricature. Maybe you can explain what makes it so? As for "suggestions"- I don't have any. People do what they are wound up to do and that is why it is so easy to manipulate them. There have always been people in every time who see where things are headed, but they rarely have an audience, much less a following. Surely, there were many who could see the folly of WW I before the carnage, but like Charles Lindbergh in WW II his understanding gave way to participation because patriotism, like love is blind.

PAUL: Would you say that skepticism, talk about psyops, as well as the possibility of false flags and a general belief in conspiracies could possibly be false flags and psyops themselves? It seems the psychology can and does work both ways. As in the question, "who benefits form the San Bernardino shootings"? From most accounts I've heard, Donald Trump has capitalized on it more than others. Is he using the "event" in these manners?

Psyops and false flags are todays current terms for opinions and viewpoints that we disagree with, and little more. If I disagree with what I perceive Obama's "real intent" to be, this doesn't make me correct or incorrect. My viewpoint simply points to how I view things, and that I disagree with whatever his view might really be. But to say that Obama, ". . . pretend to wipe a tear away while talking about the 'victims' . . ." might say more about you and your opinion about him than it says about him. Since you are not him, yours is mere speculation. What you suspect has nothing to do with truth because neither you or I can know. Your words and mine are directed toward the same purpose. Or intent is to persuade. Perhaps we are guilty of psyops. If the *event* should be questioned and doubted then we should also question our answers and ourselves.

"... to think that Obama would participate in ... lying to the American people."

Frankly, I expect presidents and those involved in security to lie to us. I don't expect those with security clearance to tell us through the news media *the truth*. I think it is my responsibility to realize they may (have to) do this from time to time. I accept this. I don't have to believe all of what Obama says or all of what his detractors say. I have enough responsibility for myself than to overly concern myself with the supposed *intentions* of others. Mostly because I can't know about *that* and *them*, but I can be realistic and my realism can be responsible.

"In another post you referred to my description of 9/11 as a caricature. Maybe you can explain what makes it so?"

For the reasons I just stated. I think we do ourselves harm; we harm our reason by assuming we can know what we cannot know. It leads to other errors of the ego. It is skepticism run amok. We can be realistic and skeptical without misleading ourselves. Your description is a caricature just as your sureness in your own beliefs is a caricature of truth. Everybody who puts down another viewpoint because they currently prefer another view caricatures the fact that other views have value. In example, "**People do what they are wound up to do and that is why it is so easy to manipulate them.**" And this does mean you *and* me. I, for one, at least know that I am not a prophet.

Back to the other topic at hand . . .
SHARON: Homosexual behavior, like masturbation or bestiality, is natural in the sense that it can be used to achieve sexual arousal and orgasm, but one does not "fall in love" with the object, image, or activity that eliciits sexual arousal because there is no reproductive consequence, no biological need to bond. By the same token the prostitute is objectified and used for sexual release, but love has nothing to do with

it. In the human species it is especially important for the female to feel love before engaging in sexual intercourse and she needs that assurance even if she is unable to bear children - in other words, love, for the human female, is integral to reproductive success.

It is not only possible to disengage one's behavior from the two essentials of all life forms - survival and reproduction - but given the flexibility of our instincts we can be driven to do things that are antithetical to both. For example, the instinctive desire for water can be temporarily satisfied by drinking sea water. The instinct is natural, but satisfying thirst with sea water isn't "normal" for a subset of humans. Drinking sea water is the perversion of an instinct. Homosexual behavior, like masturbation, is an adjunct to reproductive sex; it is not a defining characteristic of a subset of humans or other species. While homosexual behavior, like masturbation, has been seen in other species there are no examples of individuals that refuse heterosexual coitus in favor of homosexual sex. Nor do we see female animals that perform male mating rituals as a way of attracting same sex partners; nor do we see an occasional male standing with the females hoping to be chosen for "mating" by the male who has finished his rut. We do not see females who are excited by another female's estrus, nor do we see males who are oblivious to the estrus of their species. 'Homosexual' as an identity is a political contrivance of very recent vintage.

The love between man and woman is unique because it is integral to successful reproduction. For the same reason, love between parent and child is unique. Other loves are not as powerful as those that are driven by instinct. We can love our friends, our relatives, our teachers, but we don't "fall in love" with any of them. By the same token we would not sacrifice our own lives for any of them, but we would for our child.

PAUL: From my experience, falling in love has little to do with love. I have fallen in lust. I have fallen for my idea, my projection of love, but not for love as I understand it today. So I'd have to disagree that one doesn't "'fall in love' with the object, image . . ."

For me it has been my projection (an image of what I desire) that I have fallen for. Luckily I have grown beyond myself.

Either way, lust, regardless of love, has always presented reproductive consequence. If it did not, birth control wouldn't be an issue. "Reproductive consequence" has nothing to do with love. Somehow my wife and I seem to understand this. Or perhaps we misunderstand that we love each other although there can be no reproductive consequence for us.

". . . the prostitute is objectified and used for sexual release, but love has nothing to do with it. In the human species it is especially important for the female to feel love before engaging in sexual intercourse . . ."

Or not. Take a survey of women. Your sentences seem incoherent here. Current everyday reality fails to bare out your claims.

"It is not only possible to disengage one's behavior from the two essentials of all life forms - survival and reproduction - but given the flexibility of our instincts we can be driven to do things that are antithetical to both."

Then survival and reproduction are not so necessary because we are reproducing quite well in our ignorance of the proper process. I would think this would devalue the importance you put upon such process.

"Drinking sea water is the perversion of an instinct."

No it is not. It is simply drinking water that isn't good for you.

"Homosexual behavior, like masturbation, is an adjunct to reproductive sex; it is not a defining characteristic of a subset of humans or other species."

The fact that nearly all humans masturbate, defines it as normal. Homosexual behavior is not adjunct to reproductive sex if you don't engage in sexual relations with the opposite sex. It is simply a behavior. A behavior shared by many species.

"While homosexual behavior, like masturbation, has been seen in other species there are no examples of individuals that refuse heterosexual coitus in favor of homosexual sex."

Yes there is; between homosexuals.

"Nor do we see female animals that perform male mating rituals as a way of attracting same sex partners."

Some female homosexual behavior might indeed be like this but frankly I don't know. The fact that they may do it differently doesn't mean anything to me. It doesn't prove or disprove anything that I can see.

". . . nor do we see an occasional male standing with the females hoping to be chosen for "mating" by the male who has finished his rut."

Actually, in humans, many women do get tired of being rutted and will go for the outlying, sensitive male waiting in the wings. The idea that the alpha male is the physically strongest is not of as much value in humans as it used to me. The geeks (sorry for the generalization and stereotyping; it is only to demonstrate a possible point) are often found to be quite attractive today (I hear).

"We do not see females who are excited by another female's estrus . . ."

Except perhaps for homosexual females. There is a market.

". . . nor do we see males who are oblivious to the estrus of their species."

Perhaps ditto.

"'Homosexual' as an identity is a political contrivance of very recent vintage."

Yet it is a real identity and has been likely for human existence, let alone animal existence which have no formal politics to hide behind. Your denial of reality doesn't make reality unreal.

"The love between man and woman is unique because it is integral to successful reproduction."

I disagree. It is unique because of the complex values it repre-sents. These values are represented by homosexuals as well as those who will not reproduce.

"For the same reason, love between parent and child is unique."

No, it is a different reason. It does not involve an image of re-production, we might hope.

"Other loves are not as powerful as those that are driven by instinct."

Neither love nor falling in love are instinctual. Sex is. As you say, "We can love our friends, our relatives, our teachers, but we don't 'fall in love' with any of them."

"By the same token we would not sacrifice our own lives for any of them, but we would for our child."

I can't say this about myself. I might sacrifice my life even for a stranger.

"Other loves are not as powerful as those that are driven by instinct."

History and news is replete with contradictions to your claim. Perhaps others some see important relations where you don't.

Meanwhile, back to a different politics . . .

SHARON: My description of 9/11 is a shorthand reiteration of the information the public was given to explain what happened; how it happened; and by whom it was perpetrated. None of it is my speculation. Are you saying that the government's story about 9/11 is, itself, a caricature designed to satisfy the public's curiosity while leading us to take a view that benefits those in power? Is it impossible to know the truth about 9/11 or any other thing that is not within our direct vision and examination? Are you saying that because of one's subjectivity it is impossible to know truth and that one's confidence in what he believes is true is an illusion made manifest by that selfsame confidence? Perhaps what you are saying is that as long as one is comfortable and secure there is no purpose in troubling oneself with questions or doubts about anything that is remote from one's direct experience? Isn't that precisely the reason why nearly everyone falls quickly into one belief camp or the other rather than asking questions and raising doubts? Is it not a gross error of the ego to let personal comfort determine one's view or to pretend that every view is of equal value simply because it is one's view. Two people are back to back, one looking north and the other south. What each sees is "truth" from his vantage point. While one is looking south he sees a man with a hatchet kill a man out for his morning walk. When the police come to the scene they take the statements of the two. One saw a murder and the other did not. Is the one who saw the murder or the police who just heard about it out of place in devaluing the statement of the one who did not see it? How can the police get to the truth without raising questions and weighing evidence?

PAUL: I would call the government's description an example of how a government responds when it is explaining a terrorist attack. It is not truth but not all lies. I would call your description a caricature of the government's curious description.

"Is it impossible to know the truth about 9/11 or any other thing that is not within our direct vision and examination?"

Yes, we cannot learn *"the* truth", but there are methods (processes) that can aid us in getting closer so as to make reasonable judgments or at least to question reasonably. Our methods are important because they should align with the processes relating to truth. If we do not understand these complexities we will not learn about truths, we will only zero in on that which supports our preconceived notions, prejudices and fears.

"Are you saying that because of one's subjectivity it is impossible to know truth and that one's confidence in what he believes is true is an illusion made manifest by that selfsame confidence?"

Unfortunately, this is pretty much the case. Too often people believe they are being objective by looking outside themselves to other objects and subjects and then making determinations, but the reliance and value they place upon their subjective views too often proves to be illusory due to their selfsame confidence. If people were to devalue their egoism, they might truly question the value of their viewpoints. I can kid myself all day long that I can look at something from my limited view and come out with a conclusion that doesn't challenge my views. Generally speaking, we grow up in a community that believes in *this* religion and holds *these* political views and then we congratulate ourselves and call ourselves open minded when we find the religious and political views of our community true. Those others who grow up in a different community in a different part of the world then believe their religion and political views to be true while congratulating themselves for finding *the* truth. Sure, we see how obviously mistaken they are, but we absolutely refuse to see this in ourselves. Why? Because we *know* we are right.

"Perhaps what you are saying is that as long as one is comfortable and secure there is no purpose in troubling oneself with questions or doubts about anything that is remote from one's direct experience?"

Exactly the opposite. We should argue with ourselves, and

refuse to accept the answers we come up especially with when they just happen to fit with our preferred views. Otherwise, yes, "nearly everyone falls quickly into one belief camp or the other rather than asking questions and raising doubts." And they aren't even aware of it or they wouldn't find the idea the least bit astonishing.

"Is it not a gross error of the ego to let personal comfort determine one's view or to pretend that every view is of equal value simply because it is one's view."

All views are of equal value, but what they might mean to us alter their value. And too often we coincidently value the views we prefer. We prefer their comfort to their truth.

"Two people are back to back, one looking north and the other south. What each sees is 'truth' from his vantage point."

I am hesitant to define a point of view as *true*. To do so is to devalue *truth* if every view is *true*. A point of view is convenient, and since viewpoints are infinite in number, any a singular viewpoint obviously falls short, extremely short of truth. A vantage point is merely that. Ignorance of it is ignorance. An intent to be ignorant of a viewpoint might be deemed as foolish. You and I intend to look at each other's view. We ask questions. Do we learn?

"While one is looking south he sees a man with a hatchet kill a man out for his morning walk. When the police come to the scene they take the statements of the two. One saw a murder and the other did not. Is the one who saw the murder or the police who just heard about it out of place in devaluing the statement of the one who did not see it?"

Of course not. One saw something, the other did not. One is worth asking about the issue, yet even this person won't possess the "truth", he merely possesses information. He saw something relevant from his viewpoint that may be relevant to the investigation. Some people see absolute nothing and wish that their words will have the same impact as those who admit that they too didn't see and don't really know. There are those who have more credibility because their information is more obviously reasonable.

"How can the police get to the truth without raising questions and weighing evidence?"

The police must. They must at least begin by not believing

those who have no evidence or relevant view. Now, if nobody has witnessed anything and there is no evidence anywhere to be had by anyone, then reason itself turns out to be the order of the day. I think we then have to consider the process of reason and processes of reality. Do the people who have something to say only intend to support their preconceived notions or are they more skeptical of themselves than that? Do these people understand the complications of reality enough to be trusted to sort through it? Do they devalue their perspectives enough to have credibility due to an impersonal wisdom? No doubt some of these people are so sure of what they see and believe that they call this "true" in spite of a myriad of options that they are ignorant of. And the police can devalue the reason provided by those who don't or won't seriously consider broader reason once they become aware of this fact.

SHARON: What makes the government's description of 9/11 "curious"?

PAUL: Anytime I am told something that doesn't "ring true", I find it curious. But my *ringer* might be faulty too. So, is my curiosity aroused because something doesn't ring true, or is it because I simply have misunderstood something or missed something, or both? This curiosity leads me to keep my ears and eyes open. This isn't due to some negative skepticism, it is a positive curiosity of mine. The fact that I might be missing something and/or misunderstanding something is so incredibly likely that I value this aspect highly. It is a part of my personal and social responsibility to do so. In fact, what I personally lack likely has more to do with what I'm trying to investigate than with external facts or conditions. I must conquer myself while I investigate the case.

Although my internal problems don't have any direct effect upon external facts, they can make it impossible for me to know the difference let alone understand it. Without this basis, I can hardly know relevant facts from irrelevant because I'll likely find my self and my beliefs impinging upon and therefore determining relevancy *for me* in spite of reality beyond my self. Unfortunately my main basis for distinguishing and choosing will likely be my own biases. So my process has to do with checking my *ringer* (see above) too. There are so many conditions that make something ring true or false to me that have nothing whatsoever to do with facts outside of me. Perhaps you can liken it to an internal conspiracy that causes me to minimize most things external while favoring my own beliefs about them. Yet I can do something about me and my internal conspirator. From what I've observed about human disagreement, most of those participating in disagreement have failed to do their homework about themselves.

So, back to your question, I first consider what this "curiosity" means to me. Is it personal? If what I am examining is not personally directed at me, I then I remove myself from the equation. Personal or not, however, I will now consider the story from the teller's perspective to see how it might sound to their ears. What might it mean to/for them? If it still sounds lacking, I consider what perspective it might make sense from. I try my best to consider the most likely down to least likely. . . through my minimal ideas about what I can imagine to consider. Since I'm looking for context that can be separated from me or my beliefs, this can be a challenge. Sometimes I am left with more questions than clues. Sometimes my reasoned imagination gives many clues to consider while other considerations either lead to dead ends or they lead to boxes of belief that I refuse to enter because they are so convenient as to dissuade me from the process. Their convenience only serves to mislead me so I put all such considerations on the back burner. I then look to other sources for information. I have a responsibility to be well aware that these *sources* use their minds and choose their methods much as I do. I consider their biases (implicit and otherwise), just as I do my own. I then let all of this float around inside my mind while looking for relations that I might have missed or devalued. Over time I start seeing a clearer picture and so I check it against my biases again to see where I am likely to go wrong. Pretty soon, after listening and discussing with others who I often may disagree with, things begin to make some sense, and so I go on from there with my process.

Another option here is that I could simply ignore this process of reason because now we're talking about government and/or politics and this is somehow different in many people's minds. So many of us will look at government as though it is some unique creature. They will talk about government being bloated and inefficient etc. Have they never worked for a large corporation? Hell,

161

everybody talks about how stupid their boss is and how much better things would be if *they* were in charge instead. Regardless, to think that I could have skipped all of this work of reason and simply reacted to the latest news story with my own opinion. Or perhaps I could have tuned into my favorite channel or those Internet sites that I often agree with. I could have quickly found, to my amazement, that I agree with them. Done. Time to post.

As it is, I don't expect anybody to tell me *the* truth. I don't think most people even know what truth telling would involve. Just as the words faith and belief have become irrationally interchangeable, people too often equate truth with belief, yet they too are opposed. Many people are essentially skeptics of truth yet (or perhaps because of this) they know all about perspective. Viewpoint is what they value because this is what society generally values as some sort of bottom line. Few value much about any understanding that exists beyond their strongly held viewpoints. They don't see how their skepticism (as opposed to curiosity) about the value of greater reality has overruled their quest for greater understanding at the outset. For myself, I only expect people to voice their opinions, their views, or the facts as they see them from their own perspectives. And most of this is about themselves after all is said and done. I seldom expect any of them to even honestly ask what I think, and then listen to what I say. In this way I don't congratulate or condemn them for more than they are due; this would also be irresponsible of me. It is my responsibility to understand this and to do the work (sifting for value) using a different process.

But this is just my short answer to your question :)

SHARON: It sounds like you need a machine in which to enter "curious" facts and explanations so they can be handled mathematically according to the laws of probability. Without such a device one can start by asking oneself why one cares about a particular "curiosity"? I think modern communication alters the scope of that which, for millions of years, and even now for other creatures, is immediate and personal, namely one's survival and the survival of his offspring. For modern people everything is personal and nothing is personal. We are invited to view events entirely remote from us and our concerns as if they are as relevant to our lives as what happens next door. For nearly everyone the media doesn't widen his view - it actually displaces or replaces reality. This creates a problem because even though we are in an artificial environment we still retain our most primitive instincts along with characteristics that have evolved in our people over thousands of years in difficult and dangerous circumstances. An instinct like "fight or flight" is endlessly tweaked by contrived "experiences". A proper response in a natural environment is misapplied or warped in an artificial environment. That is why I ask "why one cares?" I think there are at least three different answers:

1. A person with a natural or learned capacity for scope tries to use reason and information to explain what he sees, i.e. how things work.

2. A man's instinct to protect his wife and children is activated by threats that may be remote but his imagination fills in the "possibilities" - such a man could be described as circumspect. A woman with the same approach is more likely a worry wart - torturing herself with terrible "possibilities".

3. A person who is secure and comfortable and has no skin in the game. He "cares" only insofar as he can project an image of caring.

I am the female version of #2 - the things I care about all have the potential to impact my children and grandchildren negatively. I am definitely a worry wart, for example, when Howard's family was living in Paris in a tenth floor apartment, I decided not to send the children a book about a pig who could fly because I thought it would give H - the impetuous one - ideas. That kind of circumspection would tell anyone that I am a mother. I care about homosexual activism and sex "education" in schools because both are essentially pornographic. I think it is anathema to sexualize young children and set them up for alienated sex rather than marital sex. Heretofore. we have treated sex as a private matter between adults and before I had children I simply did not care what people did to or with each other. Now, however, I see a threat to the innocence and wellbeing of my grandchildren. I care about Third World immigration into European countries and I am troubled by the fact that the French do not have guns. I imagine how it would be if two or three male immigrants invaded my son's remote home. How would he protect his family? My political views fit my concerns, but those concerns aren't beliefs - they are worries. I can try to check my tendency to worry and I can resist the temptation to see an electoral solution, but I seem unable to narrow my view if even for my own mental comfort.

PAUL: You say, "It sounds like you need a machine in which to enter 'curious' facts and explanations so they can be handled mathematically according to the laws of probability."

My thought process might sound a bit complex but most of it happens within a few seconds, but my less immediate considerations can go on for a long while. Everybody's got to have a hobby:)

So I guess the curiosity makes me care if nothing else does, and I always know why I care. As far as your three reasons about why one might care, I have fit into all three before. Oddly, perhaps, I've fit into that motherly role before too.

I have no idea if sex education in schools today is pornographic. When I was a kid it was no where close to pornographic. When Karyl's granddaughter recently had her class, I assume she didn't seem to become any more sexualized than I did.

I'm sorry you have *fears* about, "Third World immigration into European countries." Does Howard share these fears? I would agree that your political views fit your concerns and worries and fears. When you say you can, "resist the temptation to see an electoral solution." What does this mean? What do you mean by, "I seem unable to narrow my view if even for my own mental comfort."?

Sharon hadn't replied to my questions but I've come to expect this. In the meantime I had "liked" a Christmas (Dec 23rd) Facebook post about Eartha Kitt that had a picture of her when she was young with a caption that said: "Eartha Kitt was conceived by rape, born on a cotton plantation, spoke 5 languages, sang in 7, and recorded the hit song *Santa Baby*, July 1953."

SHARON: It is good she that was born before Roe v. Wade.

PAUL: This post isn't about abortion. It is a post about overcoming adversity. This one happens to be about a woman of color in the Jim Crow South. But since you brought it up . . . no matter what people think about abortion, regardless of whether people support constitutional law or not, today most people have the right to decide whether to keep a baby born of rape. But my guess would be that a woman who gets raped on a cotton plantation didn't have many rights that were being enforced in the first place, let alone the slim chance that she might see any justice at all, controversial justice or otherwise. Why? because the Jim Crow South wasn't much interested in abstract constitutional ideas such as equal rights and equal protection under the law.

SHARON: The post made a point of saying that Kitt was conceived in rape and that is not a disadvantage to the child unless the child is aborted. My point is that a child conceived in rape post-Roe v. Wade is not likely to have a chance to overcome adversity. While blacks comprise only about 13% of the population more than a third of the babies aborted in the U.S. are black. Thirty-three percent of 53,000,000 is more than 17 million black babies who never had a chance to overcome adversity. Eartha Kitt should make women think again about killing the child to punish the rapist.

PAUL: I would think most people reading this post understand it to be a feel good Christmas post. It is unfortunate that you read it as a commentary upon abortion. You and I only sully the spirit of the post through our own comments.

A week later I message Sharon:
PAUL: Although you sometimes comment on posts from a site valuing personal liberty, rather than respecting individualism, you don't speak of individual persons, rather you speak of groups. You seem to value one collective against (or at least as contrasted with) another collective: Europeans as opposed to all non-Occidentals, blacks against whites, male power as contrasted with the female's proper place, straights against gays, natives against non natives (or perhaps the current natives against prior natives), and Democrats

against Republicans. You do this knowing full well not everybody fits these molds. So, given all this, I'm wondering why is it you do this?

No reply.

But my thoughts keep flowing so I send her another message:
PAUL: Stereotyping, as a shortcut, shortchanges all individuals who don't fit conveniently into these groupings or self identify with these groups. The grouping of people becomes tantamount to propaganda. And since the stereotyper must be in error at least some of the time, the stereotyper shortchanges herself as an individual by minimizing other individuals; there is a loss of credibility. Propaganda about a group can't make individuals of less value. So, with these negatives known to those who promote this propaganda, do they value their propaganda over truth or are they skeptical of truth? Or is it simply seen as okay to devalue individuals in the quest for the objective of the propaganda?

If our discussions have made me reevaluate one thing, it would be to revalue the individual on par with the collective. As a young observer of libertarianism, I used to value the individual higher than society, but I quickly lost my fervor while witnessing the *more independent than thou* individualism that stood against society at every turn. Such reactionaries thought they could ignore society in favor of the individual as if individuals are naturally independent; or as if family isn't the first society. Over time I came to revalue social/civic values as highly as individual values primarily because, like family, we all must find ways to live together, or cut off our noses to spite our faces.

None of us are born independent. As compared with most other species, we are dependent many years longer. Every individual is long dependent upon family (or at least some sort of assistance from society) for their very survival. The basic responsibility of the family, is recognized within the family's ability to raise and socialize their children to become integral with the family and greater society. As families grow and extend, all of us are ultimately related, yet we too often treat other groups as foreign while only paying lip service to relations as well as individualism. Yet *their* process is the same as ours. There is a disconnect here that nobody has explained to my satisfaction.

So to devalue society, by extension seems to devalue the family by failing to recognize relations. We value family while decrying *socialism* within broader society. Socialism: the big bugaboo. I can't tell you how many discussions I've had with people who spout certain political beliefs and then in the next conversation about their family make it abundantly clear that they would never think about treating individuals within their own families this way. They understand their own families as if they are distinct from others and then sometimes pit their family against others while we say things like, "family is everything". Others are happy to extend their filial piety to families of others who share their religion, football team or political party. But soon enough, it comes down to some against the others. I've watched those who demonstrated such love and concern for their immediate familial relationships opposed this value next door. But at least their local socialized virtue is more admirable than no extended virtue at all.

So it is that we all praise socialism within our family; our own family. While family can become our highest virtue and our greatest responsibility, unfortunately it can become the original group-ism. We value our own group while refusing to extend this virtue to other groups. Few are allowed *in* because they are not *of* us. We take great care as to who our sons and daughters marry as if our family is more important or somehow different than other families. So much so that other groups (sometimes families) refuse to accept the invitation to relate because they more important or somehow different too. At some point one would think we all would see that we have this in common rather than keep viewing this most common trait as uncommon.

Throughout much of the history of the United States, people have claimed power for themselves and others most like them by denying the rights of individuals via groups (because it's easier to propagandize, discriminate and persecute en masse). But this reality has brought the circle to closure for me by reminding me of the value of individual rights retained regardless of group.

The individual must be respected within the family. Individualism must be fostered but not to the detriment of the family. There should be balance. Our individual *ability to respond* to the collective (family, society) amounts to our *responsibility* (personal and social). Too enamored with individual responsibility, we shirk further responsibilities like that of family or society. Too enamored with familial responsibility, we shirk further responsibilities like that of the individual. Unfortunately, as families grow large enough they finally fail to see these extended relations anymore. At this point, or some point just beyond it, anything goes. We can be as disrespectful of others as we please at some point within unseen or devalued relationships. Both are errors of responsibility. John Fowles once said, "War is a psychosis caused by an inability to see relationships. Our relationship with our fellow-men." I don't know if war is a psychosis or not, but I don't think we have to let psychosis go as far as war for us to witness the damage done not only to individuals and society but also to reason. Our failure to see relationships beyond our own groups becomes prejudice or even bigotry at the expense of reasoned values. Many reasons may be rational yet others are compelling; some justifications may be reasonable while others are important and more valuable.

No Reply.

Each weekday I receive in my e-mail an excerpt about a book or an article from a site called DelanceyPlace.com
From time to time I repost the ones I find most interesting. This day I passed along a post entitled, The Dark Side of Thomas Jefferson. *This turned out to be a summary post from the* Smithsonian Magazine *that began: "When Thomas Jefferson had the opportunity in 1817 due to a bequest from Revolutionary War hero Thaddeus Kosciuszko, he did not free his slaves."*

SHARON comments: What is missing from the article is Jefferson's reasoning and his assessment of the factors that would have affected the success or failure of such an endeavor.

PAUL: What was Jefferson's reasoning and assessment of the factors that would have affected the success or failure of such an endeavor?
Since we can't know the possible successes or failures of such an endeavor, since he disallowed it, what were the success or fail-

ures of Washington's endeavor to free his slaves?

SHARON: I can only speculate about his reasoning, but one obvious "factor" would be what his slaves wanted to do, Because thousands of slaves continued to live and work for their former owners after emancipation, it is quite possible that Jefferson's slaves preferred the security of their homes, their work, and their community to the thought of striking out for new territory that had not been settled. Such an endeavor would require leadership, organizational skill, and a comprehensive understanding of every aspect of American agriculture and meeting the needs of a population of recently emancipated slaves. I think it is significant that we don't know what happened to Washington's slaves; if it had been a success it would have served as an example for all those who were reluctant to simply free the slaves without any plan for what they would or could do. The Great Emancipator himself pledged to return the freed slaves to "their native clime" which suggests that Washington's example was not before him.

PAUL: Like you, I can't honestly speak to Jefferson's reasoning either but one "obvious" factor is that, "what his slaves wanted to do" implies that slaves were well versed in choices open to them —as if they weren't slaves. But he could have freed them and then invited them to stay if they "wanted" to.

One of Washington's fears was that freed slaves might want to attack their former owners—even after these masters had formulated such fine "plan[s] for what they would or could do." Evidently the master's vast concern for his slave's *wants, preferences and security* weren't always a big part of the slavery package.

SHARON: Many Americans, especially those who lived in slave states, opposed emancipation without repatriation because they didn't fancy the prospect of a mass of unemployed, unskilled, and uneducated ex-slaves with no clear path to self-sufficiency. The wants, preferences, and security of today's employees are not always a big part of most employment packages. Of course the employee is always free to go somewhere else, to strike out on his own, or to do nothing, but that kind of freedom can be very intimidating when the employee has a family to care for. "Freedom" shouldn't be viewed in the abstract but in the context of the practicalities of one's life. As I said, the article doesn't provide us with Jefferson's reasoning, nor does it explore the factors that might have influenced his decision to maintain the status quo and without that information we are at a disadvantage in making a judgment about Jefferson's intentions. People - even slaves often choose concrete security over theoretical freedom.

PAUL: I will agree with you on some of this, yet I'll restate and reframe much of it so as to include what we do know: We know what Jefferson's actions were. We needn't (and shouldn't) limit our discussion to your reasons, my reasons or speculation about Jefferson's possible reasons and intentions. We must consider actions as well as the real situation of slaves in general.

The slave states indeed created a terrible problem for themselves as well as problems for the rest of the states of America. Worse was the terrible problem of slavery and those enslaved. The slave states refused to take responsibility for this situation let alone "fancy" repairing it. Slave owners enslaved rather than employed. Slaves remained "unskilled" because their masters held the whip and enchained them while refusing to educate them. There were laws forbidding education of slaves. Why? Because these people were *slaves,* and the states as well as the slave holders chose to ignore the (abstract?) idea of freedoms, rights, and full humanhood as being applicable to slaves. Slaves were denied a path toward self-sufficiency. They were denied education.

"[B]ut that kind of freedom can be very intimidating when the employee has a family to care for."

Free people can and do make the decision to quit and/or take another job everyday but you seem to keep making, or trying to make some link, parallel or whatever it is, between being a slave and being an employee. We can't think of slave owners as employers. We can't draw a line between being a slave and employee. We can't link living on the same piece of ground with being like family members. I am not being abstract here. "'Freedom' shouldn't be viewed in the abstract but in the context of the practicalities of one's life." I agree. But the practicalities of a slave's life weren't terribly practical for them. The practicalities of a slave's life is that they are not family, they are not employees. Slave families were broken apart by slave traders and slave owners. No respect at all was shown for family.

"As I said, the article doesn't provide us with Jefferson's reasoning, nor does it explore the factors that might have influenced his decision to maintain the status quo and without that information we are at a disadvantage in making a judgment about Jefferson's intentions. People - even slaves often choose concrete security over theoretical freedom."

We don't know Jefferson's reasoning but I can argue with yours. *Slaves, by definition cannot choose. They are slaves.* They made few life decisions by and for themselves. These decisions were made for them and to them. By law they are refused education, and their families are torn apart. Many slaves were forbidden to or forced not to make the rational decisions such as what you describe. Jefferson had free choice and he made his status quo decision, like he always had. The slaves did what slaves had to do; they went along because they were forced to do so under the penalty of death, or worse: to live in slavery, live in fear of being raped, live with the reality of their families torn apart and being further torn apart. We are pretty sure Jefferson fathered children with at least one slave woman. Was a slave able to consent to sex? I say no. I will call this rape. On the other hand, Jefferson knew these realities and had many options (as the privileged always do). As this article that I reposted the link to pointed out, he was provided a very specific way out; it was thrust upon him. He could stop being so conservative. Instead of promoting (and protecting by way of constitutional law) the life, liberty and the pursuit of happiness for black people as he had done for white people he refused.

Even without knowing Jefferson's reasons, I can make a moral judgment about his actions. And I am not skeptical of my ability to do so. I can judge his actions in lieu of knowing his thoughts. Unlike his slaves, Jefferson is the one with the knowledge, resources, privilege and the power to make this change. And so rather than considering Jefferson's reasons as primarily relevant to this discussion, I consider his actions, not only from his point of view or from my point of view or from your point of view, but also from the point of view of the slaves (or at least from the point of view of the reality of slavery). I feel comfortable with casting this form of moral judgment.

Going back to a question I posed a couple replies back . . .
SHARON: "So, given all this, I'm wondering why is it you do this?" (Speak in terms of groups rather than individuals.) How does one talk about race without reference to racial groups based on genetic, phenotypical, psychological, and cultural differences? How does one talk about men or women without reference to the biological complement of male and female. that is to say, both men and women have characteristics unique to their biological differences and complementary nature.? How does one talk about sexuality without reference to reproduction? How does one talk about Western Civilization without reference to Europeans? It seems to me that you cannot very well deplore the settlement of North America by Europeans without recognizing the difference between those who inhabited the land and fought against the Europeans. Many ignore the fact that the "natives" were collectives of warring tribes that not only fought against the English and French, but against other native tribes both south and north. I don't often categorize people by Democrat or Republican but rather by terms that mean more to me, e.g. liberal, neo-con, liar, criminal, bought, controlled, and fabricated. My first election was in 1964 and I voted Democrat. After that I voted for Eldridge Cleaver, George McGovern, Jimmy Carter, and then there is a hiatus in my recollection which makes me think that I wrote in non-candidates until Pat Buchanan in 2000. Ralph Nader, Chuck Baldwin, and I wrote in Ron Paul in 2012. With the exception of 1964 and 1976 I never voted for a winner and those I voted for that did win were very disappointing. Individualism isn't a political force and when a people is threatened they either join together to fight or they die.

PAUL: I understand that we group. We all do. But in doing so we should admit that we run the risk of reductionism. Running this risk, I still wonder why you insist upon it? Why not discount it?

We minimize the outstanding individual when we group. We generalize about individuals by attaching this individual to a group instead of valuing the individual in her own right. Therefore, we minimize the individual as we maximize generalizations about a group they belong to. In this way, people can talk about *me* without ever actually referring to me: A white, male, liberal, living in a middle class American neighborhood, in Utah, who drives a Chevy, etc. We can employ all of these groups as if it describes me in lieu of me. Yet I'm definitely not your typical white male in Utah. I am not a Mormon. I don't have any children. *White* might refer to a shade of skin and yet ignores many other aspects of me. As it is, white makes me a minority in my middle class neighborhood. Mormons are also in the minority on my street. My "American" car is assembled in Mexico with an engine from Canada and a transmission from Austria using many Chinese and Japanese sourced parts and electronics. Having liberal tendencies doesn't make me a Democrat. I am not nor have I ever been a member of the Democratic party :) But I have been a card carrying member of the ACLU, and, here in America, I've been lambasted for my concern for civil liberties, equal rights and equal justice. My self-confessed liberalism refers back to something closer to the classical liberal tradition of Locke and Adam Smith (although my own version differs in certain ways). My voting history, like yours, is varied, except that I walked away from my brief (four year) involvement with the Libertarian party when they nominated Ron Paul for president in 1988. He was merely a right-winger with some libertarian leanings.

So, these groupings fall extremely short with regard to their value for generalizing about me, yet you constantly fall back upon generalizations about others as if they make some necessary determinations for you. Since these determinations often fail, the presumptions you rely upon to tell you something about others shortchange you and me and everyone else. Their value is not only limited, it is often plain wrong. Yet when you talk about race you speak as though race is a determining character trait of the individual, then make determinations about the individual due to your racial considerations. I think this is reductive. It reduces complex individuals to some lowest *common* denominator; all under the guise of definition.

You don't have to rely upon this one value so heavily. You could try enlargement for example, i.e. why not consider the whole *human race*? This has its problems too but it also provides some balance. Without knowing my race, sex, or locale, how is it that anybody can you read or understand my words? Do you or they have to make assumptions about me in order to understand the words? Will this "context" explain my words or only prejudice them due to your own overlay? If this is the case then they are reading at least as much about themselves when they are reading me. Yet they don't realize this.

Quite a while back you said "**Humans are capable of distinguishing between the major racial groups and that ability has been observed in babies as young as fifteen months-old. Unlike the word 'race', the words 'racism' and 'racist' are very recent inventions used as pejoratives against people who admit to perceiving racial differences. (The toddlers in the study were already racists at 15 months!)**"

I would guess that what you call *race* here refers to skin color (since toddlers have no idea what *race* means or implies). It has been shown that these same toddlers simply show a preference for the familiar. It appears that babies prefer looking at their mother to looking at a stranger. They also seem to prefer their mother's voice to any other. But even more generally babies seem to prefer the skin color of their mother to others. Yet they also prefer the sound of their own language (a language they don't understand) to the sound of another language. And in very diverse multicultural societies, babies are so used to seeing different skin colors from birth that they do not show this preference.

Now, the fact that you might minimize this may speak to your bias. The fact that I might maximize it may speak to my bias. The fact that either of us do this might speak less to our political inclinations as it does to our reactionary tendencies. Perhaps reaction *v* action *v* non-action might speak more toward our intents than politics or religion. But many of us may be too self-involved in racial, political and religious biases to want to choose another group-ism to consider. Some of us might temper this tendency by enlarging the group to include more, or many of us might reduce the conversation to individuals. None of this is right or wrong but each method leaves us lacking. Why do this to ourselves? What is the gain we expect. What should we expect? Aren't we getting exactly what we should expect? . . . Meanwhile in Oregon . . . *

*My comment about Oregon refers to Sharon's last line, "Individualism isn't a political force and when a people is threatened they either join together to fight or they die." Because I thought she might be referring to this recent incident: Washington Post - 1/3/2016: An armed militia took over a building at a national wildlife refuge in Oregon late Saturday and vows to occupy the outpost for years to protest the federal government's treatment of a pair of ranchers facing prison time.

SHARON: Why does everyone "group"? I would say that it is natural - that is to say, it is a biological phenomenon. Humans are social animals and their social relationships are integral to their personal identities and maturation. I suppose It would be possible to raise humans in an institutional setting that could be controlled to limit attachments to and identification with others. Both caretakers and other infants could be selected for "optimal" diversity of race, sex, affect, intelligence, and skill. Perhaps by the time the child reached puberty his experience would have precluded bias. Wouldn't we have the makings of a dystopia? Artifice replacing natural human characteristics? Humans like all other creatures need their powers of discrimination for survival and for reproductive success. What is the purpose of disarming any creature by hampering his ability to make judgments about others? The races of mankind evolved because of thousands of years of intrabreeding and avoidance of interbreeding. Race would not exist without a high degree of long-term racial exclusivity. We share a high percentage of DNA, not because we have interbred, but because we have a very distant common ancestor. Is our ability to discriminate no longer necessary? Is it racist to avoid walking in South Side Chicago at night? Is there a reason why there are signs that say "Don't feed the bears"? Some people have had to find out the hard way.

And before I can reply, back to the previous subject:
SHARON: Slavery was ended in the U.S. 150 years ago, so

what is the point in moralizing about Thomas Jefferson's attitude toward slavery and the treatment of his slaves? At the time only about 1% of U.S. population owned slaves so what is its relevance today? Are white people as a "group" expected to atone for the sins of George Washington and Thomas Jefferson or are we supposed to see the descendants of slaves as a "group" defined by their ancestors experience and deserving of apology and reparations in perpetuity? What about the free blacks who owned slaves in the U.S. and the Africans who owned and traded in slaves then and now? It is estimated that 20% of the population in the Islamic State of Mauritania is held in slavery today. Do they get a pass because they are black and wouldn't have been allowed to eat at the Woolworth's lunch counter if they had been in Biloxi in 1950? The continued speculation and preoccupation with Jefferson as slave owner is like straining at a gnat and swallowing a camel.

PAUL: First off, the grouping question:

When I ask why we group, it isn't because I have no understanding of why we group. What I wonder is why we group yet refuse to see or take responsibility for the problems inherent in doing so? It may well be as you say; it relates to some sort of "biological phenomenon", perhaps emanating from our reptilian brain. But we have more brain than our reptilian complex. We are more than our genes/DNA. We have evolved; or our brains have. We are more than our breeding. We are more than race. We should strive to be more than mere instincts and prejudices. Or have we evolved as far as we have merely to gain enough reason to argue in favor of our most base instincts rather than something greater and hopefully better?

"Is it racist to avoid walking in South Side Chicago at night?" Never been there. But I've been attacked several times in my life; always by "white" people.

"Both caretakers and other infants could be selected for "optimal" diversity of race, sex, affect, intelligence, and skill. Perhaps by the time the child reached puberty his experience would have precluded bias. Wouldn't we have the makings of a dystopia?"

Or, as the study I mentioned suggested, life can just go on with all colors and sounds of people intermingling and it seems to have the natural effect of precluding bias without interference. The results of the study seemed to suggest that this was the natural course.

"What is the purpose of disarming any creature by hampering his ability to make judgments about others?"

I don't think you have to worry about this ever happening. We all judge and we all will. Some will discriminate more reasonably and make better judgments than others.

"We share a high percentage of DNA, not because we have interbred, but because we have a very distant common ancestor."

Who is this ancestor? Where they white or black? How did races become distinct? Might the idea of race (since it is an idea) begin when the same brothers and sisters are separate long enough that we begin to call our brothers and sisters a separate race.

And so, "what is the purpose of [making] judgments about others?"

On to the Jefferson question, you say, "Slavery was ended in the U.S. 150 years ago, so what is the point in moralizing about Thomas Jefferson's attitude toward slavery and the treatment of his slaves?"

I, for one, merely passed along (without comment) a post that I found in my feed. I'm not overly concerned with Jefferson's slave ownership. Recently you commented on a post about Hitler and Nazi Germany. Are you overly concerned about Hitler? The history surrounding each personality happened many years ago but I passed mine along because I learned something about history that I had forgotten, or never really considered. Perhaps you and I would like to see if others might benefit from the articles too. The beginnings of our ideas about race began many years ago and our thoughts about it have influenced morality ever since. I often read history and I read books I've previously read. Sometimes I read them in a new light the second time around. Sometimes I learn something new.

Commenting on another DelanceyPlace.com *post I passed along about* The Culture of Fear *by* Barry Glassner. . .

SHARON: I think a preponderance of "fear" is simply the process of giving shape to amorphous anxiety. The source of anxiety can be personal, but is more often related to one's responsibility to protect one's children. Such concern for their health and safety is normal but it makes people vulnerable to media suggestion and the media is not a trustworthy source when weighing risk. The article gives the example of asbestos that was put in schools to protect children from fire, but taken out to protect children from asbestosis. Are fearful parents really to blame for asbestos removal? Or isn't it likely that the 10 billion dollars spent in removal was driven by a deal between contractors and politicians while fear was simply used to justify it - if anyone were to ask. Asbestos removal wasn't driven by public fear, moral repugnance, or a hatred of technology and industry, but by money. You can be certain that there was no public examination of the science and the relative risks; there were no questions asked and no vote taken. Fear is used to manipulate people. It is important to look at who benefits from that manipulation.

PAUL: As one who suffers from anxiety, and as one who has no children, I've pretty well learned to how to separate anxiety from fear. Fear is a negative outgrowth of anxiety that can firmly outline everything I view. As such it can become the driver of a vehicle out of control. I've not feared asbestos but I've learned how to harness my fears of science, money and government. In the realm of psychology as well as propaganda and psyops, fear and repugnance are the two prime manipulators..

SHARON: Glassner's book says that people are afraid of the "wrong" things which implies that there are some "right" things that we should fear. What are those things?

PAUL: I don't know what the book says, I've not read it. My first inclination, however, is that by simply being aware of our tendencies to fear the "wrong" things, this awareness might help us filter them out and/or at least question them. To be serious about our awareness of all of this helps us to make better judgments. This is not a bad thing or a thing to fear.

I, for one, have several irrational phobias/fears. And although I know this to be true about myself, my phobias don't go away but at least I'm not in error about the facts regarding them.

To be more concrete about more reasonable fears: Automobile accidents as opposed to plane crashes. Serious illness as opposed to contracting the bird flu. Pain caused by injury or resulting from major surgery. Not being able to maintain my health/physical and mental abilities as I age.

But the less concrete notions apply not only to the book's premise but to our discussions here as well. Many people fear the government taking away their guns. It isn't happening. I'll pay anybody I know $1,000 for every gun Obama has taken away from them. I can't even foresee this eventuality happening anywhere in the near future from where we are today. The fear is imaginary. People fear Obama declaring Marshall law just before his term expires so he can have yet another term in office. I'll bet $10,000 this won't happen. People fear that we'll soon allow people to marry animals. Same bet. Some people fear the new money and think the Federal Reserve is going to _____. Fill in the blank. Most people are too afraid of crime in general. Crime rates have declined over many the years. Many Democrats fear guns too much. Some Democrats seem to be too afraid of religion. The left and right are far too afraid of each other. And this is *the* case in point. Perhaps what can and does result from all this fear is fearful to me.

SHARON: Glassner says that to blame the media is to oversimplify, but none of the "misbegotten fears" could have been generated or countered without the media. It is simple - without the media "fears" are immediate and personal. With the media we are vulnerable to manipulation in the guise of information. Without the media people would still make judgments about risk, but those judgments would be instinctual and experiential. "Common sense" would tell us that young children need a high degree of supervision; that machines can be dangerous, that there are hazards in nature, that other people can be hostile, irrational defensive, or predatory; that there is safety in numbers; that a society's rules for behavior are meant to protect the individual, the family, and the wider society. Glassner's list of "fears" tells us what what "news" in 1999. In 2015 Glassner has to contend with the media-driven notion that Lewis and Clark College is not "diverse" enough for its white students though not a one of them or Glassner himself, offers his position at the college to a black, a Chinese, or an Indian. Misbegotten fears brought up to date.

PAUL: Yep. Without *the media* we are still left to our own fears; still right or wrong.

SHARON: Who is to judge whether one's fears are "right" or "wrong" especially when the fear has some basis in both instinct and reality? Is it wrong to fear spiders because most are harmless? Should we second-guess nature because an instinctive fear often proves needless? Should we take measures to override instincts that lead to bias? We can know that statistics show automobiles to be more dangerous than regularly scheduled airplane flights, but that doesn't make us stop driving or prevent one from thinking about what it would be like to fall from 60,000 feet. The word "fear" is often used to de-legitimize or mock the views of others, e.g. "people fear that we'll soon allow people to marry animals". Whether or not Obama has made good on his rhetoric about quelling gun violence he has participated in psyops that supply justification for gun control. Paradoxically (or not) what was meant to justify disarming the public has made thousands of Americans who never owned firearms think about what it would be like to be attacked with no way to defend oneself - and that has resulted in record gun sales.

PAUL: You ask, "Who is to judge whether one's fears are 'right' or 'wrong' especially when the fear has some basis in both instinct and reality?"

Evidently you; unless you are arguing for something you believe to be wrong. Evidently me; like everybody else I make judgments everyday. I think we've been through this before. Fears have many bases. Some are irrational or unhelpful. Some, like phobias may be out of our own control to some degree except to recognize them as they are *irrational*. Some people think they live in a *reality* that is *out there* but their fears exist only inside their mind. Our instincts have basis prior to thought. Often we are startled, and then upon momentary thought we realize the reality of things. News has basis in reality too. And we can all think beyond our instincts whether natural or not. Yes, I said we can do better than our natural instincts. We can reason through our fears even if we can't conquer them. We can know better.

"The word 'fear' is often used to de-legitimize or mock the views of others, e.g. 'people fear that we'll soon allow people to marry animals'."

Is the word "mock" is another way of saying I shouldn't question the illegitimate fear that people fear that we'll soon allow people to marry animals?

"Paradoxically (or not) what was meant to justify disarming the public has made thousands of Americans who never owned firearms think about what it would be like to be attacked with no way to defend oneself - and that has resulted in record gun sales."

Nobody is or has been disarmed and they won't be with Obama's speech. Your fear of what isn't true, and what will not be, is illegitimate. End of story. Certain illegitimate fears are engendered in people by who? The media? By scared people whose fears are unfounded? If (and this is a big if) anyone can't buy a gun due to anything that comes of this proposition, it will be those that the president of the National Rifle Association agrees should be hampered in these ways. The president of the National Rifle Association gave this speech in 1999 speech on the subject. https://www.youtube.com/watch?v=M-oqfPojhec *

Like you correctly point out, I can buy guns now just like the many people who are now purchasing and keeping guns. As you say, nothing has changed except the salesman. And one thing that has remained the same in this equation is *fear*. How do I know it is illegitimate? Because I can buy a gun today, legally and I have no fear of anybody prying it from my cold dead hands (to use the language of fear which I got through the media, that was provided by a large, rich organization, the NRA, who is just one of the beneficiaries of this fear).

Should we follow this money trail to see if it determines *the* truth about gun control?

*What we're talking about: President Obama recently gave a speech reiterating the need to enforce and improve upon existing gun laws. Some years earlier the president of the NRA gave a speech in favor of what they now say they are against. The main points are listed below.

    1. That all gun dealers need a license and need to do background checks.

    2. Hire more folks to process applications faster.

    3. Help the mentally ill get treatment.

    4. Boost gun safety technology; you can keep your phone from being used by some-one else, we can do the same with guns.

SHARON: I'll put up $1,000 if you can show me a person who "fears" that "we will soon allow people to marry animals." That particular reason for opposing same sex marriage is a childish expression of opposition to what one sees as unnatural or perverse. People don't "fear" a man engaging in intercourse with a sheep, nor do they "fear" that legalizing bestiality in the U.S. military will lead to an increase in soldiers' liaisons with farm animals. Revulsion and fear are not the same thing. I think there are legitimate reasons for opposing same sex marriage that have nothing to do with fear.

PAUL: Childish or not, some people do fear that same sex marriage will lead to people marrying animals. Some fear that it will lead to legalizing polygamy and/or incest and bestiality. Many people are afraid that it's all a slippery slope of one thing likely leading to another. "Revulsion and fear are not the same thing", but they do go hand in hand with psyops. Revulsion and fear are *the* primary keys to swaying people psychologically.

BTW, how many Internet links will I need to list in order to claim this $1000? :)

SHARON: The primary purposes of making judgments about others are protective and selective - protection to afford survival and selection to produce good offspring. Characterizing instinct as reptilian suggests Homo sapiens has advanced beyond those instincts that promote survival and reproductive success – apparently for some higher or more advanced purpose. What is that purpose and how does such a leap comport with our understanding of evolution?

When you refer to "we" as having evolved are you referring to all Homo sapiens or are some more evolved than others? Is the ability to "discriminate more reasonably and make better judgments..." a description of morality and what is the source of such ability? What makes a judgment "better" or discrimination "more reasonable"? Is it unreasonable to use our senses – our powers of discrimination to pick a mate? Isn't it reasonable to know and weigh the risks of venturing into a non-white neighborhood? If there is value in overriding our instincts to preclude discrimination, perhaps we should be assigned mates by lottery without regard to race, gender, ethnicity, national origin, religion, education, disability or deformity, and sexual preference. Random and copious mating might bring enough "color and sound" to the "family" that it would not be necessary to create an institutional environment to supply optimal diversity to curb bias in children.

Race is a taxonomic category that could be termed subspecies in Homo sapiens. It is based on the varying and measurable physical, physiological, psychological and behavioral differences and similarities among the genus Homo. Racial characteristics are evolutionary products resulting from environmental adaptations, natural selection, along with varying degrees of physical and social isolation. In other words, race is a zoological taxon: animals are grouped by measurable similarities and differences.

The concept of a common ancestor is basic to the theory of evolution and when studies show that another species is very closely related to Homo sapiens the evolutionary explanation for the similarity is that of the common ancestor. Recent genetic studies support the idea that Pan troglodytes – the chimpanzee should be classified in the genus Homo. All the species of the genus, Homo, have a common ancestor, including erectus, neanderthalis, and the chimp. One recent study of 97 important gene sequences shows that within important sequence stretches of these functionally significant genes, humans and chimps share 99.4 percent identity. Long before Homo sapiens appeared the species Homo erectus was widespread in the world and at least one subspecies of Homo erectus – Peking Man had a Mongoloid skull shape, suggesting that elements of racial difference were apparent before Homo sapiens evolved and replaced H. erectus. Races became distinct through evolution in situ. In other words there was a high degree of racial exclusivity caused by physical and social isolation during the period of adaptation to a specific environment. It is useless to speculate about the skin color or hair of ancient remains because all we have to study are bones, teeth, and in some cases cultural artifacts.

It isn't simply separation that gave us the idea of race, but the myriad of differences that evolved during that separation. Those differences in many cases make interbreeding impossible which, in turn, reinforces differences. Doesn't a respect for nature require us to protect racial and cultural differences?

Before I could respond:
SHARON: Obama participated in the Sandy Hook psyop, apparently, to generate a better political climate for gun control. If that is not what the Democrats had in mind, what was it?

PAUL: You say, "Characterizing instinct as reptilian suggests Homo sapiens has advanced beyond those instincts that promote survival and reproductive success – apparently for some higher or more advanced purpose. What is that purpose and how does such a leap comport with our understanding of evolution?"

Our understanding of evolution is that, *"our cultural and linguistic complexity, dietary needs and technological prowess took a significant leap forward at this stage, our brains grew to accommodate the changes. The shape changes we see accentuate the regions related to depth of planning, communication, problem solving and other more advanced cognitive functions."* According to an article from the *Scientific American*: *How Has the Human Brain Evolved?*

Or, like I have said before, maybe our evolution has only served to help you explain the greater value of our base instincts as opposed to the value of an evolving brain.

"When you refer to 'we' as having evolved are you referring to all Homo sapiens or are some more evolved than others?"

I meant we as Homo sapiens.

"Is the ability to 'discriminate more reasonably and make better judgments...' a description of morality and what is the source of such ability?"

No, but the source appears to be the evolution of the brain.

"What makes a judgment 'better' or discrimination 'more reasonable'?

One aspect is when it corresponds best with reality outside our preferred, more common views. To explain this requires reasons. Better reasons are often understood due to their correspondence.

"Is it unreasonable to use our senses – our powers of discrimination to pick a mate?"

No, we all do this. Some of our reason extends beyond our senses. We all discriminate with everything. Some discriminate differently than others. Some discriminate better than others. How? See previous question and answer.

"Isn't it reasonable to know and weigh the risks of venturing into a non-white neighborhood?"

Speaking for myself today, it is reasonable to know the risks of venturing into any neighborhood, white neighborhoods included. Most crime is committed by whites in America. I'm a minority in my neighborhood but I have no fear. But then again, I don't check the map to find out where the non-whites live. Most murders are committed by men, as are most rapes. So I try to stay out of the male dominated neighborhoods :) Now, if I am black and living in the Jim Crow south 50 to 100 years ago, I wouldn't venture into the white neighborhoods. If I'm black and living in New York, perhaps I'm not so afraid, except in poorer neighborhoods. I for one don't seem to have an instinct for "race, gender, ethnicity, national origin, religion, education, disability or deformity, and sexual preference." These all seem to be things I've learned about. I have my preferences but they aren't instincts.

"Race is a taxonomic category that could be termed subspecies in Homo sapiens. It is based on the varying and measurable physical, physiological, psychological and behavioral differences and similarities among the genus Homo.

Racial characteristics are evolutionary products resulting from environmental adaptations, natural selection, along with varying degrees of physical and social isolation. In other words, race is a zoological taxon: animals are grouped by measurable similarities and differences."

Sure, a very few people see it this way. Even experts disagree with this list. For most people, race is simply a way to put others down and discriminate against.

"In other words there was a high degree of racial exclusivity caused by physical and social isolation during the period of adaptation to a specific environment."

Some things don't change much. But now some us simply isolate ourselves away from "others".

Now as for your other note: "Obama participated in the Sandy Hook psyop, apparently, to generate a better political climate for gun control. If that is not what the Democrats had in mind, what was it?"

What would I know about what Democrats have in mind? And I can't seem to read Obama's mind or know what his motives are. Democrats as well as non-whites vary in many ways no matter how much you try to group them into stereotypical sameness. In fact you and I differ in many ways and we're kin who resist, sometimes on purpose, being labeled. We should afford others this dignity too.

SHARON: I'll give you the $1000 if you can find a real person who genuinely FEARS marriage between an animal and a human. Some people bring up that possibility because it is preposterous, not because it is dangerous. It is a common way of mocking the idea of same sex marriage, not an expression of alarm or fear. That is probably why you picked that rather than the genuine arguments that can contain an element of fear, e.g. the effect on children of the ambiguity of sexual identity and the fracturing of the relationship between love, marriage, sex, and procreation. Same sex marriage didn't "legalize" sodomy - that was accomplished in Lawrence v. Texas. Same-sex marriage simply made sodomy the equivalent of conjugal love and procreative sex.

Because polygamy is illegal only in respect to the previous definition of marriage, i.e. one man/one woman - it is reasonable to revisit polygamy with respect to the new definition. It could be argued that any of the restrictions on marriage, imposed by the states, could be deemed unconstitutional under the equal protection clause - so restrictions on the age, blood relationship, disease and/or vaccination status, and marital status of those seeking a marriage license may have to be reconsidered as well. The slippery slope is usually a weak argument, but its use doesn't mean there are no good arguments or that any and all arguments are based on an irrational fear.

PAUL: I picked this fear because I overheard an argument about it at work. As preposterous as it might sound, it was between real people. But I doubt I can prove a genuine FEAR. I'm not sure it is even doable scientifically.

"That is probably why you picked that rather than the genuine arguments that can contain an element of fear, e.g. the effect on children of the ambiguity of sexual identity and the fracturing of the relationship between love, marriage, sex, and procreation."

I've been aware of the fears that some people have throughout most of my life, and although they may scare others, I've never been confused about my sexual identity. Neither have gay people effected my relationships. Yet you have these fears, just as you fear the government coming to take away our guns. But these are not fears of mine, and so I find them preposterous (sorry but you prompt the comparisons here).

"Same-sex marriage simply made sodomy the equivalent of conjugal love and procreative sex."

Same sex marriage addresses policy inequity issues while it acknowledges political and social realities. And the reasons that we employ in one case are likely to reflect upon another case. Our reasons can support the upholding of restrictions of polygamy. Marriage, along with gay marriage, helps the institution to be seen as egalitarian just as spouses finally became equals under law in the 1970's. There can be no equality in polygamy.

Now, I know you don't agree with spousal equality in either of these cases but we live within a system of liberal constitutionalism. Inherent within our citizenship is a tension similar to the tension built into the executive, legislative and judicial branches of government. Our citizenship requires each of us to moderate our beliefs to the degree that we can coexist with quite a bit of liberty under the umbrella of equal rights. It is a difficult mission but one I have come to accept and embrace.

Going back a few pages, Sharon replies. . .

SHARON: The quote from the Scientific American suggests that there are identifiable and measurable differences in the brains of humans and that those differences (? volume, weight, size, conformation of the lobes, and the brain product as measured by testing) can be seen to have evolved in tandem with "our" cultural and linguistic complexity and technological prowess. Not every racial group has shown technological prowess or advanced cognitive functions. Doesn't that imply a racial difference in the rate of brain evolution? And what does that difference mean in respect to discriminating more reasonably and making better judgments? It makes sense that most crimes are committed by whites in the U.S. because whites are the majority (63%) While blacks are only 12.4% of the population they are the attackers in 84% of the violent crimes involving blacks and whites. Those are the statistics you should use since your instinct doesn't work to alert you to important differences.

PAUL: Brain size isn't the whole story (and we understand precious little about this). There is much to be learned about how the synaptic connections are made and how they work etc. In addition to this, there seems to be some evidence to suggest that human brains are now getting smaller. But not only are relative measurements in question, it is unclear if the brain grows larger in support of greater learning or if more learning makes the brain grow larger. Causal relation is unclear in all respects.

"Not every racial group has shown technological prowess or advanced cognitive functions."

Regardless of groups, have any individuals? Should we minimize them in accord to some belief (valid or not) about their group? Chinese innovations include gunpowder, paper making, printing and the compass. The first tools were made and used in Africa. There we find the oldest astronomical devices. Egyptians developed a 365-day, 12 month calendar and the Lebombo bone is the oldest mathematical artifact to date. I guess I could go all the way around the world but it would make little difference to you. And you have your reasons why none of this counts for much.

Also from the *Scientific American*, "Not every person in any group has shown technological prowess or advanced cognitive functions. A recent study by Kim Dietrich, a professor of environmental health at the University of Cincinnati, found that individuals who suffered from the highest lead exposure as children had the smallest brain sizes—as well as the most arrests." As it is, there are many things that may be causal. Many things may not be. One study isn't science. Scientific method requires many more studies and testing.

"While blacks are only 12.4% of the population they are the attackers in 84% of the violent crimes involving blacks and whites."

Can you imagine any other possible factors besides race that might account for this? Anything? You are correct, my instincts seem to tell me nothing about race. And statistics are numbers that are neutral and need context. Unfortunately we provide the context and our context says at least as much about our prejudices as it does anything else. We pick and choose what we see, what we want to see, expect to see, how we see, how we interpret what, want and how we see. Where we live, the direction we face, who we know, what we know, our preferences, and perhaps more importantly, what we think we know and what we believe.

"Those are the statistics you should use since your instinct doesn't work to alert you to important differences."

I do wonder how I've survived so long. I minimize both instinct as well as stats. But I don't minimize others by them either. I don't approach the world according to statistics. My life doesn't seem to proceed by statistics. I don't match many of the statistical likelihoods of others in my locale and age. But I can lie with statistics as well as the next person. As for myself, my questions have always taught me more than my answers. I find it best to work on myself and because I can't do much about others. Also, I look toward the

best in others, regardless of skin or hair color while taking the opportunity to learn from them.

So we come down to the larger questions: What should the US
do with these non-whites? Do half breeds count? Quarter breeds?
How about other gray (or tan) areas?

No Reply.

SHARON: I think your preference for individualism as opposed to "grouping" is artificial. Man is a social creature and
everything about him from his evolution to the creation of
culture cannot be understood without reference to the
groups to which he belongs. Reduced to one individual we
find that the male or female cannot be understood without
reference to his/her reproductive complement. At the other
end we see that culture is a collective creation of like-minded
individuals. No matter how large the individual's brain or rich
his synaptic connections, if he is born a Bushman he will not
be a Beethoven, a Tesla, or a Kurosawa. By the same token,
if the baby Mozart had been adopted by Chinese, Zulus, or
Eskimos he could not have been a composer of Western
music. The expression of genius requires a social and cultural setting which includes others who are able to respond
to that expression. Genius, like the fabled tree falling in the
forest must be heard to be realized. Individual genius that
cannot be appreciated by the group to which the genius belongs will be lost. We can imagine that there have been individuals of great genius in every race in all times and places,
but without any evidence the notion is fantastical. After you
ask about the genius of the individual you proceed to list accomplishments of racial/geographic groups – so that is the
answer.

What does the Lembobo bone mean in this context?
Wouldn't we expect the first mathematical instrument to have
an unbroken line of development evidenced by an increase
in sophistication as artifacts are found nearer the surface,
culminating with the most sophisticated existing in the hands
of the descendants of the maker of the breakthrough device?
If Swaziland is the birthplace of mathematical instruments

why is it that only the first five numbers can be historically reconstructed for proto-Bantu language, the base language of the black inhabitants of Swaziland? And why is it always Europeans who make these discoveries and develop the scientific disciplines for their study? Why is it important to say that "the first tools were made and used in Africa"? What can that possibly mean in relation to the peoples currently inhabiting sub-Saharan Africa or so-called African-Americans? Is it supposed to make them feel proud or to make Europeans humble and contrite? It is easy to imagine that 30,000 years hence remnants of the Panama Canal could be uncovered but like the Great Pyramid at Giza, it would be wrong to assign the design and building to the ancestors of the extant populations, especially if those populations showed no understanding of the technology involved. The question would be, "What happened to these people to cause a loss of technology and a reversion to a primitive state?"

There is no evidence that the brain grows in size in response to "greater learning". If it did an MRI would be a better measure of one's education than a written exam. I suspect the idea of growth in response to learning comes from the wish to explain racial differences in average brain size and IQ as being the result of cultural deprivation or prejudice rather than genetics and evolution. That wish to make nature bend to social and political theory should be examined, in part, because it is now so prevalent and unexamined. Politicization of race has gone so far that the biology of race is denied while new words like "racist" and "racism" are invented to denigrate those who would refer to the biological facts of racial difference. Some even wish to control the social environment and/or teach self-censorship in an attempt to short-circuit our senses that inform us of difference. Babies don't apply the word "race" to the differences they perceive, but that doesn't mean they don't understand that there is a profound difference between a Bantu, a Tibetan, and their Irish parents. To ignore the biology of racial differences one has to disregard over a hundred years of physical anthropology, paleontology, comparative studies of phenotype, physiology, psychology, and culture, and now the genetic studies of the last 50 years.

When there is statistical evidence that blacks commit a disproportionate amount of violent crime compared to whites the statistics are about a racial difference so the only thing that could account for a racial difference is race or some racial attribute. You might have a point if the statistics involved black males compared to white females, but for a statistic to be valid it can't compare apples to oranges.

A while back you posted an article discussing Barry Glassner's book about misbegotten fears. A primary technique Glassner's suggests to counter irrational fear is the use of statistics. One might make some progress in overriding an instinctive reaction to racial differences, but if one also refuses to make use of statistics because she doesn't want to exhibit prejudice then she may be whistling past the graveyard. About once a week we hear some horrific story about a young white woman who didn't see it coming.

PAUL: Rather than preferring individualism over group-ism, I have said that when it all comes down to it I don't see how group-ism or a reductionism to individualism can serve us well. Perhaps the humility of an expansion outward might serve us better. Yet I also have mentioned that our tendency to want to discriminate against groups of people reminds me of the relative value of preferring the idea of individuality over group-ism. I'm quite practical.

Individualism and group-ism are artificial to certain degrees because groups consist of individuals, and individuals cannot exist without at least a couple (a group) to precede them. I can't honestly be reduced to belonging to certain groups although aspects of me might fit into many varied categories. We are varied and social creatures; our society consists of many different types of people. Various skin tones, eye shapes, accents. (For some reason we tend to ignore eye color.) All societies have people who look different and all societies will. Some of us prefer to focus upon differing physical appearances while they ignore or devalue class distinctions. Others will disparage people due to their perceived income brackets or femininity or masculinity. Many people seem to need somebody to look down on. In the past I've been termed by some people as "stuck-up", while others thought me a "hood". I can't possibly imagine how I've been either or both at the same time so to categorize me these ways seem to speak more to the categorizers than to me. To distinguish me as a male only defines what might be my biological gender. This doesn't tell anybody anything about my biological complement. (And one can't speak to my reproductive complement since I have not and will not reproduce, yet I am not valueless.) So one must find some other way to define me (for whatever reason I can not know) in some sort of way that suits them because it is their definitions that suit them regardless of how accurate it might actually be about me. After all, like the Bushman, I was not born Spanish. What do I mean by this? I don't know. But something like this seems to mean an awful lot to some people. As for myself, I seem to be part Scottish, English, German, Danish, and (somewhere along the line) very likely milkman. Because, after all, some of my genealogy may be in error if not actually intended to deceive others. Some people find it so important, for some reason, and this notion spreads. It causes many people to hide who they are or at least who others think they are. Why, because they will be boxed in by other individuals who love to box groups yet hate to be placed in most groups by others.

I don't know much about expression of genius. Like you say, it's a cultural prejudice rather than objective. I'm probably the expression of the average; in general (average) group terms. To **"imagine that there have been individuals of great genius in every race in all times and places"** is in no way **"fantastical"**. It only points to our obvious ignorance of such extremely likely events. I've been able to read history of other cultures that I can acknowledge as genius, both from within their own context as well as from my own culture today. And I don't have to point to their culture as genius. Nor do I have to find any further value with this person's culture. And I don't have to feel contrite in order to feel humble. I can admire openly without guilt.

But speaking of **"[g]enius, like the fabled 'tree falling in the forest' [that] must be heard to be realized.** Whether it is heard or not, the tree indeed falls, because reality exists whether anyone realizes (or wishes to realize) it or not. So here we value either our perception of reality or we value reality as it surely exists; mostly beyond our meager comprehension. To value our slight comprehension should humble our opinions. But we prefer to overvalue ourselves as if we are something special; as if our kids are something special. We much prefer to be better than, even if reality demonstrates than we're on average, quite average with our average lives. (The only reason you never heard of the Chinese baby Mozart is because his name was 伯牙 and you've never looked him up:)

"And why is it always Europeans who make these discoveries and develop the scientific disciplines for their study?"

Because Europeans are superior?

"Why is it important to say that 'the first tools were made and used in Africa'?"

Because Africans are superior? This knife cuts both ways. Why is this competitive for you? I can appreciate contributions from all sorts of people and my appreciation takes nothing from me . . . not even my appreciation. I don't mind if Europeans or Africans did this and that. It is not a competition for me as it is for you. You look for cultural superiority or reasons for inferiority, I look for value. I can find the contribution of all kinds of cultures within the one that I live. And I find this to be nice. None of this has to do with contrition, for me at least.

"The question would be, 'What happened to these people to cause a loss of technology and a reversion to a primitive state?'"

This is your question and not mine. And if I were to conjecture, neither my answer or yours will be true, conjecture often simply masquerades as facts while facts masquerade as truth . . . while we kid ourselves.

"There is no evidence that the brain grows in size in response to 'greater learning'."

And there is no evidence for most of what you say or from the conclusions you draw from this lack of evidence. But this seldom stops people from arguing as if their evidence or conclusion is true.

"That wish to make nature bend to social and political theory should be examined, in part, because it is now so prevalent and unexamined."

I have heard people "examine" it everyday on talk radio or Internet posts. They examine it from their own perspective while devaluing all others.

"Politicization of race has gone so far that the biology of race is denied while new words like 'racist' and 'racism' are invented to denigrate those who would refer to the biological facts of racial difference. Some even wish to control the social environment and/or teach self-censorship in an attempt to short-circuit our senses that inform us of difference."

Indeed what I read and hear from most people is politicization rather than examination; all the while calling it examination. Some people thought they could talk about culture rather than race, since this is supposedly the real point. But talk about race rather than culture allows others to point to the problem; the color, the eyes, the accents (via our senses; such as sight and hearing). And it conveniently ignores the fact, the reality that we are stuck with the culture and world we have, and the most likely result of pursuing the race *problem* is discrimination and separation at best, violence and genocide at worst. Our senses, like those of sight and hearing are not our problem. Our senses don't inform us of racial differences. Skin tone and accent aren't what you're concerned with. The "short-circuit" is elsewhere.

"To ignore the biology of racial differences one has to disregard over a hundred years of physical anthropology, paleontology, comparative studies of phenotype, physiology, psychology, and culture, and now the genetic studies of the last 50 years."

The biology, physical anthropology, paleontology, comparative studies of phenotype and physiology, psychology, and culture tell us next to nothing outside of the context that we ourselves provide through our own psychology and culture.

"When there is statistical evidence that blacks commit a disproportionate amount of violent crime compared to whites the statistics are about a racial difference so the only thing that could account for a racial difference is race or some racial attribute. You might have a point if the statistics involved black males compared to white females, but for a statistic to be valid it can't compare apples to oranges."

Are these the blacks in China, Africa? No. This is not an issue with "blacks" so much as it tends to be a problem of SOME blacks and some whites, and some liberals and some conservatives and some rich and some poor within *our* culture. Our culture serves as context. The issues are different in other cultures.

"About once a week we hear some horrific story about a young white woman who didn't see it coming."

And we seldom hear about the black, Hispanic or Chinese women. Why is that? We seldom hear that they are missing or found dead. But we are certainly told of the "young white woman". The media loves to sell its news to their likely consumers.

Change the channel.

No reply.

A while later I reposted a DelanceyPlace.com *book blurb about Italy in the 1700 and 1800's entitled:* Most Italians did not speak Italian.
From a book entitled, The Pursuit of Italy: A History of a Land, Its Regions, and Their Peoples - Author: David Gilmour
SHARON: I remember reading about the language differences many years ago in a Harper's article. Another interesting thing is the genetic evidence of the Etruscan presence in Liguria a people that disappeared two thousand years ago. Ancient legend tells that the Etruscans came from the North and if that is true it would explain their genetic distinctiveness. The area of Liguria is isolated and protected by mountains and that would support a concentration of an outlying genetic group. The language they spoke was not Indo-European. There is another group on the Adriatic coast are also genetic outliers as compared to other areas of Italy. It is very interesting that the genetic distinctions have persisted in that area to the present day.

I replied with a question and a similar book posting from DelanceyPlace.com *about ethnic Romans:*
PAUL: Was this story part of the legend?
There were no ethnic Romans, from a book entitled, *Rome* by Robert Hughes.

No reply.

A few weeks later:

Following one of my general DelanceyPlace.com *posts about books that began by noting: "At the dedication of Washington, District of Columbia's spectacular Lincoln Memorial in 1922, the few blacks that were invited were required to sit in a roped-off, segregated 'colored' section."*

SHARON: Abraham Lincoln said, "Let us be brought to believe it is morally right, and, at the same time, favorable to, or, at least, not against, our interest, to transfer the African to his native clime, and we shall find a way to do it, however great the task may be."

PAUL: Lincoln's words seem like they could be reasonable and moral sentiments for one to have had back when many Africans had been more recently plucked from their homes to serve as slaves in a foreign land.

I've read your words about this concept before. You've spoken of the words of Marcus Garvey on this same subject. Would you consider their words as being a reasonable and moral "solution" today?

African descendants today are not from another land. We are all Americans living under a constitution with rights and laws to be applied evenly. No longer is an African considered 3/5 human. What would you like to do today? Fences? Walls? New laws? Constitutional changes? What is *your* moral "solution"?

SHARON: The importation of slaves was outlawed in the U.S. in 1808, fifty years before Lincoln gave the speech from which the quote was taken, so there were no recent arrivals. Before emancipation there was an effort to repatriate free blacks who made up about 2% of the black population in the U.S. The American Colonization Society was set up in 1816 for that purpose. At that time Liberia was founded along with a British colony in Sierra Leone. I think that Lincoln was exceptional in thinking that repatriation was a moral issue, for most proponents saw it as the only solution to the problems associated with manumission and eventual emancipation. People feared race-mixing and viewed racial difference as an impenetrable barrier to social assimilation. A major reason for the retention of slavery was the very real concern that freed blacks would not be able to find a place in white society or be able to fend for themselves because most of them had been born into slavery in a foreign land, a foreign culture, among a people who had traveled a very different evolutionary path. I think Lincoln must have understood this and that is why he viewed a return to the black man's "native clime" as a moral imperative. An interesting questions are who fought against the ACS's efforts to repatriate blacks and why? Because Marcus Garvey was able to tap into the wishes of several million displaced Africans to go home a hundred years after the cessation of the trans-Atlantic slave trade, it is clear that Africans who had been born in the U.S. for several generations still wanted to go back to their "native clime." So the interesting question is who worked against this plan and why? Who wanted to keep Africans here and why?

PAUL: Lincoln's words seemed like they could be reasonable even when Lincoln had been uneven in his words and actions regarding slavery. But his intentions did move in a certain direction over time.

"A major reason for the retention of slavery was the very real concern that freed blacks would not be able to find a place in white society or be able to fend for themselves because most of them had been born into slavery in a foreign land, a foreign culture, among a people who had traveled a very different evolutionary path."

I'm sure some people felt they were protecting these poor African souls by keeping them in bondage because they saw themselves as good people. Some "whites" feel the same way today. Yet I doubt the slaves generally saw them this way. Slaves wouldn't have seen them this way. Had they been free, like you and me, I doubt you and I would view our captors this way.

Yet, as it was then it is for some now; some people still fear race mixing (as if we had not become mixed anyway, coming from common ancestors). Yet some still consider "others" to be "foreign" and on a "different evolutionary path", meaning that "whites" are superior to those of African decent genetically. Correct me if this isn't your essential position.

". . . it is clear that Africans who had been born in the U.S. for several generations still wanted to go back to their "native clime." So the interesting question is who worked against this plan and why? Who wanted to keep Africans here and why?"

Free people of African decent could and can travel anywhere they would like, as long as they have had an opportunity to work and earn the fare to make the journey. Of course they may have to be rich enough to bring generations of family with them. Yet some did make this journey while many others (had they wanted to or even could) had/have never been afforded such opportunities to go "back to" a place they had never been before; where their ancestors were taken as slaves in "an economic program of a relatively small minority of traders." I think issues such as this pose more interesting questions about just what it means to be free. Is freedom simply the condition of being physically unshackled or does it involve something more? Is there a moral dimension to one's liberty or is liberty simply a fancy term for those strong enough not to be bound?

No reply.

It had been a while since I'd heard from Sharon.

A friend of mine, JE, alerted me to a brief tongue-in-cheek article from the New Yorker *magazine entitled* "Scientists: Earth Endangered by New Strain of Fact-Resistant Humans".

I responded to him with a serious tongue-in-cheek reply:

PAUL: Hi JE. Further studies have found that people suffering from this malady are not stupid; they simply too often have a subcondition called *narrow factioditis.*

It seems to be spread by claiming one group, i.e. Democrats, Republicans, racists, Christians, atheists, ad nauseam, are wrong by virtue of their associations rather than their values. This tendency to put down people via "*group*" somehow causes the spread of this malady. Luckily there are two well known, time honored treatments: Respect others enough to ask questions first rather than accuse. The other treatment is to simply change the channel. The lesson of the first should be obvious. The latter is somewhat more vexing. It seems that too often we get out information from single sources like "talk radio" or *MoveOn.org*. The Internet at once gives us the ability to communicate cross-culturally while also allowing us to pick and choose only the exact points of view we wish to acknowledge. Researchers have found that single source listening, reading and watching increases the spread of our dis-ease. Rather than wearing a mask of righteousness, we should first ask questions to determine the extent of the malady and then take steps to change our own single source news gathering. Finally, respect is the only known cure. Nobody is a dumb as they tend to sound; it's just the malady talking. But are we really listening or just paying lip-service?

JE: Yes. That is exactly why I thought of you with that lovely piece of satire. Especially after our conversation the other day.

SHARON: What "facts".
No one is immune to the facts of his own existence, but facts that are many steps removed from one's existential reality are easy to ignore, dispute, or disbelieve. Modern communication has created a problem of alienation so that many misperceive reality. I think the satire meant to draw attention to people who reject what scientists establish as the "facts" as if scientists are the final arbiters of reality.

Context: Evidently the article was about climate change but never mentioned this in words. Instead of addressing climate change, I responded to why my friend had shared it with me. I assume Sharon doesn't like or believe the idea of climate change but she also doesn't say.

PAUL: You ask "What 'facts'?"
Then you say, "**No one is immune to the facts of his own existence.**"
So I guess *I* must ask, what facts?
You mention "**existential reality**". Define existential reality for me? How does it differ from other types of reality?
You say, "**Modern communication has created a problem of**

alienation so that many misperceive reality."

I would say that all communication creates problems of alienation and misperception of reality. It has been a common topic of philosophy (and perhaps religion too) for thousands of years. So, who or what is or should be the final arbiter of reality? It seems to me you value the science of genes and DNA. But don't we all pick and choose? We never come upon facts in a vacuum. Few of us regard science without regarding how it's evidence or even implications might bear upon our values. We pass what we hear and read through these value filters before we decide how to regard these facts. Where does this leave us?

SHARON: The facts of one's own existence are what one perceives directly. The facts contained in a scientific work are not perceived directly. One can apply scientific facts to what one perceives directly, e.g. the earth orbits the sun; the sun does not orbit the earth. A person with access to scientific facts can "explain" what he sees, but it doesn't alter his perception - i.e. it still looks like the sun moves from the eastern horizon to the west. Is the person who doesn't think about the earth's movement "immune" to facts? Or isn't it the case that such facts are irrelevant to most people who can and do live their lives without that knowledge? One can "value" scientific facts without closing one's mind to the possibility that the facts or the theories based on those facts are wrong. Science is not the final arbiter and scientists, like all people, behave in accord with their own interests. We have enough experience with "science" that has proven wrong that to mock those who have doubts and questions or those who take a wait-and-see attitude as "immune" to facts is partisan.

Before I could send off a reply:
SHARON: You mention genetics and DNA and that presents one of the strangest notions of our day. Rather than using science to explain how something works we are told we cannot use science to explain racial differences. Our senses directly perceive many of these differences but we are told that science does not support our perceptions even though that

same science can identify and classify genetic differences that can be traced to their continental origins. The single nucleotide polymorphism can be used in forensics to show the racial makeup of an offender who has left his calling card. However, the concern that the perception of difference equals racism "scientists" have taken the lead in self-censorship. This is counter-intuitive for all those who are not immune to "facts".

PAUL: So, the facts of one's own existence are those subjectively perceived. These are obviously incomplete. The facts of science are more objective and incomplete in their own way.

So how do we *apply* scientific facts? Facts become subject to us during our application of them; we subjectify them. Yet the scientific method (objective?) of considering things can enlighten our selves by attempting to take us out of ourselves. Although we can never remove our selves from ourselves, we can temper the value we place upon our subjective views by valuing the strength of another way of seeing. So scientific method can and should alter the value we place upon our points of view. This method, this process, has something to offer even though it is not absolute. Values that are recognized by way of this process could alter our views enormously if we allowed or adopted its value.

You ask, "Is the person who doesn't think about the earth's movement 'immune' to facts?"

Well, I've not mentioned the term "immune", although it was used in the tongue-in-cheek article to which you refer, but I will say that the strength of, and the value we place upon, our personal viewpoints are narrow and often exclusive and so tend to *inoculate* :) us from other facts for the very reasons mentioned.

We can all live without a lot of knowledge and we do. And some of us seem to well practiced at keeping away from understanding. Perhaps they haven't closed their minds; they just fail to value views beyond their own current ones (their existential reality?). Sure, they are "free" to do so but I don't see how ignorance contributes to their freedom. Why? Because we can freely close our minds to that which we believe to be untrue without understanding that is our own subjective views that have blinded us and bound us to our ignorance. But when this happens, it is hard, if not impossible, to tell because we are bound and blind. This happens with regular folk as well as scientists. So although scientists have been wrong with their theories, regular individuals have proven to be at least as susceptible in their ignorance. If both groups were to be a bit more ego less by valuing scientific method, we all would be better off.

So, scientists shouldn't be the final arbiters of reality? Neither should we? Who or what should? Where does this leave us? *Doubt* can keep us searching but should we really value personal viewpoint and opinion above all else? Should we throw out scientific method because the result of human application have often been wrong? There are clues here. What are they?

PAUL: You believe in the science of genetics and DNA because you point to a portion of science that seems to support your belief in the superiority of the "white", "Northern European" *race* as compared to the other races. You believe this while you disbelieve the scientific fact that we cannot tell race via genetics. The closest we can get to determining anything close to this is a general idea about a continent where a certain portion of genetic material might have come from. But even if there were more to *race genetics* than this incredible generalization, this has little to do with what our narrow perceptions and prejudices will lead us to determine about what race means to us in the world in which we live together day to day.

"Our senses directly perceive many of these differences but we are told that science does not support our perceptions even though that same science can identify and classify genetic differences that can be traced to their continental origins."

Our senses can't, and have never been able to, perceive race. Our sense of sight, sound, taste, smell and touch cannot tell us any- thing about race. An 18 month old child can recognize skin color differences but this child knows nothing about what people mean by or imply with the term race. The babies just notice skin color. And continental origin is not race. This might be especially true if one agrees that all human life began in a single location.

"The single nucleotide polymorphism can be used in forensics to show the racial makeup of an offender who has left his calling card."

This is not true. It is not science. Although "there are variations between human populations, a SNP allele can only be shown to be more common in one geographical or ethnic group and rarer in another." Wikipedia - *Single-nucleotide polymorphism*.

To claim more than this from genetics distinguishes our *concepts* of race from science. This is why making such determinations from some facts could amount to something that smacks of racism to many people. We know that facts are not born, nor do the live, in a vacuum. We *apply* our subjectivity to every single "fact". With this understanding, we could do better.

So here we are back to the beginning: Should scientists be the final arbiters of reality? Should we? Who or what should? Where does this leave human understanding and our lack of it? There are clues here. Can we see them? What are they? I'll offer up a clue: The last sentence to the preceding paragraph.

Continuing to add my own thoughts . . .
PAUL: Perhaps it's time for some DNA testing. DNA testing can trace my real history back whereas we commonly accept our family ancestry as told to us. I learned rather late in life that you were my half sister. Furthermore I remember being told time and time again that my skin was so much more "olive colored" . . . than . . . who? Blond, blue eyed, fair skinned, left handed sister Jan. Or my parents? You? I also remember hearing that I was often called "the little Indian" due to my skin tone. This knowledge combined with the olive colored skin comments might point toward clues that I've never scientifically investigated.

I also learned rather late in life that dad was absent several times (sometimes for extended periods?) during my childhood (up until I was 6ish?). Perhaps my father isn't my father as he wasn't your father. Perhaps a DNA test might tell me *the* truth and locate the recessive? gene responsible for my skin tone. Perhaps this test will point *one* possible continent of origin. But if I truly am a "little Indian", will we find this genetic marker pointing toward India or to North America, South America?

Being born in Utah may add a complication to my heritage that might not concern many other people. Polygamy was legal here and polygamy *is* part of, and current to, Utah culture, legal or not.

It was actively practiced in these parts for generations up to this day. Even if my immediate ancestry is not found to be in question, the chances of it being misunderstood or even lied about in past generations is enormous.

Now, if I find out that I have a gene from a continent that isn't Europe (or specifically Northern Europe), will this discovery make me inferior to you? At least I assume you have investigated your DNA markers. And if we find out we are both of the same Northern European ancestry should I then agree with my friend's *Facebook* comment that I "come from good stock"? And if you and/or I find out otherwise, do we resign ourselves to our genetically predisposed fates?

No reply.

My wife, Karyl, liked a post called "Turn Ignorance Around", *that was posted by members of the Latino community who don't appreciate the rhetoric demonstrated by Donald Trump in his presidential campaign. Although my wife's post wasn't intended for Sharon, she seemed to feel it her duty to defend him and/or herself.*

SHARON: Illegal aliens crossing our border with Mexico are not synonymous with "the Latino community". That is why Trump gets much of the Latino vote. Latinos who have become citizens "by the book" resent illegals who have not, but are here taking advantage of social services, crowding our schools and hospitals, and getting tax credits for children that live in Mexico. I live three miles from the woman Trump has used as an example - a woman who was "raped, sodomized, and killed" by an illegal alien together with an anchor "baby". The "Latinos" I have known over the last thirty-eight years agree with Trump's proposal to deport illegals and build a wall to control who comes into the country.

KARYL: These members of the Latino community see Trump's sweeping generalizations as ignorant. To say that Latinos think this or that is just as silly as saying that Republicans think this or that.

I don't think even Trump thinks he has the Latino community in his pocket: In a speech at the 2015 Conservative Political Action

Conference, he warned conservatives that a growth in the Latino population would result in the demise of the Republican party, saying, "But of those 11 million potential voters, which will go to 30 million in the not-too-long future, you will not get any of those votes no matter what you do."

His rhetoric seems directed at some people's base fears.

SHARON: Aren't the actors in the video giving a sweeping generalization about what Latinos think? What makes you think Latino citizens feel like they belong to the same "community" as illegal aliens? If there were no truth in Trump's characterization of illegals then Latino citizens would have no need to dissociate themselves from the thirty million illegals, some of whom are drug dealers, rapists, and murderers, but all of whom are taking advantage of the American taxpayer. Trump warned the Republicans about their collusion with the Democrats on amnesty. The Democrats have allowed, even encouraged, the deluge because they expect to add these people to their coalition of blacks, homosexuals, feminists, college students, and what is left of their control of labor unions. Trump warned Republicans that there was no way they could compete with Democrats for that vote because the immigrants know who has facilitated their immigration and impeded all efforts to control the border. Trump isn't competing for the illegal vote, he is competing for the votes of people who are bewildered by the treachery of the two political parties on the issue of immigration and that includes many Latino citizens who see themselves as American taxpayers, not a part of a "community" here illegally, whose only connection is language. A country 20 trillion dollars in debt cannot afford to support 30 million illegal immigrants at the expense of their own citizens. Mexico is a rich country; they should take care of their own people.

KARYL: Oh come on. Two people can talk about race and not be racist. Two people can talk about a generalization without becoming the generalization itself. This makes as much sense as your saying "If there were no truth in Trump's characterization, etc." If there was no truth in what I said about your fears then you wouldn't have replied to them either so let's cut the crap. Everything you say about the Latino community can be said of any group of people. You want segregation, I enjoy integration. Trump supporters seem to want to be their own community. Another Utopian dream. But in any community some individuals are good neighbors and others aren't. Nothing is new under the sun.

What is your personal disconnect that makes it so difficult to understand basic human or humane connections? Language? Really? Your comments are simply a list of your fears. You are afraid of illegal aliens coming in from the rich land of Mexico, Democrats, blacks, homosexuals, feminists, college students, and labor unions. Your fears drive your attitudes. Trump gives your fears a platform. And unless you kept track of your contributions and withdraws, you too are probably taking advantage of the American taxpayer through social security and medicare checks. There are individuals who don't think we should support these programs either so be ready to pull yourself up by your bootstraps. But immigration isn't a problem with the US budget. The military takes up much more of the budget but nobody wants to cut it because of fear. And what are you afraid of? Individuals who are not enough like you in your community. What makes someone a good citizen within their community? Segregation of that community?

My two granddaughters are part Mexican and they have felt the repercussions of your fears.

I don't want to write or respond anymore. Write to Paul. He has the patience of Job.

My wife found she had little patience with Sharon's immigration arguments but a niece of mine finds some time to jump in of this one:
TIFFANY: Aunt Sharon, there are nine immigration reform Acts that have been put into law during Donald Trump's lifetime. The most recent, the 'Border Security, Economic Opportunity, and Immigration Modernization Act' of 2013, was a bipartisan effort approved by the Senate Judiciary Committee. Donald Trump had nothing to do with this Act, or any other legislation---ever---because he is a private citizen who has never held a

political office. Donald Trump may have warned Republicans in his sleep about the perils of improvements to immigration reform, but in real life they would not have listened to him because the majority were voting FOR these bills----not against---or they would never have been passed. Yes, if you read a summary of each Act, parts may appear to be against or push back on immigration. However, economists do their jobs and provide the government with positive factual data that support the continued influx of immigrants. Supply and Demand: Immigrants have to feed themselves, feed their children, buy clothes, buy a car so they can go to their job that pays them, so they have more money to demand more goods and services. Yes, many of these workers are illegal. Here in Palm Springs, many of the workers that took care of the lawns and gardens in my parents' community were illegal. But these reform Acts and good employers obeying these Acts, over the years, have helped them so they have proper jobs and can support their families. Economists site the basic laws of supply and demand as having a positive effect on job growth for all races, not job loss for whites---a positive effect for the economy if more immigrants are put through proper education because then they will continue to pay more into the system. Yes---Mexico IS a wealthy country and if they were taking care of their citizens and providing them with an economic process that would allow them to take care of their families instead of living in constant fear that their women and girls will be raped or their men or sons will be hanged naked by the highway scaffoldings, or being shot by random stray bullets---- then certainly many would not be fleeing towards a better life in the north. And frankly, if one professes the argument that no immigrants should be allowed to enter our country and that we should get rid of anyone that is not white----then the only race in our country that would have a factual claim to this argument would be the Native Americans, not the Whites.

SHARON: I live in a town that was a majority white when we moved here in 1977. The grade school two doors away was 85% white, as was the neighborhood. Now the elementary/middle school district has 16,026 students and of those students only 534 are white. 48% do not speak English. If I had young children I would not send them to school here because they would be neglected in a system that puts all of its energy and resources into bringing immigrant children up to speed. When my children were growing up I was very active in the community, in PTA, Brownie Scout leader, youth soccer coach, Little League, American Field Service Student Exchange, etc. I knew my neighbors, and the parents of my children's friends. About twenty years ago the city bought up a block of houses on either side of our street to be used as Section 8 housing. Those receiving subsidized rent also get gardening service and free city utilities - water, trash pickup etc. We kept our house because we had just finished remodeling and re-doing our yard. Living here now is like living in a foreign country. I went for a walk a while back and saw a little girl coming toward me with what looked like her little brother. She looked to be about 8 or 9 and as she got closer I saw that she had a baby on her back and was the mother of both. She was not Mexican, but Oaxacan and her children will speak neither English nor Spanish. When school lets out there is a flood of women pushing strollers and trailing toddlers as they pick up their older children and head home. One never sees a white mother with a bunch of little kids. Those who support open borders are those who benefit from cheap labor and retail sales. As taxpayers we are subsidizing those businesses by giving illegal immigrants schools with free breakfast and lunch, health care services, and often food stamps, and rent subsidies. We live in an agricultural area and when my son was in middle school he went out to a nearby strawberry field and asked for a job picking berries. He was denied a job because he "didn't speak Spanish". So much for jobs Americans won't do. What most people do not realize is that the immigration laws were changed in 1965 to favor Third World Immigrants over the quota system that had favored Europeans. Since 1965 many of our cities have deteriorated, our public schools are bad, and people are alienated in their own neighborhoods. All countries need borders, have always needed borders because people need to protect and care for what they and their ancestors have built.

TIFFANY: It would be easier for me to understand your arguments if every single person in our country, excluding Native

Americans, couldn't trace their ancestry to another country. We are a "melting pot", always have been. Do you believe that only white people should receive government help, e.g., food stamps? Even if whites are continually documented as receiving more government assistance than any other race?
SNAP Graph deleted.

TIFFANY: The Economix blog at the New York Times reported the following in February of last year: "Blacks comprise 22 percent of the poor, but blacks only take in 14 percent of government benefits. Conversely, whites make up 42 percent of the poor, but take in a disproportionate 69 percent of government benefits."

TIFFANY: "Seventy percent of counties with the fastest-growth in food-stamp aid during the last four years voted for the Republican presidential candidate in 2008, according to U.S. Department of Agriculture data compiled by Bloomberg."

TIFFANY: Department of Commerce Welfare Demographics: White 38.8% verses Hispanic 15.7%. Research Date: January 23rd, 2016.

TIFFANY: The organization, Aid to Families with Dependent Children (AFDC), states that, "Among the poorest of the poor – single mothers, living below the poverty line with minor children to support 39.7 percent of AFDC clients are Black single mothers and 38.1 percent are White women with children. Food stamp recipients are 37.2 percent Black and 46.2 percent White. Medicaid benefits are paid to 27.5 percent Black recipients compared to 48.5 percent White clients."

SHARON: The government you speak of is supposed to be a government of, by, and for "the people". The people Lincoln referred to were not all the people of the world, but the people of a specific nation - a nation with a white, European culture, a nation with a constitution, borders, laws, and government that applied to its citizens only. There is no nation on earth without borders and no nation that gives the advantages of citizenship to any and all who cross its borders. There was no American nation before Europeans established it after the struggles of 150 years as a small minority against hundreds of thousands of hostile natives. Consider for a moment why we have a black population in the U.S.today. They are here only because slavery was an economic benefit to a small number of landowners - it was the "cheap labor" of that time - but at what cost? Just looking at your SNAP graph tells us that the cost of "cheap labor" will never be paid. Blacks are only 14% of the population but are over-represented in all categories of welfare, unemployment, educational failure and crime. With slavery the plantation owner fed, clothed, provided shelter, and health care for his "cheap labor" but today those who benefit financially from illegal immigration do so only because the citizen taxpayer subsidizes food, shelter, education. health care, and crime. If this program is not addressed what will the country look like in fifty years?

And again . . .

SHARON: One can justify Third World immigration into white countries as atonement for the ruination of aboriginal cultures, for slavery, and for colonialism, but while that may work to induce guilt in Americans, Englishmen, the French, and the Dutch - what are Icelanders, Norwegians, Finns, and Swedes atoning for? Iceland has never been a "melting pot" but the birthrate of Asians in Iceland is higher than that of Icelanders. It appears that just being white requires that we pay reparations to those who are not.

PAUL: I hope I can butt in and say, Happy Easter!

You say, "The government you speak of is supposed to be a government of, by, and for 'the people'."

And it still is of, by and for the people. The people just aren't as white as you'd like. I'm okay with them not being so "European".

You say, "The people Lincoln referred to were not all the people of the world, but the people of a specific nation - a nation with a white, European culture . . ."

I don't know how Lincoln got involved :) but please direct me to Lincoln's quote.

You say, "There is no nation on earth without borders and

no nation that gives the advantages of citizenship to any and all who cross its borders."

And there still isn't. Although some areas, by law, allow some advantages that others don't.

You say, ". . . **Europeans established it [this nation] after the struggles of 150 years as a small minority against hundreds of thousands of hostile natives.**"

And considering yourself a native, you sound hostile too.

You say, "**Consider for a moment why we have a black population in the U.S.today.**"

Hum, let me see . . . much of the early black population was brought over in chains as slaves.

You say, "**They are here only because slavery was an economic benefit to a small number of landowners - it was the 'cheap labor' of that time - but at what cost?**"

Many of these landowners became our venerable founding fathers who praised liberty and settled upon considering the black population 3/5 of a man. That in itself cost many blacks plenty. Cheap? They were slaves. And our nation is still paying for it because some people hang on to the idea that it was right to treat people with a different color of skin like they were 3/5 human. Many seem to still think this way, and the attitude causes untold harm.

You say, "**Just looking at your SNAP graph tells us that the cost of 'cheap labor' will never be paid.**"

You are correct. How can we ever repay a population that we enslaved for hundreds of years and then applied Jim Crow laws to them for another hundred, and never voted for a civil rights bill until I was 6 years old?

You say, "**With slavery the plantation owner fed, clothed, provided shelter, and health care for his 'cheap labor' . . .**"

Those kind plantation owners, taking such good care of their slaves. Perhaps they deserve metals.

You continue, "**but today those who benefit financially from illegal immigration do so only because the citizen taxpayer subsidizes food, shelter, education. health care . . .**"

First, not all illegal immigrants commit further criminals. Not all receive subsidized food, shelter, education and health care. And there are plenty of legal "white" folks, even Northern European

Icelandic white folks who benefit from government programs. Correct me if I'm wrong.

You say, "If this program is not addressed what will the country look like in fifty years?"

I would say it will likely look much like it does today.

SHARON: Happy Easter to you, too. The "people" referenced by Lincoln did not and do not include non-citizens. Lincoln "got involved" when I paraphrased the Gettysburg Address - which we memorized in junior high school. "Natives" are always protective of that which they consider to be their own and that is true of the individual, the family, the clan, the tribe, the nation, and the race. Wariness usually precedes hostility for we are endowed with instincts that allow us to make distinctions and assess danger; we are cautious with strangers and strangers are cautious with us. Abandonment of caution is disordered and militates against survival. I am not hostile to non-whites - on the contrary, I think I would be judged by my many non-white workmates and patients to be exceptionally friendly, kind, generous, admiring, and interested. However, that doesn't mean that I don't feel keenly the loss of comfort and camaraderie of a racially, culturally, and intellectually homogeneous neighborhood, workplace, and town and would never have moved here in the first place if my children had been a small minority in the schools. The U.S. would not have a black population had it not imported slaves for "cheap labor". No matter who the slaveholders were, they benefited financially from a socially destructive program, the disastrous effects of which plague us today and far into the foreseeable future. Do today's beneficiaries of the "cheap labor" of illegal immigrants differ in some way from those who benefited from slavery? Today's beneficiaries don't take any responsibility for the sustenance of the people they are exploiting, but are given a free ride by the American taxpayer. It is like slaveholders imposing a tax for slave maintenance on the 99% who did not own slaves.

PAUL: If you mean, *a government of, by, and for the* white European cultured *people*, I guess I had missed that part when I learned it :)

"'Natives' are always protective of that which they consider to be their own and that is true of the individual, the family, the clan, the tribe, the nation, and the race."

This explains why the native Americans were upset. Now the tables are turned; you consider your *race* to be the natives. Does native now equal the strongest? The victorious? Is abandonment of caution the same as fear? Or are you simply cautious of Mexicans, Democrats, blacks, homosexuals, feminists, college students, and labor unions?

"The U.S. would not have a black population had it not imported slaves for 'cheap labor'."

I doubt this since we have all kinds of immigrant populations here today that weren't imported as slaves.

"Do today's beneficiaries of the 'cheap labor' of illegal immigrants differ in some way from those who benefited from slavery?"

Yes, but net gain or loss of benefit is not a main consideration of mine, nor should it be a consideration of justice.

"Today's beneficiaries don't take any responsibility for the sustenance of the people they are exploiting, but are given a free ride by the American taxpayer."

I agree, and this fact is incredibly disturbing.

SHARON: Continued. As for the 3/5 designation, that was not a formula applied to physical and/or mental character of the black man, but a formula to adjust the population numbers that favored the more densely settled North. The fraction is preposterous as the basis for "treatment" of the African. e.g. For the African I will shave off 2/5 of my usual regard - only 3/5 of a nod, a wave, a smile. Only 3/5 of a thank you, The Democrats today would like to enhance their numbers by adding illegal immigrants and their offspring to the party and they are confident that immigrants know to whom they owe allegiance. Slaves were fed, clothed, given shelter, and care, not because the slave owners were kind, but because the slave was useless unless well cared for. Slaves were valuable and only a fool would neglect or mistreat them (and that fool was more likely to be an employee than it was to be the owner himself). Cheap labor implies substandard and unreported pay. Substandard pay implies a deficit for necessities - rent, food, clothes, and health care especially for needs of a family with four or more children and only one wage earner. One of the reasons the statistics show a relatively high number of unwed mothers among Hispanics is that they deny they are married in order to get the welfare benefits. Mexican and Oaxacan women have large numbers of children, close together, so they do not work and that keeps on welfare. The cost of slavery will burden the tens of millions of descendants of those who never owned a slave as well as the descendants of slaves. Lincoln was correct in his assessment that the only moral and practical course to repair the damage done by transporting Africans away from their culture, their kinsmen, and their evolutionary home was to return them to their "native clime". Those who tried to do it were thwarted by those who thought the Africans could be a useful political tool. They have been and continue to be a useful political tool, but it is clear 6-7 generations away from slavery that there is no law or policy or reparation that can fix the foreign nature of white men and their culture to make them compatible with the African. Evolution is an exceedingly slow process and the two races have, over hundreds of thousands of years, followed very different evolutionary paths.

PAUL: I know what 3/5 refers to, and I think both you and I know that people regarded slaves as less than human, so unfortunately the 3/5 designation has insidious implications. Would you say that Africans are 5/5 of your Northern European ideal? Isn't it true that you regard their "evolutionary path" as deficient to yours?

"The Democrats today would like to enhance their numbers by adding illegal immigrants and their offspring to the party and they are confident that immigrants know to whom they owe allegiance."

You simply assume the "Democrats" intentions as if they are all the same. All Democrats don't believe the same things just as all Republicans don't. Is this not obvious to you? Can you not accept the fact that Democrats might see, "[t]oday's beneficiaries [who] don't take any responsibility for the sustenance of the people they are exploiting . . .", as unjust and therefore requiring of some defense and justice? Just as various Republicans believe different things, so do Democrats. You simply imagine the intent of a Democrat as simply many Democrats imagine what a caricature of the quintessential Republican believes. Unfortunately, your overriding determination to group all similar people (Mexicans, Democrats, blacks, homosexuals, feminists, college students) together as a matter of convenience than truth. And the ignorance of reality this demonstrates cheapens any and all you apply this to.

"Slaves were fed, clothed, given shelter, and care, not because the slave owners were kind, but because the slave was useless unless well cared for. Slaves were valuable and only a fool would neglect or mistreat them (and that fool was more likely to be an employee than it was to be the owner himself)."

And there were many fools. I hear this same mistake in reasoning applied or misapplied everyday. People say that *people wouldn't act this way, it is against their interests etc*. But people are often foolish. Everybody knows this and still speak of how illogical it would be if . . . Well, people are foolish or illogical. We all know this. Otherwise smart people will even claim things like, "[s]laves were fed, clothed, given shelter, and care . . ." as if the protection of their investment in their slave ownership somehow points toward their virtue. At best it can only point toward their ignorance.

"Cheap labor implies substandard and unreported pay. Substandard pay implies a deficit for necessities - rent, food, clothes, and health care especially for needs of a family with four or more children and only one wage earner."

And slave labor is slave labor. They were not cheap labor or receiving substandard wages. They were slaves. Assuming the slave owners were at least intelligent enough to know the differences as you and I do, they have no excuse for claiming virtue. Nor do you have any excuse to apply it retroactively.

"One of the reasons the statistics show a relatively high number of unwed mothers among Hispanics is that they deny they are married in order to get the welfare benefits."

If this is true it is true for all groups other than Hispanics. So the term "Hispanic" has no relevance within this sentence.

"Mexican and Oaxacan women have large numbers of children, close together, so they do not work and that keeps on welfare."

This is true it is true for all groups other than Mexican and Oaxacan women. So the terms "Mexican and Oaxacan" have no relevance within this sentence. And in past discussions you have complained about women working, and that "Millions of healthy women have been denatured and have traded fulfillment for rather dubious 'rights' of voting, abortion and birth control." "Motherhood has been devalued as the nuclear family is coming apart." So it seems that motherhood must take a backseat to economics. Nothing is as simple as race and motherhood. There are many dependencies to be considered.

"Lincoln was correct in his assessment that the only moral and practical course to repair the damage done by transporting Africans away from their culture, their kinsmen, and their evolutionary home was to return them to their 'native clime'."

I disagree. Lincoln was wrong. Many descendants were born here and therefore had no "native clime" to return to. I think I've asked you this already: Is this your solution today? The issue I mentioned has only multiplied. What would you say if a group of people wanted to send you back to your 'native clime'? Where would this be?

Before I could send the reply above . . .

SHARON: Of course the aboriginals of the Americas were "upset" with the advent of Europeans, just as they were "upset" by the presence and competition of neighboring tribes. Tribes laid claim to territory, and battled to maintain what they believed was theirs. The tribes of Virginia, Canada, and New England fought genocidal wars against Europeans and came very close to annihilating New Englanders in King Philip's War of the 18th Century. Europeans won the battles with the aboriginals and they now have rightful claim to those territories. Victors never walk away from what they fought and died for - that would be insanity, not altruism. The natives had the advantage of numbers for at least 150 years, but they were not unified nor organized. "Native" does refer to the descendants of the victors - they got to the land on their own steam and fought to claim it. That is how the world has been populated. So-called Native Americans became natives by invasion and laying claim. The abandonment of caution in social situations is to abandon one's abilities to "read" others. This is considered a mental defect. Didn't you mean to ask if caution equals fear? I was a little confused by the question and the list you attached. The list referred to the new coalition the Democrats have pulled together to substitute for the hemorrhage of ordinary working people who don't believe they have interests in common with feminists, homosexuals, blacks, immigrants, college students, etc. I not only have no interests in common with that group, I think the "issues" that have been assigned to them are socially destructive. There was no black immigration into the U.S. until the quota system was repealed in 1965. Up until that time the system favored a proportional assignment according to the demographic model existing at the turn of the century. That model insured that most immigration would come from Western Europe. The 1965 legislation subverted that model and began to favor Third World immigration including African. Why Africans would want to come to a white, "racist", KKK, land of Jim Crow to live among the ruined descendants of African slaves and the descendants of slavers is hard to fathom. Perhaps they think they will be paid reparations on the basis of skin color. What do you think?

And again . . .
SHARON: My point about slave owners providing life necessities - food, shelter, clothing, and medical care was not to praise the slave owner, but to show that the owners were not subsidized by the taxpayer as are today's beneficiaries of cheap labor. That doesn't make slave owners virtuous, but it does show how taxpayers are unaware of the fact that they are subsidizing the low wages paid by businessmen. You do realize that Africans were not the only slaves. Children were

often indentured by a widowed mother who could not support her younger children. Children were kidnapped and forced to work on ships and then sold to someone in America. President Andrew Johnson was an indentured servant who escaped from his owner, learned to read and write on his own and became president when Lincoln was shot. Child labor in our country continued into the twentieth century and nearly all of those children were white. The trans-Atlantic slave trade was just an offshoot of the immense trafficking in slaves within Africa. Even today about 20% of the population of Mauritania is enslaved - many of them born into slavery. Rather than speculating about the character of American slave owners of the 18th and 19th centuries or the indignities of having to drink out of a designated fountain in the Jim Crow South shouldn't you turn your attention to the ongoing slavery in Africa?

And again . . .

SHARON: I don't think anyone thinks of slaves as less than human or they would not have any objection to slavery. Less than human would correspond to the way we view draft animals. Difference doesn't imply greater or lesser, that's why I consider a reference to "white supremacy" as a pejorative, not a descriptor. I don't think in terms of a Northern European "ideal", but the designation is a type with definable characteristics. It is my type and that of my family both forward and back. I know of many characteristics that define racial type, but trying to rank them by assigning value to particular traits is a useless exercise, e.g. scent glands add value, their absence subtracts. It is likewise preposterous to assign value to an evolutionary path. The path is a rough description of evolutionary changes that respond to the physical and social environment, natural selection, and some degree of isolation over time. Success in evolution is measured by survival. Whatever the various races and sub-races of mankind have done to survive into the 21st century is obvious success. With that measure one would have to say that the aboriginals of Tasmania did not succeed for they did not survive. Was their path deficient? Perhaps, since it did not allow an adequate number to survive to continue reproducing. On the other hand a sub-race may have been obliterated by a natural disaster and while nothing was wrong with their path they were not numerous enough or widespread enough to avoid extinction.

Some context for Abraham Lincoln's quote about "native clime" that Sharon keeps referring to. . . .

The quote comes from a speech made by Lincoln before he was president. His 1857 speech derided the then recent Supreme Court Dred Scott decision. Dred Scott was a slave who tried to sue for his freedom and the freedom of his immediate family because they had lived in Illinois and the Wisconsin Territory where slavery was illegal. But the Supreme Court decided 7–2 against him because, among other things, Scott's temporary residence outside Missouri did not bring about his emancipation under the Missouri Compromise (which the court also ruled as unconstitutional) because it would "improperly deprive his owner of his legal property." Immediately following the passage that Sharon quotes are the last two paragraphs of Lincoln's speech:

> "How differently the respective courses of the Democratic and Republican parties incidentally bear on the question of forming a will—a public sentiment—for colonization, is easy to see. The Republicans inculcate, with whatever of ability—they can, that the negro is a man; that his bondage is cruelly wrong, and that the field of his oppression ought not to be enlarged. The Democrats deny his manhood; deny, or dwarf to insignificance, the wrong of his bondage; so far as possible, crush all sympathy for him, and cultivate and excite hatred and disgust against him; compliment themselves as Union-savers for doing so; and call the indefinite outspreading of his bondage 'a sacred right of self-government.'
>
> "The plainest print cannot be read through a gold eagle; and it will be ever hard to find many men who will send a slave to Liberia, and pay his passage while they can send him to a new country, Kansas for instance, and sell him for fifteen hundred dollars, and the rise."

Next I paraphrase, in italics, what I seem to keep hearing from her. (Some of this is from her public comments on other posts unrelated to what I've represented herein.)

PAUL: We seem to be in the same circle here again.

Slaves were not paid but were housed and fed and clothed but the idea of paying reparations is against your beliefs. No solution.

The corporations don't pay enough to the people from south of our border, but get these temporary workers back to Mexico (or wherever) ASAP, not because you care about them but because it's really the government's (primarily the Democrats) fault that farm owners got away with taking advantage of those you want the heck out of America because they have the wrong culture or perhaps different DNA (not worse of course, just different enough to classify "them" as a culture that can't ever blend adequately with our "white" one).

A few blacks had slaves and some Mexican people are as bad as "white" people and so how can we talk about morality; whatever that is?

Child labor is bad but God forbid the government (a group) or labor unions (a group) or mothers (a group that should be home and not working yet who don't make enough money and so their family suffers) intervene. And yet all these problems are too big for a single person, but three is a crowd, aka, a group.

If a certain portion of the world is still enslaved then nobody can say anything bad about slavery without being hypocritical or hypercritical. That is just political correctness fomented by the Democrats (a group). There is no such thing as morality, probably no God; we all just make it up and we're all hypocrites (as a group) anyway. Furthermore DNA (a group of cells) is the real driver of culture (a group) here.

"Upset" obviously isn't a strong enough word for you but "genocide" is too strong? Can't win. And don't talk about Hitler and genocide because some others committed it too. Hitler was, after all on the defensive due to all sorts of geopolitical conditions so it wasn't his fault. After all, the whole holocaust has been blown way out of proportion, and is probably the "Jews" fault anyway due to (insert your historical point here that somehow excuses or minimizes the holocaust).

We can't hold any individual responsible because then you will have to feel some responsibility for morality, humanity and justice rather than pointing the finger at nameless, faceless politics, ge-

netics and economics. Groups are easy targets. They don't have brains or hearts. They are simply evil unless it's the Trump campaign. (Of course his campaign is not a group, he is self financing, while still dodging responsibility for his own words.)

I ask questions of you, as an individual that you refuse to answer. You talk about nameless, faceless groups that you can demonize without any human connection. Groups seem to be DNA transportation devices who are all so imperfect that nobody can put a humane face on any one. It's all purely academic. The people are just patches of color and inferior (no, just different than yours (no value judgments here)) DNA that belong to certain continents that they should never stray from (for their own good, bless their hearts); they have imperfect governments and cultures and we can refer to "them" as a group by using arguments that never end due to the imperfections in all our individual arguments. Perhaps you don't assign value to an evolutionary path, you just point is out as a natural way of discriminating. And discriminations are valueless . . . meaning they lack all value.

Please excuse my oversimplifications here. I should have made them appear scientific and complicated but I'll take personal responsibility for my errors, and apologize in advance for not taking the time to nail down every seeming inconsistency of semantics.

Now, what if we didn't talk about discriminating but spoke about commonalities instead. Or is this beyond the pale? Can you speak of people without referring to DNA, race, political parties; groups of any sort?

SHARON: Let's go back to the beginning. I responded to a video that used Trump's comments about some illegal aliens to support the "Donald Trump is a racist" meme. How did we jump from the question of illegal aliens to race? I am told that the "Latino community" is offended by Trump's comments about illegal aliens – that is to say, Latinos see any criticism of Mexican criminality as an affront to their "race." Once the connection is made all ignore the question of thirty million people illegally in our country. So we go for pages without ever addressing the open border and the millions of non-citizens using our taxpayer-funded, public services. Is it racist to have borders and to have requirements for citizenship? Is that why no one wants to talk about it? Or is it the case that borders are an anachronism of a time when men armed themselves and fought to defend their people and their lands? There were 17,000 American casualties in the Mexican-American War that created the boundary between the U.S. and Mexico, a border that is now to be nullified - because? Mexico is the 14th largest economy in the world with a GDP of $1,178 trillion. However, the wealth stays at the top – the top 1% of Mexico's distribution has an average annual income nearly 50 times that of the poorest 10%. The Mexicans are more than happy to send their poor to the U.S. – so what we are doing is helping the wealthy in Mexico keep their wealth and avoid the consequences. It isn't the wealthy in our country who pay the cost of caring for and educating the poor of Mexico. Does this have anything to do with "base fears" of those with a different "skin tone"? No. At the top of my list is the ruination of the neighborhood schools – schools that are paid for with property taxes but that no longer serve the needs of white children.

PAUL: You ask, "How did we jump from the question of illegal aliens to race?"

We got onto *race* because you said, "The Democrats . . . their coalition of blacks, homosexuals, feminists, college students, and what is left of their control of labor unions. . . I am told that the 'Latino community' is offended by Trump's comments about illegal aliens – that is to say, Latinos see any criticism of Mexican criminality as an affront to their 'race'."

So, there you are at *race* again.

"Once the connection is made all ignore the question of thirty million people illegally in our country."

Once again, "all" is a group. Once you say "all", If one disagrees, your generalization is, by definition and by reason, untrue.

"So we go for pages without ever addressing the open border and the millions of non-citizens using our taxpayer-funded, public services."

None of these public services are exclusive to non-citizens. All people receive public services.

"Is it racist to have borders and to have requirements for

citizenship?"

No.

"Is that why no one wants to talk about it?"

Lot's of people talk about it.

"Or is it the case that borders are an anachronism of a time when men armed themselves and fought to defend their people and their lands?

No.

"There were 17,000 American casualties in the Mexican-American War that created the boundary between the U.S. and Mexico, a border that is now to be nullified – because?"

No :)

"Mexico is the 14th largest economy in the world with a GDP of $1,178 trillion. However, the wealth stays at the top – the top 1% of Mexico's distribution has an average annual income nearly 50 times that of the poorest 10%."

Unfortunately many economies go this way. We feel much of their pain.

"The Mexicans are more than happy to send their poor to the U.S. – so what we are doing is helping the wealthy in Mexico keep their wealth and avoid the consequences."

"Mexicans" is a group. Once you say "Mexicans", if only one disagrees or doesn't fit with your generalization, it is by definition and by reason, untrue.

"It isn't the wealthy in our country who pay the cost of caring for and educating the poor of Mexico."

What do you suggest we do to get the wealthy to pay more?

"Does this have anything to do with 'base fears' of those with a different 'skin tone'"? No. At the top of my list is the ruination of the neighborhood schools – schools that are paid for with property taxes but that no longer serve the needs of white children."

Once again, "white" is a group. Once you say "white children", if one disagrees or doesn't fit with your generalization, it is untrue.

SHARON: My statement about the Democrats' new coalition isn't about race. But then a coalition is a group and once one says "coalition" if one disagrees or doesn't fit with the generalization it is untrue. Oh, and "Democrats" is a group, too, so once I say "Democrats" if one disagrees or doesn't fit with the generalization, it is untrue. And then we have, blacks - a group, feminists - a group, college students - a group, homosexuals - a community - a community - a group....How can my statement allude to "race" or anything at all if all the elements are a priori untrue?

PAUL: So, you and I both know what a group is. I think I've been quite clear. You say, *Democrats* are *this*. If there is one person who is a registered Democrat who doesn't agree with *your characterization* of her, then your characterization of her is untrue. You have simply characterized a group, Democrats, in error. We can replace *Democrats* with *blacks, Mexicans, homosexuals, labor union members, college students, feminists,* ad infinitum, and the error is still an error. There are very few ways of characterizing individuals that belong to any of these groups that are common to all of them. This is a point of reason. I can speak about homosexuals without being homophobic or homosexual. It doesn't make me a Democrat or anything else. One can't attribute characteristics me that don't belong to me, prejudice does that. Even if I "honestly" attribute characteristics to a Democrat because I "believe" them to be true, my belief doesn't change reality of what "Democrat" means. My belief simply makes me mistaken (at best) about reality.

I am not a Democrat. Anything else that might be believed or said about me as an individual that is any broader than my own narrow statement, is untrue at least, and prejudicial in general . . . because it is general. This is the nature of generalities.

SHARON: The "Democrats' coalition" doesn't refer to Democrats but to those who devise election strategies for the Democratic Party. The coalition is not accidental, but deliberate and knowingly cultivated. The party strategists "group" people and assess their strategies by calculating probabilities. How to appeal to feminists? "The War on Women". How to appeal to homosexuals? "Marriage Equality." How to appeal to blacks? "Trayvon Martin and Black Lives matter"?* How to appeal to college students? All of the above.

*A reference to local police killing unarmed black men.

PAUL: Well, you can now shift from "Democrats" to the "Democrats' coalition" but you've just changed terms to point to the same grouping that is dishonest.

The liberal side of me can find sympathy with the struggles of women without calling them "feminists" for having a struggle. I can also empathize without participating in what you and some others conservative coalitions brand a "war on women". Yes, conservatives and the right-wing have coalitions just as the Democrats do. I can sympathize with homosexuals and not participate in what some factions brand as a *war on marriage*. I can sympathize with blacks and have concerns about Trayvon Martin. I can find sympathy with college students and not be against liberal education.

When you characterize "feminists" as "this or that" you are often pointing to an extreme case while representing this case as common and imminent. Your characterization becomes a caricature in the same way one draws one. Take a portrait of someone with a rather prominent nose and make it so bulbous that it dwarfs the size of the eyes which, in turn, makes the chin jut out so as to look menacing. But we must never forget that this caricature arose out of an unfair characterization that was exaggerated from extreme cases.

Perhaps it's easier to speak of an individual. Pick on me. I will stand-in for the Democrat, homosexual, Mexican woman who is a college student going for my nursing degree in America. Now you tell me all about me. Let's see if you can tell *the* truth about me, as an individual, rather than painting an ugly, unlikely caricature of me. I am human after all.

SHARON: You are grouping women by sympathizing with "the struggles of women." The Democrats' election strategists group women in their "War on Women" rhetoric, but the only "struggles" assigned to the group are abortion and free birth control. (and in his speech to female supporters Obama apologized for not including "dry cleaning") Because the "issues" of this group are so narrowly defined it is fair to say that the group being addressed is more narrow than all women and for want of a better description I use the term, 'feminist'.

PAUL: You tell me, "You are grouping women by sympathizing with 'the struggles of women'."

Very good. Now, by your words here you seem to admit to the problem of such grouping. Am I correct? Or is it only a problem for others and not a problem when you do it? Such as when group-ing all feminists together according to your definition. I asked a feminist that I know and she disagrees that your characterization applies to her. Therefore your definition is untrue. The only way to make it true would be to address "some" feminists.

SHARON: The Democrats' strategists imply that all women are under threat of losing the right to abortion on demand, and subsidized birth control. But not all women feel threat-ened by either possibility, so what does one call the more narrow group the strategists are appealing to? What do the strategists call them? Does the group agree on abortion and birth control? Does your feminist friend agree? Would any feminist disagree? Does the group not exist because there is no name for it and no characteristics that define it? If I say that the Democrats' election strategists have built a coalition of victims groups is that untrue because some homosexuals are not victims? Is it untrue because some women are not victims? Is it untrue because some blacks are not victims? Is it untrue because some immigrants are not victims? And then there is the problem of liberal college students who are part of the coalition, not because they are victims, but be-cause they sympathize with the victims. So if election strate-gists can group people for purposes of getting votes, why can't I recognize that grouping in my critique?

PAUL: I can see that it is difficult for you to speak about individu-als. Throughout your grouping, you've tried to minimize it by go-ing from "Democrats" to "Democrats' strategists", then to "strategists", and from "group" to "narrow group", back to a group tag of "feminist", and then back to "group".

As it is, my self-identified feminist friend is now confused and lost. So I asked another feminist friend and *he* thought the argument didn't apply to all the feminists he knew either. He preferred to call them "humans" however. He saw nothing more definite or widely agreed upon within his group. I am pretty sure that a single individual feminist can be found to agree however. So let's talk about this individual. But it seems extremely difficult for you to speak about an individual. You are back to "coalitions", "homosexuals", "victims", "immigrants", "college students". Just as Democrats became "Democratic strategists", later they become a grouping called **"election strategists"**. The name change doesn't solve the issue of your grouping.

"So if election strategists can group people for purposes of getting votes, why can't I recognize that grouping in my critique?"

Because you think you are simply acknowledging the existence of a group. You are not. You are asserting that every individual agrees with the group. To make matters more complex, you are applying your own definition of what you believe the group is while ignoring what individuals themselves think. This is not honest. It shows them no respect for their own perspectives. To condemn an individual due to the actions of others in a group (with whom they disagree) is not just. The (your) definition is proven untrue.

Many people who try to form coalitions want their followers to follow within the lockstep of group-think rather than thinking like the individuals they are. Now, you have often noted such problems when you refer to some people. Yet when you desire to group, you ask me what's wrong with it?

We must not forget that it is you who applies "your definition" of any group, let alone applying it to individuals who may not agree with your definition. Even when certain individuals may agree with your definition, they may not agree with what other members of a group or group-think.

SHARON: Illegal aliens may not share any views, subscribe to the same ideology, possess any human characteristic in common, have the same needs or behave in the same way, but they do share the status of non-citizen in the U.S. illegally. The video at the beginning of this interminable thread grouped all "Latinos", legal and illegal, into something called "the Latino community" for purposes of charging Donald

Trump with racism because he referred to some illegal aliens as rapists, murderers and drug dealers. That is dishonest. And when Tiffany refers to the rapists and murderers IN Mexico who make other Mexicans feel unsafe and drive them northward, she is not called a racist. How does that work?

PAUL: Maybe you mean that *undocumented immigrants :) may not share some of your views*?

My use of the term *undocumented immigrants* is not simply me trying to be politically correct. I am trying to be accurate. Many individuals migrate for work etc. They might then stay. At this point of decision I'd call them undocumented migrants, perhaps undocumented immigrants. Also, my use of the term is by one who views individuals as humans first, countrymen second; just as our forefathers did.

Since undocumented immigrants are human beings (I assume you agree) and you are a human being, undocumented immigrants share physical and mental perspectives as do most other human beings, and therefore share similar needs and behaviors as many other human beings. And, yes, if they have entered the United States illegally they share a non-citizen status and have broken the laws that are applicable. But none of this removes their humanity. They are human beings who have rights that I, for one, will respect as natural and inalienable.

Back to the video. "The video at the beginning of this interminable thread grouped all 'Latinos', legal and illegal, into something called 'the Latino community' for purposes of charging Donald Trump with racism because he referred to some illegal aliens as rapists, murderers and drug dealers. That is dishonest."

You have the power within you to end this thread anytime you would like to stop replying.

I would agree that this video "grouped all 'Latinos', legal and illegal, into something called 'the Latino community.'" That is how they see it. I don't have to see it that way. I see the community as a community of human beings who have rights that I, for one, will respect as natural and inalienable.

Who knows what "their" purpose was? One thing we are sure of is that they at no time called Donald Trump a racist. As one who knows little about racial distinctions, and has not studied and defended it, I never thought Latino was considered to be a race anyway. The video was about these members of the Latino community viewing Trump's generalizations as ignorant. Many generalizations are because they are ignorant of individual differences. In this admittedly edited clip, Trump doesn't say **"some illegal aliens as rapists, murderers and drug dealers." He says, ". . . when Mexico sends its people, they're not sending their best. They're bringing drugs, they're bringing crime, their rapists . . ."** (Hold on, is it "their rapists", "they're rapists"? I, for one, can't tell what he means by what I heard.)

I also don't know what Trump means by "Mexico sends". Don't some immigrants come of their own volition? Or is it all a conspiratorial plot orchestrated by the Mexican government? If a few Mexicans do cross the border without the Mexican government sending him/her, then this generalization is untrue and dishonest.

"And when Tiffany refers to the rapists and murderers IN Mexico who make other Mexicans feel unsafe and drive them northward, she is not called a racist. How does that work?"

I didn't follow all of these posts and I also can't speak for her but I can tell you what I think. Every culture has rapists and murderers. This malady is not restricted to countries, cultures, skin tones, or race. People (all kinds and *un-kinds*) travel east, west, north and south, and if one feels unsafe in the east, one might travel west etc. The direction one flees has nothing to do with race. And once again, how are Mexicans a specific race? What distinguishes "Mexicans" from "Americans"?

But here's what I read on the Internet, so accept it for what it may be worth (next time I'll quote *Encyclopedia Britannica* on subjects such as these:)

The three main races are said to be:

"1) Caucasian (Aryans, Hamites, Semites),

2) Mongolian (northern Mongolian, Chinese and Indo-Chinese, Japanese and Korean, Tibetan, Malayan, Polynesian, Maori, Micronesian, Eskimo, American Indian),

3) Negroid (African, Hottentots, melanesians/Papua, 'Negrito',

Australian Aborigine, Dravidians, Sinhalese."

Since the idea of race is subjective rather than scientific, some say there are five races while some say there are seven.

"The term 'Hispanic' as an ethnonym emerged in the 20th century with the rise of migration of laborers from the Spanish-speaking countries of Latin America to the United States. Today, the word 'Latino' is often used as a synonym for 'Hispanic'. The definitions of both terms are non-race specific, and include people who consider themselves to be of distinct races (Black, White, Amerindian, Asian, and mixed groups). However, there is a common misconception in the US that Hispanic/Latino is a race or sometimes even that national origins such as Mexican, Cuban, Colombian, Salvadoran, etc. are races. In contrast to 'Latino' or 'Hispanic', 'Anglo' refers to non-Hispanic White Americans or non-Hispanic European Americans, most of whom speak the English language but are not necessarily of English descent."

This might be why I would not call someone a racist when referring to individuals feeling forced to flee from one location to another.

SHARON: No, I mean "illegal aliens" defined as people who belong to another nation and are breaking the laws that control who enters and stays in our country. If documentation is required by law and they don't have it - they are breaking the law; they are in the country illegally; cf. If a driver's license is required for driving, one is breaking the law if he drives without one. The legal status of lawbreakers has nothing to do with their "ideologies", what they think, or the reason they are breaking the law. I suppose you don't like the reference to law because it is definite, while "undocumented" is open-ended - slippery. You prefer the word, 'immigrant', because it indicates a fait accompli.; e.g. "These people are immigrants who just haven't gotten around to the paperwork" Our travel and immigration law do not treat people as nationless humans, but, rather, all humans are identified by the nation under which jurisdiction they live. All lawbreakers are human beings but their humanity does not invalidate the law or the statutory penalties for breaking the law. The most obvious penalty for entering a country illegally is deportation. I rather doubt that one could justify an inalienable right to enter a foreign country any more than there is an inalienable right to enter your neighbor's home.

PAUL: I don't "belong" to this nation. I am not enslaved or forbidden to travel. I simply live here and abide by the laws that I find reasonable or would rather not pay the price or fight over. This could change.

Laws are made, laws are changed and unmade. Laws are not absolute. Some people like some laws and some people don't like other laws. We alter our laws all the time. There are consequences for violating them, often even if we are unaware of them. Yep, I get it. The laws in this country are an ongoing conversation. People might want a law, it might be voted on and put in place. The law might be be broken and then there is a trial. The verdict might be challenged. The law itself might be challenged. This goes to a higher court where it may be reviewed. There might be problems found with the law and it might be handed back down for lower courts, legislatures or citizens to re frame. Or it might be struck down immediately. The Constitution might have to be amended in order to change the basic framework of our laws. We do this because laws are not written in stone. They are a part of (or should be) our civil conversation; from human being to citizen to cop to lawmaker to judge; and the process keeps going around.

What is illegal today, like chattel slavery, was once legal. And, yes, the status of lawbreakers sometimes does have to do with ideologies. In the 1950's, Senator McCarthy got many people in trouble by simply branding them as Communists. Communism is an ideology.

All law might be considered "slippery" because humans make and apply laws that we disagree about. Our conversations make this obvious. Although one might call a sort of open-ended-ness "slippery", I don't; it is a conversation. The "fait accompli" I will cop to here is that humans are humans first. We are humans prior to the laws we enact. I am guilty of holding this value.

"These people are immigrants who just haven't gotten around to the paperwork." Who are you quoting here? Not me.

"All lawbreakers are human beings but their humanity does not invalidate the law or the statutory penalties for

breaking the law."

At one time in the United States some humans were branded as slaves without human or civil rights Some broke their bonds and violated our laws. Other humans assisted them and thereby broke other laws. Yet we can to apply a moral component to justice rather than simply a political one. We can decide which we value more: morality or politics. We can begin this process by accepting the fact that we are humans first.

"The most obvious penalty for entering a country illegally is deportation."

We can and do do that. We might also want to consider the morality in what we do due to human complications such as "family" bonds that might be damaged in the process. Perhaps we can mitigate such things within the bounds of the laws we enforce.

A human being has a human right to travel. A reasonable human being might want to be aware of, or quickly learn, the rules of the borderline they cross. They might cross a line where law (not morality) has determined that the violator might be held in lifelong slavery as punishment, never to return home again. This might be a law but it might not be moral. Laws that seek to stress a moral component of essential humanity might offer more humane options to the violator. As moral agents, we are in charge of the laws we desire to enact, and we can improve them, make them worse, violate them ourselves, or be ignorant of their implications for justice or morality. We are still learning. The conversation goes on, or I hope it will.

SHARON: Alien means "belongs" to another esp. of a foreign nation; under foreign allegiance. Travel to foreign nations requires documentation that identifies one's nationality. Laws change, but while a law is in effect the person who breaks the law is a lawbreaker; is acting illegally and is liable for the consequences. There are, at the very least, 11 million aliens in our country illegally, it is that status that defines them as a group. Beyond that status we do not know who they are and it is preposterous to assume that they are all good people who do not need to be vetted and will not be a burden on our social services. The other thing that we know about illegal aliens is that they, and all their "complications" belong to another country, it is that country's responsibility to care for its people, not ours. As an individual you can devote yourself and your resources to help humanity, and with a passport you can take your pick of humans from Tibet to Tierra del Fuego, from Mexico City to Johannesburg, but our nation has no obligation to use our people and our resources to aid the poor of any other country. Likewise, there is no other country in the world that is expected to care for poor Americans - if there were it would free up resources and perhaps then it would be possible to take care of the poor of Mexico - possible, but ridiculous. Our country has a 19 trillion dollar debt and we have our own poor; it simply is not practical to add a burden of millions of additional poor people. So who wants to take them in, and why? Humanitarians? It is easy to "sympathize" with the "struggles" of others and petition the government to alter laws to help the millions of poor Mexicans, but will that humanitarian take a poor Mexican family into his own home? And if he would do that for a Mexican family why doesn't he do that for a poor family living in a homeless shelter across town? Can a government be humanitarian? Our government will represent its actions as humanitarian to satisfy those who like to think of themselves and their countrymen (To do otherwise "is not who we are") as humane, but the real motivation behind flooding the country with a Mexican underclass is business. Who we are is the Chamber of Commerce.

PAUL: Our "nation" may have no political or legal obligation but many individuals feel obligated to humanity. It is not expected of me. Some of us just do what we think is best. You don't have to. That's not your thing. That's your right.

Of course I'm pretty sure you feel you have no choice in these matters since your taxes go to support others that you wish not to support. Yet my taxes support your social security and medicare, while supporting many other people of our native clime, regardless of race. I suppose, like you, I don't like supporting corporations or imperialistic wars either, but we don't always get what we want. But if we try, sometimes we might just find, we get what we need. :)

You say, ". . . but the real motivation behind flooding the country with a Mexican underclass is business. Who we are is the Chamber of Commerce."

Yep, corporations and individuals make money off those who can be exploited. And those without legal status can be much more easily exploited by business. The Chamber of Commerce as well as businesses have reason to keep the laws as they are. If the laws making and keeping "illegals" illegal helps support the situation. So it seems that these businesses like this stream of exploited humans. They employ these workers and they don't pay taxes, there is no reason to provide them health insurance. They can be like slaves without the obvious moral repugnancy of slavery ever being raised. Too many people are too busy being mad at these people for taking their jobs. This situation is quite reminiscent of how many within the US who migrated from the dust bowl to California during the depression. Most of these migrants believed in the promises of work for pay but instead they were exploited by business. Are humans not humans no matter their "nationality"? Who is to be the defenders of humanity in this fine US justice system? Perhaps we should address the laws that mistakenly and immorally support businesses at the expense of people we can exploit "legally". Even if we can put them down by labeling them "Mexican underclass".

What is your solution?

SHARON: You only look at one side of the incentive of business to welcome illegal aliens and it's not the most important reason. They are importing consumers - big time consumers. If American men - even college-educated American men can't find jobs that will pay enough for them to marry, buy a house, support a few children, and pay back their student loans they will not marry, buy a house, and have children. With an influx of illegal aliens there is high demand for rentals which keeps the rents high, and illegals with several children and no income or low income get subsidized rent, food stamps, the WIC program, Medicaid, etc. If those illegals were deported the reduced demand for housing would reduce rents and other prices making it possible for young men to marry and have some confidence in their ability to start a family. Businessmen in retail sales love the millions of illegals because they are great consumers. The grocery store doesn't lower its prices because there are a lot of people too poor to pay. No, the government steps in with food stamps (they aren't stamps anymore - it's like a credit card), so the four foot tall Oaxacan woman ahead of me in line uses a card just as I do, but she never gets a bill. Does the government really give a shit about a family of six illegals - no, they are concerned with keeping the grocer's prices up. That is what I mean when I say, The Chamber of Commerce is who we are. Liberals pretend not to see the business reality, as they hide it behind a facade of humanitarianism. Liberals only need to support the continued influx of illegals to feel good about themselves. Well, it also helps to denigrate those who don't support that influx by calling them racist, xenophobe, bigots and insinuating that the social security they've paid into since beginning to work at age 14 wasn't really a savings account, but a form of welfare that every immigrant grandmother will get even though she's never worked a single day in the U.S. and hasn't contributed to the account with fifty years of payroll deductions.

PAUL: I do not consider only one side of the same coin. You believe that US businesses (untrue by inaccurate generalization) and even the US government (untrue by inaccurate generalization) act as the US Chamber of Commerce, welcoming illegal aliens so as to import customers; then the customers either produce (unlikely in your view?) or live off the system. Correct me if I'm wrong. I have seen no independent data that supports your claim; there may only be prejudgment based upon prior held beliefs. Undocumented workers are not taking the jobs of college educated American men who refuse to marry, have children or buy houses, either directly or by proxy. To observe a correlation is not to accurately judge causation. These issues are not connected unless you group them together in order to claim that "we" should first take care of "our own". I'm an American man who has been to college, and yet I am married, own a house outright, support my family, and I have a number of jobs that no "illegal" has taken from me. And I don't think I'd be better off or have more "confidence" if those illegals were deported so as to reduce demand for housing or reduce rents.

The confidence factor your speak of, ". . . **making it possible for young men to marry and have some confidence in their ability to start a family . . .**" as far as I know had to do this. The great recession caused it by a lack of laws and/or enforcement of irresponsible large lending institutions.

"**Does the government really give a shit about a family of six illegals . . .**"

If the government doesn't care about the six "illegals", why would it care about the six legals? Legality or illegality has nothing to do with the caricature you sketch.

"**Liberals pretend not to see the business reality.**"

Once again, I reject the accuracy of your grouping. I am a liberal and a conservative too. As a liberal I am not a Democrat. As a conservative I am not a Republican. Your label fails as does your argument, for much the same reason.

"**Liberals only need to support the continued influx of illegals to feel good about themselves. Well, it also helps to denigrate those who don't support that influx by calling them racist, xenophobe, bigots and insinuating that the social security they've paid into since beginning to work at age 14 wasn't really a savings account, but a form of welfare that every immigrant grandmother will get even though she's never worked a single day in the U.S. and hasn't contributed to the account with fifty years of payroll deductions.**"

I am not a humanitarian in the sense you speak of. In fact, I merely find it my duty and responsibility as a good citizen of a diverse nation to be self-critical so as not to overvalue my own personal or socially provincial viewpoint. I think that justice is complicated I think society is complicated. Easy answers based upon inaccurate groupings does not strike me as the sort of citizen I want to be. And I, as a liberal, don't support the continued influx of immigrants any more than I support the influx of iPhones. I, as a liberal or conservative don't need to feel good about myself due to my denigration of others, whether they be American citizens, Mexican migrants or immigrant of any nationality, legal or illegal. It would do no good for me to call you a racist, xenophobe or bigot, and I haven't. In my own mind, your status on these matters does not make any difference. Your status within your own mind has never been made known to me, even when I've asked if you might agree with a definition. In your own mind you will happily agree or unhappily disagree no matter your or my status on the question. Your status is not up to me. You have your own right to conscience even if that right and those words are not in the US Constitution.

I don't see how calling someone racist, homophobic, anti-semitic, xenophobic, bigoted, or any other term is helpful. If others agree with my characterization they will simply do so. If they dis-agree, they will argue with it. And there are many other responses between the extremes yet few can get anybody anywhere they want to go. The best I can do is to ask questions and listen to the an-swers. I might disagree with how others regard themselves but I am unlikely to change *my* own impressions of *them*, let alone their own impression of themselves.

I haven't insinuated that, "**the social security they've paid into since beginning to work . . . wasn't really a savings ac-count, but a form of welfare**", I have stated it outright. To the best of my knowledge, this is exactly how the system works and always has. All of our payments are thrown into a pool and this pool has been paid into and out of and it has been borrowed against. Correct me if I'm wrong. And yet, I will defend your enti-tlement to such disbursements even if I might not fight for my own because, for me, you and others have a moral expectation at this point, rather than this primarily being a matter of law.

I don't know "**that every immigrant grandmother will get [Social Security benefits and Medicare] even though she's never worked a single day in the U.S. and hasn't contributed to the account with fifty years of payroll deductions.**"

I don't know this generalization to be true. The fact might well be true for some immigrant grandmothers. Unfortunately, It is dif-ficult for me to entertain the validity of your claim due to your ten-dency toward groupings has been too general to be accurate.

Speaking of individuals, families and businesses I personally know of, the businesses I have worked for have not welcomed ille-gal aliens into this country as an incentive or otherwise. None have imported "illegal aliens" as customers. Nor have any of these busi-nessmen have ever expressed their love of "millions of illegals" because they are great consumers or otherwise. This has been more the norm within my experience; quite far from your claim that this is business as usual.

Your claim that "illegals" receive subsidized rent, food stamps, WIC aid or Medicaid is untrue in my experience and from the reasonable statistics I have read because the *majority* of undocumented workers don't receive all these subsidies. Legitimate studies show that most work hard for a living and provide for themselves. If they didn't, they couldn't be such fine consumers.

I have never taken out a student loan but if I had, I would have certainly paid it back. This is simply good honest citizenship. Many "illegals" are good *citizens* too. Even with several children, the few I've known have satisfactory income so they don't get subsidized rent, food stamps, the WIC program, Medicaid, etc.

And when you ask if ". . . **the government really give[s] a shit** . . .", the government has many individuals within it who might agree with some of what you think and some of what I think. This is how government is. Individuals making decisions (sometimes what you like, sometimes what I like) for everybody. And still, most laws begin at the local community level by the democratic process. And you seem to think of justice primarily as law, enforcement and following the law. I think of law primarily as justice and equal rights first with enforcement following from this conception of justice. You tend to view people as races, nations, allegiances, factions, coalitions opposing each other with no common connection; especially in an increasingly multicultural country such as ours. Correct me if I'm wrong.

And I don't know what the average four foot tall Oaxacan woman thinks, feels or how she behaves. But she is human so I'll bet she does her best for herself and her family much like you and me. Very much like the six foot tall white Northern European that is fifth generation American who pays for his groceries using the same method of payment. Method of payment has no direct correlation with ones height, sex, nationality or status.

The fact that you group individuals into groups and that your application does not apply to many individuals within those groups, makes your assertions lack any credibility they might otherwise have.

SHARON: I didn't say illegal aliens take jobs from American men, (though they do in some areas like the building trades) I said their presence creates high demand for goods and services that keeps rents and prices high, and many young people including college graduates delay or forego marriage and family for economic reasons. All of our children had thousands of dollars in student loan debt upon graduating and a B.A. degree or even an M.A. as Katherine has did not provide a job with an income that could pay back the debt and support a family. The two sides of the illegal alien problem that are both rooted in business are

1) Hiring illegals for cash - off the books. This allows the exploitation of workers, but provides

2) the benefit of hiding income, making aliens eligible for subsidized rent, food stamps, and Medicaid for the whole family. If you discount the business connection then how do you explain the government's policy that has allowed millions to cross our southern border? If it doesn't benefit business, then who benefits? "Irresponsible, large lending institutions" are a major element of business and as we have seen our government bails them out when they get into trouble and also allows them to charge interest on student loans several times the rate banks charge for other types of loans and then deny the possibility of bankruptcy - another favor to business.

PAUL: I didn't intend to discount the business connection, but you are right. While rereading my reply I thought I had said more about this connection than I did. I happen to agree with what you have said about, "1) Hiring illegals for cash - off the books. This allows the exploitation of workers, but provides 2) the benefit of hiding income, . . . and allows them to charge interest on student loans several times the rate banks charge for other types of loans and then deny the possibility of bankruptcy - another favor to business."

But I'm more interested in your remarks concerning your family. I'd like to ask you some questions. When we began our arguments nearly a year ago, you said: "I don't want to annoy, bore, or alienate you, so I will wait for your okay before answering."

So far so good. I think we've kept going along quite well. But I was wondering why you said this. From some other posts I've seen you comment upon, you have not seemed to worry much about annoying or perhaps even alienating other people. I wonder if you could talk a bit about this.

You seem quite alienated and maybe even isolated where you live. How much do you figure your personal circumstance influences your ideas? What do you think about feeling alienated, surrounded by aliens, and yet tending to alienate others? Or have you ever looked at it quite this way? You don't have to answer if you don't want to.

Before she answered me. . .
Whereas my wife, Karyl, didn't really want to discuss politics with Sharon anymore, Karyl liked talking about family and so they had the exchange that follows:
SHARON: When it comes right down to it I don't really have any friends who are like-minded in the ideal sense, but my children fill that need better than anyone. One might think that is so because they are an echo of my own thoughts, but all passed me by as critical thinkers some time ago.

I grew up in Utah, with two years in Kanab as a young teenager. Everyone was white until Kanab and there were perhaps two or three Hispanic kids – all of whom spoke English and seemed to be from families that had been in the area for a couple of generations. All recent immigrants I knew in Salt Lake seemed to be Scandinavians – converts to the Church. When I got married in 1966 we lived two doors away from a family of Navajos. The children were very close together and the boy was only about six when they started coming around to visit. The oldest girl was the most outgoing and fearless and she started by coming to our window and looking in. Matt invited her in and played an LP of mariachi music and danced her around to *La Bamba*. It didn't take long for the other three to get up the courage to come in as well, though another girl was still a baby and didn't come around for a year or so. At the time I was doing pen and ink still life drawings and the boy wanted to try it. I gave him the pen and he did a remarkable rendering of our Danish coffee pot. He was probably only six or seven at the time and I don't think I was as impressed then as I would be now after watching the development of my own children's artistic gifts. The parents both worked – the father as a welder during the day, and the mother as an aide in a nursing home at night. They rented a very small house and I thought at the time that they were able to tolerate such close quarters because they had grown up in hogans on the Navajo reservation in Ft. Defiance, N.M. We helped the mother when she needed transportation and I think she appreciated our entertaining her children for awhile nearly every day. When our oldest son was born she brought over a blanket for him that he slept with until he was quite a big boy and the ragged remnant of the blanket was still with us when we moved to California just after he turned ten in 1977. She also brought a loaf of Navajo sweet bread for Christmas. I told their mom that our son had first smiled that Christmas morning – he was just a month old. She told me it is a Navajo tradition that when a baby first smiles the family must kill a sheep and share it with everyone – or else the baby will grow up selfish. We moved and they moved and we never heard from any of them again. Would we be considered friends? Not really. We shared fellow-feeling and helped each other but we weren't like-minded and never would be. Why? I think the reason is that we are from very different cultures. What I learned about Navajos was very interesting and it was distressing to think that her generation was likely to be the last with a clear connection to Navajo traditions. The notion that because people are primitive they are poor or disadvantaged is shallow and ethno-centric. It is true that humans are enough alike that one can adjust to a very different culture – especially if one begins early enough, but it is also true that culture is an emanation of a particular people and its value is not in its wealth or advancement, but in its fit with the people who developed it over hundreds of thousands of years.

Captain FitzRoy of the *HMS Beagle* took four young Fuegians (from Tierra del Fuego) back with him to England in the mid-nineteenth century where they were educated and "civilized." He took them back a year later and almost as soon as they disembarked they shed their English clothes and shoes and ran to their people. They could have stayed in England and the attitude would likely have been that they were privileged, indeed, to have such an opportunity. But, as I said, people tend to be ethno-centric and they do not understand that the material things from a foreign culture cannot replace another's culture and people, no matter how primitive we think it is. All of our efforts to "help" those of another race and culture are misguided and doomed to failure. I feel the same way about the Oaxacan Indians who have begun arriving here on the Central Coast. They are natives who have maintained their racial and cultural distinctiveness over hundreds of years of Spanish colonialism but now they have come to get something from us, but will end up losing what they had. It will not end well. They are not "Latinos" and most do not speak either English or Spanish which makes it unlikely that they will be accepted as part of the "Latino community." Does this foreboding mean that I am a racist who cannot appreciate diversity? As I see it, diversity, is always a dystopia. Just because we feed at the same trough doesn't mean we can even relate to one another, maintain our cultures allowing each to culture to develop naturally, and become one big, happy, human race. I have more to say, but it's too late tonight.

KARYL: I had to think a lot about what I was possibly reading into your message, but in the end, it just seems quite inconsistent to me. You talk about the *truth* of culture as though it is a constant thing that must never change or evolve. As if the only "true" value is a state of stagnation. And yet you say its value is also that it has been developing over hundreds of thousands of years. Is there a particular point in time when ones "culture" should stop developing? When is/was that?

What I glean from your message is that you are afraid that someone is coming to take something from you. I don't think it matters who that someone is, I don't see how this is about race or culture at all. During the depression, California effectively closed its borders to the "Okies" who were fleeing starvation in the dust bowl. Of course not all the people trying to enter were from Okla-homa, but the naming of a "different culture" ensured that they were treated as something "less than", and ignoring their suffering was easier. Would this be ethnocentricity as well? As for maintain-ing our cultures, I'm not even sure I know what that means. I see culture as a continuum at its best. One big, happy human race? I'm not naive, even families of the same culture don't necessarily achieve that.

I don't accept that diversity is ALWAYS a dystopia, even dystopia isn't always dystopia. That has not been my experience. I think when you say "allowing each culture to develop naturally" you are really saying "separately", because that is your comfort zone. Assimilation has been around for thousands of years as well.

I haven't referred to you as a racist and I think you have re-counted interactions which do show at least some appreciation of different cultures. I'll bet those children appreciated introduction to mariachi and pen and ink. The demanded purity of culture seems to me to be as much of a problem (if not more) in the world.

SHARON: Here is a conundrum of race, culture and assimi-lation: When Europeans began traveling to distant lands, ex-ploring those lands for resources and land suitable for living as Europeans, they were not viewed by any native popula-tion as a cultural resource or population suitable for mating, but rather they were seen as interlopers – an unwelcome, in-compatible, foreign intrusion. This was so whether the Euro-peans were conquistadores from Portugal or agrarian fami-lies from England or Holland. In our country the original Eu-ropean settlers were a tiny minority among tens of thou-sands of hostile natives and they remained a minority for at least 150 years, a time during which the settlers came close to being annihilated more than once. Europeans are casti-gated for taking the land away from the Indians, but why wasn't their advent seen as an opportunity for cultural en-richment and friendly assimilation? Where in the world has a native population welcomed racial and cultural foreigners? If

Third World peoples are now flooding into European countries to be culturally enriched why didn't the natives of Africa, Australia, and the Americas see the European settlers as a positive thing? If the aboriginals in North America, Australia, New Zealand, and South Africa were hostile and fought to maintain what they claimed as their own, why are the Europeans who settled these lands and built their own cultures not allowed to protect what they fought for, built and believe to be their own? Fighting to survive and thrive is the story of humanity, just as it is for all life forms. Survival of the fittest is the evolutionary model and it is antithetical to life to suggest that those who are better endowed and fight more successfully should step aside for the losers.

The tribal peoples of North America always fought against one another and were never united even though with unity they may have annihilated those European settlers. People fight to maintain their cultures because a culture evolves to support their survival. Because culture does evolve it cannot be termed "stagnant" but it is exclusive to the people who created it. Some very primitive cultures have survived for tens of thousands of years with little change and may have gone on in the same primitive mode for another hundred thousand years. Can that be criticized as stagnation or isn't it a marvel of survival, stability and endurance?

Some things that interfere with the survival functions and stability of culture are war, conquest, colonialism, slavery, and modern day Third World immigration into European countries. Are we now to characterize these destructive actions as development, enrichment, or evolution? Who is promoting this revolution and who benefits? Is the Navajo, the Oaxacan, or the Australian Aborigine more developed or evolved now that their primitive cultures are being replaced? How much longer do we have to enjoy the cultural "enrichment" of dying peoples? And isn't all that "enrichment" a threat to the integrity of European culture worldwide? When Europeans are no longer the majority in the culture they have built and maintained for thousands of years, the culture and its people will disintegrate.

I think you make a mistake in characterizing the self-protective motive as a value judgment, i.e. thinking of interlopers as "less than" so their "suffering" can be more easily ignored. In the first place it is wrong to characterize all people who enter the country illegally as "suffering." The members of the drug cartels aren't suffering, nor are opportunists like coyotes. And if the poor of Mexico are suffering isn't that the responsibility of Mexico? Most of the people fleeing Mexico are members of an underclass in a rigidly stratified society. The correction of that inequality belongs to Mexico, not the people of the U.S.

You suggest that I am simply afraid that someone is coming to take something away from me and that it really doesn't matter who it is. But isn't that true of everyone? Isn't that why we lock our doors, fence our yards, install alarm systems, and limit our children's autonomy? My personal feeling of threat has grown with experience. When we lived in Salt Lake I don't think we ever locked our doors and we let our children play everywhere without any worry. I even let my boys go downtown on the bus by themselves when they were about seven and nine years old. Even when we moved here I had no anxiety about letting my children play unsupervised, go to the mall, the library, and the swimming pool. It's different now. One night a couple of years ago a Mexican walked right into our house and began speaking incoherently in Spanish. I was on the telephone, Matt in his wheelchair, and I could hear Matt asking the guy what he was doing. I finally left the phone and tried to get him out of the house. He seemed to be drugged or drunk and it was very disturbing. Needless to say we now keep our doors locked all the time. When I have taken Matt to urgent care the entire waiting room has been filled with Mexicans and their children and none speaking English. When we finally get to see the doctor it turns out to be a Muslim woman in a hijab. Only about a quarter or less of the doctors in town are white. Am I a racist because I prefer Peter Krause over Ramachandra Dandillaya or Mohammed Arain? We are not experiencing cultural enrichment, but the loss of community and cultural destruction. It may be even worse where Katherine lives - the ethnicities are different but whites are a minority. Our grandchildren have competed in the U.S. Open Music Competition for the past five years. It's a competition that is held in Oakland and draws on hundreds of young piano contestants primarily from the West Coast. Each group of competitors numbers about 25 and of those 22 are Chinese. Along with the occasional white child there are a scattering of Indians, Vietnamese and Thai children. When Westerners no longer play or appreciate Western classical music is there any chance that our people can produce another great composer?

KARYL: Are you saying that the hostile natives protecting their land should have built a wall to deter those exploring these lands for resources and land suitable for living as Europeans? Aren't the immigrants now exploring those same options?

You say, "In the first place it is wrong to characterize all people who enter the country illegally as "suffering." I didn't characterize any people entering the county as either illegal or suffering. I sited an example when neither culture nor race was motivation for exclusion, and not a matter of entering the country, but a State, within the United States, in which all were citizens.

And actually, I didn't make out of whole cloth that you are simply afraid that someone is coming to take something away from you. You said, "They are natives who have maintained their racial and cultural distinctiveness over hundreds of years of Spanish colonialism but now they have come to get something from us". But if what I said was out of context, my apologies. As for locking our doors, this too, in my own experience, has never been motivated by race or culture. The neighborhood I grew up in was probably 65% white. The neighbors directly across the street from us were blonde (verging on white), blue eyed children, eight of them. We named them the "white haired brats", because they were the neighborhood bullies, and thieves. It didn't make me think of my own culture as losers because of certain behaviors exhibited by them. It didn't matter what culture or race, we locked our doors.

Does it make you racist that you prefer white doctors? I recently had to change doctors because of insurance. I really liked my doctor. The new doctor was VERY young and in my opinion inexperienced, cold and not forthcoming with information. I chalked it up to age, does that make me ageist? I don't know. My newest doctor isn't that much older but he does seem more interested in addressing my questions. Still not as good as the one I liked, maybe she was one of a kind, all are white.

As for classical music, I grew up with it. My sister taught piano, it was her career. I am much more likely to recognize a classical piece than Paul is. Of my contemporaries only one embraces classical music, he plays guitar beautifully, he is much younger than I. Again, more a matter of taste than race, culture or age as I see it. A quick check of the "all-wise" Internet shows no shortage of 21st century Classical composers, and the list is rich with diversity.

"Survival of the fittest is the evolutionary model and it is antithetical to life to suggest that those who are better endowed and fight more successfully should step aside for the losers". And in 2042 when whites are the minority wouldn't we then become the losers in your scenario? Less "better endowed"? Whatever happens, you said yourself that deporting all *illegals* wouldn't change this. Hasn't the ship sailed? America, the melting pot, is diverse. Do you see your personal situation improving with a wall? Your daughter's? Is purity of European culture then secured? Or maybe eugenics?

You and I are both white, and we have completely diverse opinions because of our personal experiences. That is the human condition as I see it. It doesn't mean we can't try to see each others perspective, does it?

Karyl received no reply.

Back to Sharon's reply to me:
SHARON: I began writing online about 12-13 years ago using a pseudonym/avatar. My first posts were on Liberty Forum, which I believe was originally a Libertarian forum with a number of refugees from FreeRepublic. Liberty Forum went offline at the beginning of 2006 so I began contributing on

other forums, like the Chicago Tribune, Deseret News, and the Salt Lake Tribune. I like contentious subjects and writing helps me think. (Maybe it should be the other way around) Some would say that I just like to argue and maybe that is true in some sense, but I only argue about things I care about; I don't argue for argument's sake. When I went to your FB page on your birthday you had lately posted what appeared to be thoughts prompted by the Supreme Court's gay marriage decision. All of the things you mentioned were subjects that I had written about on Disqus so I thought that you might be interested in discussing them. I developed a reputation at the Tribune for being an opponent of nearly all "politically-correct" notions – many of which are universally accepted and unquestioned by the vast majority of people whether pc or not, e.g. women's suffrage, Brown vs. Board of Education, gay pride, circumcision, the FLDS, etc. Taking an unpopular view generates a lot of responses – many of them angry, disbelieving, and occasionally someone who thinks. So I wrote for about 4 years on the Tribune until they changed their policy to allow other posters to censor what they didn't like. One person complains and they block you forever. I have learned that there are a few topics that will get one kicked off many websites. At times I have been bewildered by what has been censored, just as I was taken aback by your strong reaction to my comment about Roe v. Wade. I still post on sites that use Disqus and for about the last year or so I have posted on FB. At times I have gotten huge numbers of replies and every once in awhile I collect 10-20 likes. The replies are usually critical. Without the anonymity of my Disqus avatar I have left myself open to bad feelings that are generated by views on contentious subjects. The thing is that those feelings and sensitivities are there whether I provoke them or not. In other words, if I present myself honestly many people are not going to like me and I will be seen as the one who has alienated others. Should I just be nice? Never react except to "like" what others post? Unlike you, I need a stimulus to get me thinking and writing and it's the energy of argument that gets me going. Perhaps it's a mistake to look to family and friends for that energy, but I think an honest representation of oneself is best. If you don't want me to engage you anymore, just say so, and I will be happy to limit it to birthday wishes in July.

PAUL: You are wrong about me. I, too, need stimulus to get me thinking and writing. I often read books that seem to come from a point of view than I might not share. I've been surprised how much I learn from them and how often they have helped me either change my mind or at least have jolted me out of an explicit mind-set or implicit bias I didn't know I even harbored. John Steinbeck's novel, *In Dubious Battle,* changed my life. At the time (23ish) I was what I would call a right-wing conservative. The book never took a side in any particular dispute. It put both "sides" in very poor lighting (in the character's own words) most of the time. But Steinbeck also did a great job at displaying the humanity of all these villains. I had always looked at ideas and the people who held them as right or wrong. I had missed their humanity. By the time I got through with the book I didn't know what to think but I began feeling I had a lot to learn.

But I found I needed more than other points of view, I needed conversation; a give and take to get me really thinking. My wife, Karyl is a good partner in this crime. I never have gone after contentious subjects simply because they are contentious; most foundational subjects like religion and politics simply are contentious without trying to be. I'm interested in people's beliefs; how they attained them, how and why they hold onto them, and why they resist other ideas and why they often have no clue themselves as to their own mind's and motives.

So, I try to carefully tread into areas that I know many people tend to be extremely defensive and protective of and get their thoughts. If I'm not careful, I can't draw them out. Instead, I'll get an argument and they will stop talking. I don't want to simply assume what and why they believe what they do. And I've found that most people know precious little about their religion or politics except that little bit that suits them.

And still, no matter how polite I am and how lightly I tread, people turn away as if shining a light on their beliefs will not illuminate them at all but rather it will put them in a bad light. And yet, I'm trying to learn by asking the difficult questions and trying to keep from stepping into a trap of my own making that keeps us apart while the distance grows. Now I could be even nicer and not even ask them, but I thought I was supposed to be searching for "truth" (to use their most common word). How can I conduct this search in ignorance? And yet, still, (how's that for a redundant, im-proper beginning of a sentence? I like it) I find myself estranged from most people. This seems to be the case partially because peo-ple don't think much about their beliefs; they don't want to think about them; they have too often fallen prey to those who question them and trap them. They have too much riding on their beliefs like, friends, family, community and perhaps church to ever change them. I don't seek out my estrangement yet, like you, I am fairly estranged.

You say, ". . . **just as I was taken aback by your strong re-action to my comment about Roe v. Wade.**"

I wasn't concerned about the abortion debate, nor did I react to abortion. In fact, the topic of abortion is an extremely interesting one about which I have more ideas than solid beliefs about. What I said was, "This post isn't about abortion. It is a post about over-coming adversity. This one happens to be about a woman of color in the Jim Crow South. But since you brought it up . . . no matter what people think about abortion; regardless of whether people support constitutional law or not, today most people have the right to decide whether to keep a baby born of rape. But my guess would be that a woman who gets raped on a cotton plantation didn't have many rights that were being enforced in the first place, let alone the slim chance that she might see any justice at all, controversial justice or otherwise. Why? because the Jim Crow South wasn't much interested in abstract constitutional ideas such as equal rights and equal protection under the law."

My comment was based upon my concern about how some peo-ple, like you here, will pick out a subject, never mentioned in the post, and talk about it when abortion doesn't even address the topic at hand.

So, my questions for you in my last comment were about es-trangement although I used variants of the term "alienation". You don't seem to mind your estrangement, you seem to relish in it for intellectual reasons? I, on the other hand, struggle for engagement yet my struggles are in vain because my mind prefers challenging questions. Since my questions are challenging to both myself and others, others feel I am too challenging or perhaps simply baiting them. I see no value in baiting them because it shrouds any possible conversation in a defensiveness that lacks honesty. Whereas you seem to enjoy baiting people (not me, I don't think) for your own intellectual "stimulus", "energy" and "honesty". Whereas you would be quite, "happy to limit it to birthday wishes in July", but that wouldn't make me happy.

While considering new ideas and then altering my views, at times I would think I had found truth. But what I soon learned was that I had simply found a different point of view that supported my previous views. As one who struggles with depression and anxiety, this may have been a nice feeling but my feelings of *good* were then more about *me* than revealing some truthful objectivity. I came to understand how my newer, more attractive ideas simply fit my personal psychology and tendencies. I was in a vicious cycle but luckily the clues to gleaning value from this cycle were begging my questions: Since my physical nature had provided me the senses of hearing and sight, I had been naturally led to value the definite points of view they furnished me. Furthermore, my mental viewpoints paralleled my physical views. So I decided that it must be my responsibility to be extremely self-critical about the strength with which I regarded my physical and mental viewpoints. Why should I want to value my point of view above someone else's point of view when they must suffer from the same malady as I? This tendency is tantamount to war rather than accord. Our viewpoints and opinions simply aren't true, they are merely convenient. This doesn't mean "truth" is only relative to disparate individuals. But it does mean that all individuals share at least this much. The fault of overvaluing our own perspective to the detriment of others is a detriment to understanding itself. We share this detriment in common and must recognize it together while acknowledging it as a base to rise from and above. We can do better than science, biology, DNA and evolution. We can do better, that is, if our minds have evolved for any better reason than this determinism and the instincts that follow from it.

No reply.

Not much is written between us nowadays. We have a rare ex-changes from time to time like the few that follow. This one is in re-sponse to a post I shared about how Bach's wife may have written some of his works.

SHARON: The question of why there have been so few great female composers, painters, sculptors, etc. is most commonly answered by blaming others for keeping them down. This suggests that if they were freed from female stereotypes and expectations and given education, re-sources, opportunities, and a level playing field for competi-tion, the number of competent females in those fields would correspond to their numbers in the community, i.e. 51% and those considered great would be of the same proportion as men. A hundred years of freedom and opportunity haven't given us those results. If Bach's wife could write the unac-companied cello suites while bearing and raising thirteen children in a society that gave no opportunities to female composers, then where are all the great female composers today who have no children, no demanding "egotistical" hus-band and ample opportunity to compose? The answer is not one women like to hear: biology.

PAUL: Biology applies to men and women, and our minds and the evolution thereof are parts of our biology. Neither men nor women must be slaves to a mindless biology. Some men can rise above the image of *might makes right* so that they may come to respect the choices of women, even if they are often able to physically over-power them. Some women might demand respect for equal rights while expecting men to grow and learn about this virtue. Of course, this may well be a great part of our biology; to raise these boys to become better men. This may well be the responsibility of men biologically; to learn how to respect women and their choices. After a hundred years, we still have a long way to go. Those of us who make choices are not less than; we are not slaves to mindless biology; we simply make different choices. We don't have to *blame* anybody. This can be good for society at large. While all of this is happening, many of us can value the best of both worlds.

Some women can have thirteen children and also be brilliant composers rather than kowtow to some narrowly focused idea of biology. I can respect all of Anna Magdalena Bach's achievements.

SHARON: Biology isn't "mindless", it is the source of mind. We are all "slaves" to our biology in the sense that we are nothing without it. Because men and women are reproductive complements they have essential differences that derive from their separate roles. Even if a person does not have children he/she still goes through all the mental and physical development to that end. That is why there is now, and always has been so few women who single-mindedly pursue excellence in demanding fields. Females mature earlier and they begin to focus on their reproductive role in their early teens. This narrows their interests and their scope, and probably limits their mental development. ....To be continued.

PAUL: You say, "Biology isn't 'mindless', it is the source of mind. We are all 'slaves' to our biology in the sense that we are nothing without it."

Depending of course on how far this slavishness goes, everybody knows this. Much of what you say seems obviously true at the level that celebrates biology while ignoring mindful choice. But there is simply more to this. We are more than animals. Supposedly humans can do more than simply evolve. Supposedly we have some free will and greater minds and greater communicative abilities. And even of it isn't free will, is biology the driver or could it be a greater combination of things? Women can and do make choices beyond the push or draw of biology and that's okay. It's more than okay. There is nothing wrong with this.

Biology applies to men yet men aren't generally known for their profound monogamous, family desires. Many men are more likely to get sidetracked by their sexual (biological) desires while seeming to lack the same biological family drive that women are said to have. I've heard some biological explanations for this difference but much more often I've heard excuses (scientific sounding or not) for a double standard rather than stressing that we take more responsibility for our choices. Family (the first society) and larger society should step in and try to regulate these tendencies yet the opposite seems to occur. Too often we politicize people's behavior. We act like this is a religious issue rather than a moral issue of responsibility. (Yes, there is often a difference between religiosity and morality.) Then some politicians and religious people spend their time shaming and punishing women for all sorts of behaviors that men are not largely given a pass for. Men are largely let off the hook. It is largely men who pass judgment as well as laws regarding women. Many people even regard God as a male figure and, coincidentally enough, God's view of sin seems to mirror that of male dominated society. Men aren't held responsible for pregnancy etc, while women are shamed. American society even seems to applaud or at least accept men's *biological* behaviors. Or is it simply men's biology? Do men have no further responsibility? Doesn't our social attitude toward male sexuality (biology) also narrow our interests and their scope, and probably limit our mental as well as our *social development*?

SHARON: You have a simplistic view of biology and evolution as they relate to humankind, that is to say, you seem to think of biology as "animal" and evolution as a lesser function in the life of man. To include biology and evolution in a discussion about differences is not to "celebrate" biology, but to give the discussion wider scope. You place "biology" in opposition to "mindful choice", suggesting that we can rise above the push or draw of our animal natures by using our "free will, greater minds, and communicative abilities." But here you get into trouble with your desire to "respect" women because you devalue the essential thing that makes the female different from the male. You didn't post the article about Frau Bach to celebrate her achievement as the mother of thirteen children – you don't consider that an achievement - but only that she may have composed music "rather than kowtow to some narrowly focused idea of biology."

We cannot escape our biology and its penetrating effects on mind and body. In addition, our biology is the product of millions of years of evolution, the singular purpose of which, has been reproductive success. Unlike all other life forms we can choose to kill ourselves, kill our offspring, and thwart nature to prevent pregnancy – but we nevertheless continue to develop and mature as reproductive beings and perform or simulate the mating rituals that are integral to reproduction. In addition, to our physical evolution our social forms have evolved to support survival and reproductive success.

Not every human culture has evolved to have a role for the male in reproduction beyond fertilization, but a culture that is built upon monogamy has a very important role for the male as protector and provider of his wife and children and in a culture with high investment childrearing he is often the primary educator as well. His role requires moral leadership in addition to his responsibility for the material well-being of his family.

The "image of might makes right" is a caricature of the male in his relation to his biological complement and evokes the cartoon caveman. Is that really the opposite of respecting a woman's choices? And why should it work only one way? Shouldn't a woman respect the corresponding choices of the man? For example, shouldn't he have the choice to kill unwanted offspring?

Because the female matures earlier than the male certain mental qualities are locked in, so to speak. She retains a childlike quality that serves her well as a mother because it allows her great patience with children – she can spend hours "relating" to a six month-old or playing with a two year-old. An occasional man might "choose" such an occupation, but that would be seen as remarkable as a mother of thirteen composing Bach's unaccompanied cello suites in her spare time. Early maturation also means that the female, early in her teens, begins to devote a major portion of her attention to her appearance in order to attract males. When not thinking about how she looks, she is thinking about some boy she has set her sights on. This preparation for marriage and childbearing is biology at work. Can she "choose" a more high-minded path? Can she "choose" neither to develop breasts nor to ovulate? Can she "choose" not to fall in love? Is the female who is born with exceptional intellect or creativity spared the "push or draw" of female biology? I don't think so. Isn't this why feminists coined the phrase, "having it all"? Women understand that they can't stop biology and they don't really want to, but because their reproductive role has been devalued they feel compelled to deny it. The girls who used to be frank about the purpose of college as the place to find a husband now pretend that they are there to prove themselves equal to men in the worlds of academia, business, and professions. Pause, it's late.

PAUL: You tell me I seem to ". . . have a simplistic view of biology and evolution as they relate to humankind . . ." Yet earlier I gave a nod to the idea that, ". . . this may well be a great part of our biology; to raise these boys to become better men. This may well be the responsibility of men biologically; to learn how to respect women and their choices." But as it is, I cannot argue for attitude changes since they are in no way measurable scientifically, and so can hardly be regarded as biology by way of scientific method.

"To include biology and evolution in a discussion about differences is not to 'celebrate' biology, but to give the discussion wider scope."

Or perhaps a narrower scope. Even science used to fall under the umbrella of philosophy; that is before science thought it could become "the final arbiter of reality." So, no, I don't "think of biology as 'animal' and evolution as a lesser function in the life of man," I just have my doubts that biology can have the first, middle *and* last words in our lives.

"You place 'biology' in opposition to 'mindful choice', suggesting that we can rise above the push or draw of our animal natures by using our 'free will, greater minds, and communicative abilities."

Yes I do. In many ways we can and do do this. In some ways we cannot and fail. Over time we have come to see that we have little free will in some areas, yet we can still alter our choices within a very narrow range. Science has come to locate areas in the brain that are responsible somehow for certain behaviors that can't seem to be altered except through physically manipulating the brain. One day neuroscience may show how many more behaviors are physically rather than psychologically based. But when this happens there will be score of people once again condemning science as if it can be thought of as "the final arbiter". They will then only be able to wish that it was still considered be the greater free will they once assumed. No longer will they be able to judge others based upon their concept of free will.

I am not in trouble, "with your desire to 'respect' women because you devalue the essential thing that makes the female different from the male." I don't have the "desire" to respect women, I just find they deserve it. Their essential "thing" exists whether I respect it or not. I understand what makes women different from men, yet it isn't merely some attitude. And even if their thing is physical attributes, some use them or cannot use them and it doesn't make them any more or less women, just as my use, or lack thereof, of my "biology" doesn't make me more of less of a man.

"You didn't post the article about Frau Bach to celebrate her achievement as the mother of thirteen children – you don't consider that an achievement - but only that she may have composed music "rather than kowtow to some narrowly focused idea of biology."

In fact, I didn't post the article nor write the article. I didn't repost it for a biological, philosophical, political or social reason. I didn't direct it at you. I simply reposted it because I prefer Bach's Baroque style of music to most other music in what people tend to regard as the Classical music genre. I had never known his wife was a composer. It made me wonder about how the influenced each other musically. I had no idea she had thirteen children, and yes, that was beside the point of my own interests. But I did note in my first reply to you that I respected "*all* of Anna Magdalena Bach's achievements", although my primary interest was in music, and that's okay too. In fact, perhaps her musical abilities are genetic, part of her biology. But, if I want to make this about politics and social commentary, back then she was expected to play a certain role as a woman and she did. She has thirteen children while also fulfilling her role (biological or not, or more, or less) as a composer. Would you disagree that, in todays world, she would have had more opportunities/options outside "biology" than she had back then? Do you find this reality to be narrowly regarded as some sociopolitical issue to be regarded on some biological-political level? Or can you simply enjoy her music and the completeness of her personhood? Why is the completeness of a person somehow lesser than biology and genetics? After all, if the completeness of Frau Bach's person is so dependent upon her womanhood, genetics and biology and genetics, then celebrate the complete person instead of making her a foil for your politics about womanhood, genetics and biology and genetics.

There are many like me who have failed in our "singular purpose" of biology, if that singular purpose (narrowly speaking) is reproduction. Yet my choice was mental (perhaps I err, it might have been subconscious and therefore genetically based) and my wife's failure was physical/medical, perhaps linked biologically due to some genetics (I'm not sure how to place political/social blame here so I'll place the blame on biology.) So, did I have a choice whereas she didn't? Did she have some sort of choice that is somehow excused whereas mine can't be. Which of us is driven more by genetics and biology? If I regard certain personality and family traits and conclude that it might be a better choice for me not to have children, is that my genes telling me what is best? Or should I look to blame the Democrats or Republicans and each of their own brands of social engineering?

You say, "Not every human culture has evolved to have a role for the male in reproduction beyond fertilization, but a culture that is built upon monogamy has a very important role for the male as protector and provider of his wife and children and in a culture with high investment childrearing he is often the primary educator as well. His role requires moral leadership in addition to his responsibility for the material well-being of his family."

But then you go on to say, "The "image of might makes right" is a caricature of the male in his relation to his biological complement and evokes the cartoon caveman. Is that really the opposite of respecting a woman's choices?"

It sounds as though you have replied to your own commentary here unless your prior commentary is also a caricature. Then you ask further, "And why should it work only one way? Shouldn't a woman respect the corresponding choices of the man? For example, shouldn't he have the choice to kill unwanted offspring?"

These are indeed good questions. A man should have input in both the choices and options, yet all too often men take a pass, and society give them this pass. In today's broader American culture, if we saw men taking care for their choices and taking care of their offspring, we wouldn't be having the same discussions that we have today. If men had to take responsibility, men would likely opt for free, on demand (demanded by them) abortion, everywhere, all the time. But men refuse moral responsibility (leadership) and would rather hide behind the smokescreen created by a political and social divisiveness of their own making. We therefore have the society and the issues we have, and neither has much to do with biology and genetics.

"When not thinking about how she looks, she is thinking about some boy she has set her sights on. This preparation for marriage and childbearing is biology at work."

Or perhaps she is thinking about her latest cello masterpiece. It seems that she, or at least, biology has often been wrong; what with many women making such poor choices today that we must have politics intervene? BTW, boys spend time upon their looks and often have their sights set upon some girl too. Yet this may or may not be preparation for marriage. So . . .

"Can she "choose" a more high-minded path?"

I would say yes.

"Can she "choose" neither to develop breasts nor to ovulate?"

I would say, "not exactly". Women have little if any choice in how their breasts develop or when they may begin to ovulate, nor how any of these things will effect/affect them.

"Can she "choose" not to fall in love?"

I would say yes. But if I were to say no, I would qualify it by saying that she may indeed decide how to handle these feelings rather than have them rule her.

"Is the female who is born with exceptional intellect or creativity spared the 'push or draw' of female biology? I don't think so."

I would tend to disagree just as I would tend to say the male can and often does make the draw of his male biology (whatever that is supposed to be composed of according to our present society) subordinate. We see this everywhere and this is what bothers many people.

"Isn't this why feminists coined the phrase, 'having it all'?"

I think someone coined the phrase but I don't know that it was feminists or if the phrase has been primarily used by or attributed to feminists or if it was from a Clairol® commercial. I also don't think the phrase means much. As it is, men can't have it all either but they will pass enough laws to work in their favor so as to try.

"Women understand that they can't stop biology and they don't really want to, but because their reproductive role has been devalued they feel compelled to deny it."

Who are these "women" you speak of. If *women* as a group thought so uniformly we wouldn't be having this discussion. What you mean is *some women*, like yourself.

"The girls who used to be frank about the purpose of college as the place to find a husband now pretend that they are there to prove themselves equal to men in the worlds of academia, business, and professions."

Once again, this statement applies to some women, just as everything you say about men applies only to some men.

No reply.

The following was in response to a Philosophy Bites *podcast that I passed along featuring the philosopher, Katrin Flikschuh.*

SHARON: One important point she made was that African-*Americans* are more focused on individual rights, while the African sees individual rights as antagonistic to the communalist character of the African society - in which one's duties to the community are essential in the structure and stability of the community. The effort to reconstruct what has been supplanted by colonialism without resorting to foreign, Western political philosophy that stresses universal human rights would seem to be impossible. There were no African philosophers before colonialism and they are using the language of the colonizer in an effort to get back to an organic society that evolved before their contact with the West.

PAUL: It is an unfortunate aspect of American society that we tend to focus so narrowly upon individualism while ignoring the value of *society* beyond our selves. The fact that Western political philosophy (or at least that part common in the United States) has tended to devalue universal human rights while overvaluing individual rights has been a problem. There should be little wonder how this selfishness has caused much of our current instability.

No reply.

In response to my unrelated Philosophy Bites *podcast post concerning free will skepticism (with philosopher Gregg Caruso):*
SHARON: What do you think is his most valuable insight?

PAUL: For me, his most valuable contribution was to inspire discussion and further thought. The interview prompted more questions than praise for his insights. I tend to be a free will skeptic when it comes to the realm of making judgments about another's moral responsibility, but ironically this forces me, as well it should, to take greater responsibility for any possibilities regarding my own moral responsibility. I might add that the ideas surrounding free will skepticism did at least as much to drive me away from modern libertarianism as did the politics of libertarianism.

No reply.

I suppose the fact that the Justice Department as well as the FBI cleared Democratic Presidential candidate Hillary Clinton of criminal charges, inspired Sharon to post the comments below as an a sort of open letter:
SHARON: Back to Hillary for a moment. It is now very clear that Hillary Clinton is a liar. FBI Director, Comey had to admit that many of her statements regarding her servers and emails were untrue. However, it seems to me that the most important question has never been asked or answered. What was the purpose in having a private server? Why did she choose to set up private servers rather than use what was available? The question is especially important because she took an obvious risk of running afoul of government security regulations. So, once again, what was the benefit or

purpose in taking that risk? I can only think of one reasonable possibility and that is to allow total access to an unseen, and likely foreign political entity. Any thoughts?

CC replies: Possibly. Definitely to hide her activities. It seems pretty clear that her main priority is amassing more wealth and power and is always willing to commit crimes to accomplish her goals.

PAUL: I wouldn't think about defending Hillary, so back to Trump for a moment:) If I could show you videos of times he has made a particular statement and then show you videos of times he has denied what he said on the previous video, would you admit that he too is a liar? Since you know I can produce these videos, will you admit it without my going to the trouble?

In response evidently to CC?
SHARON: The way she has amassed wealth and power is to sell her services and our country's interests to those entities with greater wealth and power. She is a functionary and her power is guaranteed by those she could expose if she is crossed. Her unflappable confidence in the face of Bernie's surprising popularity and her uncanny ability to lie suggest that she has serious dirt on those for who she is working.

PAUL: Do you imagine that Donald has not also amassed wealth and power? Is he now not selling his services? Do you imagine Trump will no longer regard his own great wealth and power if his function is to be president? Do you have any doubt that Donald will not expose anybody who might cross him? Do you find that Donald lacks unflappable confidence in the face of his own lack of popularity? Will he not amass serious dirt and use it against those with whom he works? Will he show fear in using it?

SHARON: I was trying to point out that to concentrate on her lies - which is what the media and the congressmen are doing - is to miss the important question of WHY she set up a private server.

Since she disregarded my other challenges, I only address her last question:
PAUL: People typically use a private email server for privacy and control. I'm sure these reasons have a lot to do with why she set up her server. Now, we can all speculate about her additional, nefarious motives (like many politicians have done for years) but another important question concerns me: Amid all the accusations, why have our representatives not yet worked out clearly worded rules with clear consequences about email use and the use of non-governmental servers? After all, almost every politician uses so-called "private", (which are often simply non-government servers) for their *personal* functions.

CC replies to me: This post is about Corrupt Hillary. It has nothing to do with Trump. Certainly, Trump is far from perfect and might have committed unethical or criminal acts, but his would surely pale in comparison to Killarys. The Hillary vs Donald thing is inconsequential regarding this and it, along with the mostly manipulated, fear of Trump phenomenon, is being used to build support for #HerRoyalCorruptness. This, even though neither one of them is a nominee. Not yet, anyway. Propaganda is at work and most, even some of those who consider them‗ selves awake, are manipulated by it.

PAUL: This post may have had nothing to do with Trump but your reply makes this thread about Donald too. Or maybe my reply made it so. It seems a thread can change with a single notion rather than by fault. So we can now share the blame or discuss the notion if you'd like.

So, what concerns you about Donald has nothing to do with his **inconsequential . . . unethical or criminal acts**? Okay, but your concern does have to do with the manipulation of our fear about Trump? Who are the manipulators? Is every one manipulated the same? Do all people act by this same motive? What are your presumptions about me? I have no fear of Trump, so what is your explanation for me and my questions?

To determine who is awake and who is asleep may depend upon which "side" you are on, rather than any more *objective* criteria.

Now, maybe you can carefully define "propaganda" for me. Let us see if one, or both of us are already guilty of it ourselves.

CC replies to me: I wish I had more time to debate, but I dont. Bottom line is Clinton is a criminal who always seems to get a free pass to continue her ways.

PAUL: Fair enough.

TIFFANY chimes in: When I worked for Microsoft, working with the government was a running joke. Their IT infrastructure was widely known as substandard and lacking basic fore-thought in their contingent or strategic planning. We laughed when they hired CGI Group to run their first major Internet presence: Healthcare-gov. But, we weren't surprised because CGI Group had been infiltrated with lobbyists with their own special interests.

The government just recently revamped State-gov and Secre-tary Kerry was the first Secretary of State to be given a single email server account for all electronic communication. Govern-ment incompetence in their IT Infrastructure and implementation goes back decades. Former Secretary Clinton sending email from a computer other than what was provided for her by the govern-ment is not surprising in the least when looked at from those with knowledge of the government's IT infrastructure. In lay-men's terms, it's a mess. And, as a result, government officials have not been trained properly or given specific protocol on how to conduct their government business electronically. These "gov-ernment security regulations" that you speak of may exist "in theory" for the purpose of congressmen to try and seem smart when they try and bash Clinton on the news or in public fo-rums, but in reality aren't implemented or understood. Clinton "allowing access to an unseen political entity" from a non gov-ernment computer is illogical, given the sophomoric hardware and communication devices that she was found to be using.

SHARON: There is no problem in government officials having a private server for private/personal use. The problem is in conducting government business on a server that is not secure and on which one mixes sensitive government correspondence with personal e-mail and does not follow the protocols for handling classified materials. Hillary may have been interested in "privacy and control" for her personal correspondence, but using a single server for sensitive government business and her daughter's wedding plans suggests that she had no concern at all for the privacy and control of highly sensitive State Department correspondence. Clinton must have had a reason to risk losing her security clearance and to risk criminal charges even if she didn't have any compunction about breaching U.S. security, endangering lives, and giving blackmail material to god-knows who. What was that reason?

PAUL:

1) There is no such thing as a secure server, and the government hasn't come to grips with any proper management of this issue yet.

2) We can't indite people when the rules don't support indictment.

3) Hillary, and all other human judgment is only part of the problem when it comes to security.

Let's at least not let poor human judgment take our eye off of numbers 1 and 2.

You ask, "**What was that reason?**" I'll bet your answer has to do with conspiracy but since my crystal ball is broken, I'll have to focus upon the complexities of the question.

When people disagree about the meaning of laws, this disagreement doesn't have to point to conspiracy. Washington, Hamilton, Jefferson and Madison all disagreed about what parts of the constitution intended. When there is good reason for disagreement, we should get to work improving the rules and the penalties that follow from their violation.

Now all this seems simple enough until you try. During the process you have to get past the partisan bickering before anything can be started let alone implemented. And God forbid we allocate the necessary funds and the other resources required to set out on such a massive, long term project. Even if we do, incoming law-makers, or their adversaries are likely cut this budget as soon as they can because smaller government is better don't ya know. Do you see a conspiracy here? Or is it human nature and perhaps the partisan nature of politics? But we can't even get this far. If and when we do, we will be faced with the complications of having a body that is charged with setting up rules and penalties that it must apply to itself. Such a body is sure to maintain some vague lan-guage and maybe even include a hidden back door. Why? Because they are crooks? In fact it's a lot like designing a secure server. It is a difficult and ongoing process.

Humans write rules for humans, and we have to allow for hu-man input because justice tells us that one rule cannot be applied across all people. Some people are too young, too old, or lacking in the mental abilities for a given law to apply to them without our judgment intervening. Computers do not have the capability of judgment. We are imperfect people and computers are no better. This is our world. And there is precious little anybody can do to change reality except maybe to try to work very hard together. But I don't see this happening in our government. This just isn't what we value.

Your issue really has nothing to do with any of this. You don't like Hillary, and so no matter how many agencies can't find her guilty, even if a Republican heads the agency, you believe in con-spiracy. It can't be anything like I've said. There's no sport in that. No Monday morning quarterbacking, no damned refs to complain about. All that is left is a bunch of complicated work that *still* needs to get done.

It seems we want to elect someone who, above all, has with the will and the power to fight. Hillary and Trump are running for president. Each have the money, the will and the power to fight. We will see how this works for us, and how much difference they can make when we are the people.

SHARON: There is no evidence that Hillary Clinton pre-sented an argument for setting up and using private servers. She did request permission to use her BlackBerry, but the

NSA refused the request. It appears that the only argument she could have used was not very Jeffersonian, and that was "convenience". In what respect did Clinton show poor judgment? If security is impossible then her decision to circumvent what the NSA deemed "secure" isn't poor judgment, but a reasonable choice to avoid useless and ineffective regulations. There is no indication that Clinton pushed to change the rules or that she refused to sign SF 312 - the non-disclosure form for handling classified material. How do you suppose Clinton was able to carry out her work as Secretary of State if she could not send and receive classified material on her private servers or her BlackBerry? Why did she risk censure and why did she choose to lie rather than expose the ineffective security regulations that she was avoiding? The FBI did find that she had mishandled classified material and Comey exposed her lies about that mishandling when he was questioned by the congressional committee. What Director Comey did not do was to recommend indictment. It isn't a question of whether she violated the rules and lied about it, but rather how those violations and lies will be addressed. It is quite possible that these things, along with what we have learned about the Clinton Foundation will be addressed by the voters Conspiracy is real and it is foolish to reject conspiracy as an explanation just because you have been persuaded to believe that people who see evidence of a conspiracy are paranoid or nutty. Crystal balls are designed to tell the future, not to assess the truth of something in the past.

PAUL: Okay, Hillary's reasons for a private server are privacy, control and now convenience (even though it is inconvenient to set up a private server, and having setup that private server she ended up inconveniencing herself.)

Rather than Jeffersonian ideals; she was thinking of herself. In her myopia, she didn't worry of how it might end up inconveniencing herself and the rest of us. And when someone doesn't look beyond themselves and their beliefs this reveals the same bad judgment.

"There is no indication that Clinton pushed to change the

rules or that she refused to sign SF 312 - the non-disclosure form for handling classified material."

Hilary wasn't interested in changing the governmental rules. Like most people, she worked in and around the rules the as she saw fit. Many of us point out problems with the systems only to go back to the job at hand; we normally just keep working. She may have thought that her workarounds were fine but she displayed poor judgment. But rather than casting people as either crooked or honest, few people short of prison or sainthood might appear all bad or good; even that devil Trump:)

Most of us think that we are doing what is best. Some of us seek to do our least but few of us strive to do our worst. Throughout the process, we all rationalize our decisions the best we can. We rationalize our own behavior in our own defense because nobody else is going to do it for us. It is easier for us to point out the flaws of others than to see them in ourselves. This is all pretty normal stuff. What isn't good is for all extremely partisan Republicans to convict all Democrats (and visa versa). This can't bring justice; it only serves our obvious biases. We could also do away with investigators, judges and all the discretion they offer but that won't give us justice either. When things don't go the way that seems perfectly obvious to us, this may speak more to our biases than something else. But when our biases are large enough, we can't even see past them. I therefore question the judgment of anybody who fails to place ample value upon this reality within their remarks about judgment or value.

"It isn't a question of whether she violated the rules and lied about it, but rather how those violations and lies will be addressed." And now Comey has ". . . exposed her lies about that mishandling when he was questioned by the congressional committee. What Director Comey did not do was to recommend indictment."

And what is your solution?

"Crystal balls are designed to tell the future, not to assess the truth of something in the past."

And they can do neither.

It has been said that if we fail to learn from the past we are bound to repeat the same mistakes. But this is only a small part of the problem. In our attempts at using the past to direct our future, we *view* the past we want to improve upon with the same *eyes* as we view the present with. And we may not realize how much our current biases build into the improvement we wish to impart. The past may also be presented to us by others who exhibit the same faults as our own. And then sometimes the past is known to us by our own memories and still that past is colored by the biases we had then as well as by the biases we have today. We then remember the past through both these biases. Without recognizing and valuing these facts, we can't help but have a future that suffers from the same faults as our past and present.

Since we don't know the Clinton/Comey past, any evidence you present may be based upon conjecture and the biased sources who happen to see the world the same way you do. Could their evidence be biased? Could it be in error? How can one tell how biased their information is? What is the conspiracy based upon? A vicious circle of information and misinformation that simply becomes self supporting within its own circle that can never be proven to be true or disproven. We will then view all future information through the lens of what we know or prefer to think. This circumstance is indistinguishable to me from fortune telling (or the *past telling*). If there is a difference, you'll have to explain the real world differences to me rather than the semantic differences.

"Conspiracy is real and it is foolish to reject conspiracy as an explanation just because you have been persuaded to believe that people who see evidence of a conspiracy are paranoid or nutty."

Nobody has persuaded me, and I understand how you see the evidence. I wouldn't say that an attempt to explain everything political by basing it upon conspiracy is paranoid or nutty. I also wouldn't say conspiracy is unreal. I also don't think that I am foolish to reject conspiracy in light of other more pressing values. But after I note the possibility or reality of conspiracy, what then? Should I just throw up my hands and complain about it while we fail in our responsibilities to work on the issues that we can actually do something about? Most people interested in conspiracy seem to *know* the *truth that others are too blind to see*. But in focusing on conspiracy/conjecture as the issue, we end up dodging the tough questions and the realistic solutions.

I may not be able to offer up any easy solutions but I can offer up ways of regarding situations that hopefully don't suffer from unexamined bias and conjecture. I can't change Clinton. I can't convict her. But I will not rely upon conjecture (yours, hers or my own) as if conjecture would help my reasons or reasoning. What can my belief in a conspiracy and my dependence upon conjecture avail me? Make me feel better that I know some truth that others don't know? At best it can only show me that some people got together to affect a certain end. But we are all involved in this sort of conspiracy; from political parties to a neighborhood watch. Beyond this, conspiracy seems only to want to point to who not to trust. But even when I trust someone, that person can do things I don't like. At some point I still must still decide what to do or how to think about the matter, and conjecture doesn't help me; it merely muddies the waters. If there is an indictable offense or conviction to be had, it should be done regardless of conjecture or belief in order for it to be just.

If my thoughts merely end with my portrayal of conspiracy, I've shirked my responsibilities. And isn't it the shirking of responsibilities part of what bothers us about this affair? If it is, shouldn't we take the responsibility of not assuming things that can't be known or proven?

What worries you about conspiracy? Is part of your solution to be suspicious of certain groups? Is this because groups of conspirators can seem insurmountable? Is this why you tend to distrust certain groups?

No reply

AFTERWORD

It has been a year long conversation that more or less fizzled out. Our *Facebook* banter has dwindled down to about one brief exchange each month. I now generally let Sharon's reposts and comments speak for themselves. Perhaps we both lost interest in each other's arguments. Sharon believes her notions to be right and true, and can rationalize that these notions are *best for* all parties involved. But when your main argument begins and ends with condemning groups of people because they are not like yourself, I see more problems are being created than being addressed.

Our main philosophical disagreement might be seen as one of means *v* ends. By *best for*, she presumes beginnings that we can have no real knowledge of. Specifically she seems to assume an idillic time that if we cannot go back to we should at least strive toward its recreation. For her, this point in time should be maintained or somehow fixed in time. But this concept of time ignores the reality of time. My concept of *best for* inheres within the *process* of life. I see people living day to day within a dynamic, ever changing reality. My view of both time and change seems to better comport with reality as it is and as it goes.

But Sharon has little interest in philosophy and how we might apply such notions to everyday situations. I do want to thank her, however, for the opportunity to learn so much that I never knew about race. I, like most people I've since discussed the issue with, had simply assumed there was something to it. Now I know that science has precious little to tell us with regard to race. Race is mostly a sociological phenomenon. And though science can't help us much in dealing with the sociological study of race, cultural studies simply get brushed off as political correctness. It is then that talk about race itself gets derided as racism. Attempts to deal with our blindspots get branded as reverse discrimination. Yet when corrective measures are branded as reverse discrimination, prior discrimination has been admitted to, and so this still requires us to address the circumstances without branding them simply as political correctness. We may debate about how best to improve, but we shouldn't hide from or excuse our responsibilities to each other.

At the end of the day, our arguments were ends within themselves, never moving toward resolution. I repeatedly asked her to offer up solutions that move her toward her ends but she didn't or couldn't. And yet paradoxically we seemed stuck in a loop of too many answers; answers so sure that we couldn't move past them. Since she couldn't question her answers, we were damned from the start. On the sidelines were left so many topics I'm sorry we couldn't have explored in depth. But her notion that *if we could only keep these people here and keep those people away* (or even put those people back over there) ruled the day. Too much time was spent upon these issues when even totalitarianism, eugenics, and genocide won't stop immediate families from generating members who differ from the rest (physically or mentally) and so are intent upon finding their own path. We will always disapprove of at least one of our neighbors while our son or daughter finds engagement with them. Sharon and I are a prime example of brother and sister who share family, race and culture yet this commonality is foreshadowed by our differences that we focus upon instead of valuing that which we have in common. We can coexist happily ever after if we accept and value this reality for all it provides us. Differing people have never been separate. The family of man is intertwined. We come together for love and for war. In the process we will become something we never really were but we might also become more than we currently are.

Our largest practical disagreement, the problem of employing terms like: *these people this* or *those people that,* when this grouping and the generalization that accompanies it obviously isn't true by way of reason, yet certain people, not just Sharon, seem to insist upon making this error. And since these errors of reason are what might be called the *easy cases*, how can we expect anybody to seriously reconsider other errors of value when they are much more difficult to recognize? The free exchange of ideas can't hurt, even when they seem to find no anchor, or produce no fledgling *anchor babies*.

In one of our first exchanges I told her that I didn't see our disagreements as necessarily being about right *v* wrong but rather about values. She dismissed this thought and wondered how this could be said when we were raised in the same family, the same community during roughly the same era. I re-asked this question of her several times and received little input.

Sharon has much to say about biology. She maintains that everything begins with biology. Unfortunately she also believes that too much ends with biology. Biology knows nothing of society. Our society is up to us. Each of us are born into a society. We are dependent upon some sort of society for many years if we are to survive. We then live within a society that each of us is partially responsible for the maintenance of. So it is that our regard for civics should precede the advancement of our politics.

In the end, like many people, Sharon complains but offers up few workable ideas. Once we accept the responsibility of addressing these issues, we find it altering our mindsets. The search for ideas is inherently a positive one; a progressive one. More negative or regressive thought styles seem to separate us and keep us separate.

Suffice it to say that Sharon has always been quick to share her beliefs but seldom have I heard her give voice to any reality beyond belief. The closest she has come to this is when we were reminiscing, but I'm sure Sharon would disagree :)

Paul R. Gibson, July, 2016